THE LANGUAGE OF THOUGHT

The Language & Thought Series

THE LANGUAGE AND THOUGHT SERIES UNDER THE GENERAL EDITORSHIP OF
JERROLD J. KATZ, MASSACHUSETTS INSTITUTE OF TECHNOLOGY AND THE GRADUATE
    CENTER, CITY UNIVERSITY OF NEW YORK
D. TERENCE LANGENDOEN, THE GRADUATE CENTER, CITY UNIVERSITY OF NEW YORK
HARRIS SAVIN, UNIVERSITY OF PENNSYLVANIA

The Language of Thought
   Jerry A. Fodor, *Massachusetts Institute of Technology*

An Integrated Theory of Linguistic Abilities
   Thomas Bever, *Columbia University,* Jerrold J. Katz, *Massachusetts Institute of Technology and the Graduate Center, City University of New York,*
   and D. Terence Langendoen, *The Graduate Center, City University of New
   York,* Editors (in preparation)

Introduction to Linguistic Semantics
   Charles J. Fillmore, *University of California, Berkeley* (in preparation)

Propositional Structure:
A Study of the Contribution of Sentence Meaning to Speech Acts
   Jerrold J. Katz, *Massachusetts Institute of Technology and The Graduate
   Center, City University of New York* (in preparation)

Semantics
   Janet Dean Fodor, *University of Connecticut* (in preparation)

THE LANGUAGE OF THOUGHT

JERRY A. FODOR

Massachusetts Institute of Technology

THOMAS Y. CROWELL COMPANY · NEW YORK · ESTABLISHED 1834

Library of Congress Cataloging in Publication Data

Fodor, Jerry A.
   The language of thought.

   (The Language and thought series)
   Bibliography: p.
   Includes index.
   1. Cognition.   2. Languages—Psychology.   I. Title.
BF311.F56   153.4   75-4843
ISBN 0-690-00802-3

Thomas Y. Crowell Company
666 Fifth Avenue
New York, New York 10019

Typography by Jules Perlmutter

Manufactured in the United States of America

CONTENTS

Only connect
E. M. FORSTER

The wind is changing
MARY POPPINS

Much of what appears here emerged from discussions that I have had at odd times (and in, for that matter, odd places) with my wife, Janet Dean Fodor. This book is dedicated, with love and gratitude, to her.

PREFACE

There used to be a discipline called speculative psychology. It wasn't quite philosophy because it was concerned with empirical theory construction. It wasn't quite psychology because it wasn't an experimental science. But it used the methods of both philosophy and psychology because it was dedicated to the notion that scientific theories should be both conceptually disciplined and empirically constrained. What speculative psychologists did was this: They thought about such data as were available about mental processes, and they thought about such first-order psychological theories as had been proposed to account for the data. They then tried to elucidate the general conception of the mind that was implicit in the data and the theories. Speculative psychology was, by and large, quite a good thing: William James and John Dewey were speculative psychologists and so, in certain of his moods, was Clark Hull. But it's commonly said that there aren't any speculative psychologists any more.

Insofar as it's true that there aren't, the fact is easy to explain. For one thing, speculative psychology exhibited an inherent hybrid instability. The distinction between first-order theories and higher-order theories is largely heuristic in any but a formalized science, so speculative psychology tended to merge with straight psychology. The elucidation of general concepts is a typical philosophical concern, so speculative psychology tended to merge with the philosophy of mind. In consequence, speculative psychologists had trouble deciding what department they were in and were an embarrassment to deans.

There were, moreover, fashionable epistemological theories—theories about the proper conduct of science—which suggested that no respectable inquiry *could* be partly conceptual and partly empirical in the way that speculative psychology was supposed to be. According to such theories, matters of fact are distinct in principle from relations of ideas, and their elucidation ought thus to be distinct in scientific practice. Philosophers who accepted this epistemology could accuse speculative psychologists of psychologizing, and psychologists who accepted it could accuse them of philosophizing. Since, according to the epistemologists, psychologizing and philosophizing are mutually incompatible activities, these accusations were received with grave concern.

There was, in short, a period when speculative psychology was viewed as a methodological anomaly and an administrative nuisance. Yet the speculative tradition never quite died out either in psychology or in the philosophy of mind. Empirical psychologists continued to design their experiments and interpret their data in light of some conception, however shadowy, of what the mind is like. (Such conceptions tended to become explicit in the course of methodological disputes, of which psychologists have plenty.) Similarly, though there are some philosophers who claim to practice pure analysis, there are lots of other philosophers who don't. For the latter, a general consonance with the facts about mental states is an acknowledged condition upon theories of the logic of mental state ascriptions. And, even analytical philosophers are sometimes to be found reading the empirical literature and laying down the law on what the data mean. Indeed, it is often the avowedly atheoretical psychologist who turns out to have the most grandiose philosophical pretensions (see, e.g., Skinner in *Beyond Freedom and Dignity,* 1971), just as it is the methodological apriorists in philosophy who often have the strongest views on how the data must be read (see, e.g., Malcom in *Dreaming,* 1962).

This book, in any event, is unabashedly an essay in speculative psychology. More specifically, it is an attempt to say how the mind works insofar as answers to that question emerge from recent empirical studies of language and cognition. The attempt seems to me to be worth making for two reasons: first, because the question of how the mind works is profoundly interesting, and the best psychology we have is ipso facto the best answer that is currently available. Second, the best psychology we have is still research in progress, and I am interested in the advancement of that research.

The last ten years or so have witnessed a proliferation of psychological research activities predicated on the view that many mental processes are computational processes, hence that much of 'higher cognitive behavior' is rule governed. Techniques for the analysis of rule governed behaviors are now familiar to scientists in a variety of disciplines: linguistics, simulation psychology, cognitive psychology, psycholinguistics, etc. There can be no argument but that the employment of these techniques has revolutionized both the practice and the theory of the behavioral sciences. But while it is easy to see that things have changed, it is less easy to say where they have gotten to. My impression is that many practitioners feel increasingly unclear about the general character of the theoretical framework that they are working in and quite uncertain what should happen next. An attempt at consolidation would therefore seem to be in order.

That, I take it, is one of the things that speculative psychology is for.

One seeks to provide enough insight into the drift of current research to aid in guiding future inquiry. This is, of course, quite a different matter from merely *summarizing* the research. One wants to say: 'If our psychology is, in general, right then the nature of the mind must be, roughly, this . . .' and then fill in the blank. Given the speculative elucidation, the experimentalist can work the other way around: 'If the nature of the mind is roughly . . . , then our psychology ought henceforth to look like this: . . .', where *this* blank is filled by new first-order theories. We ascend, in science, by tugging one another's bootstraps.

Speculative psychology, so conceived, is fraught with fallibility. For one thing, since it seeks, fundamentally, to extrapolate from the available scientific theories, it is in jeopardy of those theories proving to be false. It may, after all, turn out that the whole information-processing approach to psychology is somehow a bad idea. If it is, then such theories of the mind as it suggests are hardly likely to be true. This sort of thing has happened before in psychology. It now seems reasonably clear that the whole learning-theoretics approach to the explanation of behavior was a bad idea, and that the theory of the mind that it proposed was ludicrous. There's nothing one can do about this except to get on with the job and find out. Making explicit the account of the mind that it commits us to may be the best way of showing that our psychology has gone wrong if, in fact, it has.

Second, there is surely more than one way to read the morals of the current psychological research. I shall sketch a theory about mental processes in this book, and I shall argue that that theory *is* implied by most of what sensible linguists and cognitive psychologists accept these days. But I don't suppose that every sensible linguist or cognitive psychologist will agree with me. Indeed, what I mainly hope this book will do is provoke discussion on these points. Some of the things we seem to be committed to strike me, frankly, as a little wild. I should be glad to know if there are ways of saving the psychology while avoiding those commitments.

Finally, *qua* speculative psychologist one seeks to elaborate empirical theories of the mind which are, if not philosophically untendentious, at least philosophically respectable. But, of course, there is more than one view of what constitutes philosophical respectability, and one has to choose. I have pursued the discussion in this book on the assumption that realism is a better philosophy of science than reductionism, and that, in general, it is unadvisable for philosophers to try to make ontological points by using epistemological arguments. I acknowledge, however, the (bare) possibility that this assumption is wrong. If it is, the account of mental processes that I shall argue for is going to be badly off the mark.

This book is not entirely my fault. For one thing, it is in large part a sequel to a book I wrote with Professors T. Bever and M. Garrett (Fodor, Bever, and Garrett, 1974). Many of the ideas that get examined here were prompted by the experience of writing, with them, an extensive review of the current experimental and theoretical literature in psycholinguistics. In the course of that exercise, we returned again and again to discussions of the underpinnings of the discipline. Much of what went on in those discussions is replicated here. My indebtedness to my coauthors probably verges on plagiarism, and my gratitude for what they taught me is unbounded.

Even so, this book would not have gotten written except for a sabbatical grant from M.I.T. and a concurrent fellowship from the Guggenheim Foundation, which, together, freed me from academic duties during the year 1973–1974. My obligation to both institutions is hereby gratefully acknowledged.

I tried out early versions of some of the material in this book in series of lectures at the Department of Psychology at the University of Oxford and the Department of Philosophy at University College, University of London. I should like to offer my thanks to Dr. Ann Treisman for arranging the former lectures and to Professor Richard Wollheim for arranging the others; also to the students and faculty at both institutions for providing useful comments and criticisms.

Finally, a number of friends and relations have read all or parts of the manuscript, invariably to good effect. Alas, none of the following are responsible for the residual errors: Professors Ned Block, Susan Carey Block, George Boolos, Noam Chomsky, Janet Dean Fodor, Jerrold Katz, Edward Martin, and George Miller. I am especially obliged to Mr. Georges Rey, who read the manuscript with great care and provided invaluable criticism and advice; and to Mrs. Cornelia Parkes, who helped with the bibliography.

The second half of the Introduction to this book is a version, slightly revised, of a paper called "Special Sciences," which first appeared in *Synthese* (Fodor, 1974). Permission to republish this material is gratefully acknowledged. Material quoted from Chapters one and two and the conclusion of *The Construction of Reality in the Child* by Jean Piaget (translated by Marjorie Cooke) is copyrighted 1954 by Basic Books, Inc. Publishers, New York, and is used with their permission. Other quoted materials are used with the permission of D. Riedel Publishing Co.; Penguin Books Ltd.; John Wiley and Sons Inc.; The Humanities Press Inc.; and Routledge and Kegen Paul, Ltd.

INTRODUCTION: TWO KINDS OF REDUCTIONISM

The man who laughs is the one who
has not yet heard the terrible news.
BERTHOLD BRECHT

I propose, in this book, to discuss some aspects of the theory of mental processes. Many readers may, however, feel that this choice of topic is ill-advised: either because they think there are no such processes to discuss or because they think there is no theory about them whose aspects will bear discussing. The second of these worries is substantive, and its consideration must be deferred to the body of the text. The best demonstration that speculative psychology can be done is, after all, to do some. But I am aware that the distrust with which many philosophers, and many philosophically sophisticated psychologists, view the kind of inquiry I shall undertake stems from something more than a jaundiced appreciation of the empirical literature. It is with the sources of this suspicion that the present chapter will primarily be concerned.

The integrity of psychological theorizing has always been jeopardized by two kinds of reductionism, each of which would vitiate the psychologist's claim to study mental phenomena. For those influenced by the tradition of logical behaviorism, such phenomena are allowed no ontological status distinct from the behavioral events that psychological theories explain. Psychology is thus deprived of its theoretical terms except where these can be construed as nonce locutions for which behavioral reductions will eventually be provided. To all intents and purposes, this means that psychologists can provide methodologically reputable accounts only of such aspects of behavior as are the effects of environmental variables.

Not surprisingly, many psychologists have found this sort of methodology intolerably restrictive: The contribution of the organism's internal states to the causation of its own behavior seems sufficiently undisputable, given the spontaneity and freedom from local environmental control that

1

behavior often exhibits. Behaviorism thus invites us to deny the undisputable, but, in fact, we need not do so; there is an alternative that frequently gets endorsed. We can acknowledge that behavior is largely the effect of organic processes so long as we bear in mind that these processes *are* organic: i.e., that they are physiological processes located, presumably, in the nervous systems of organisms. Psychology can thus avoid behavioral reduction by opting for physiological reduction, but it must opt one way or the other.

Either way, the psychologist loses. Insofar as psychological explanations are allowed a theoretical vocabulary, it is the vocabulary of some *different* science (neurology or physiology). Insofar as there *are* laws about the ways in which behavior is contingent upon internal processes, it is the neurologist or the physiologist who will, in the long run, get to state them. However psychologists choose between the available reductions, their discipline is left without a proprietary subject matter. The best a working psychologist can hope for is an interim existence eked out between the horns of this dilemma and (just) tolerated by colleagues in the 'hard' sciences.

I think, however, that this is a false dilemma. I know of no convincing reason why a science should not seek to exhibit the contingency of an organism's behavior upon its internal states, and I know of no convincing reason why a science which succeeds in doing so should be reducible to brain science; not, at least, in the sense of reduction which would entail that psychological theories can somehow be *replaced* by their physiological counterparts. I shall try, in this introductory chapter, to show that both horns of the dilemma are, in fact, blunt. By doing so I hope to undermine a number of the arguments that are usually alleged against types of psychological explanations which, in succeeding chapters, I shall be taking very seriously indeed.

LOGICAL BEHAVIORISM

Many philosophers, and some scientists, seem to hold that the sorts of theories now widely endorsed by cognitive psychologists could not conceivably illuminate the character of mental processes. For, it is claimed, such theories assume a view of psychological explanation which is, and has been shown to be, fundamentally incoherent. The line, to put it crudely, is that Ryle and Wittgenstein killed this sort of psychology some time about 1945, and there is no point to speculating on the prospects of the deceased.

I shall not attempt a full-dress refutation of this view. If the Wittgensteinian tradition in the philosophy of mind does, indeed, offer a coherent attack upon the methodology of current cognitive psychology, it is one which depends on a complex of assumptions about the nature of explanation, the ontological status of theoretical entities, and the a priori conditions upon the possibility of linguistic communication. To meet that attack head on would require showing—what, in fact, I believe is true—that these assumptions, insofar as they are clear, are unwarranted. But that is a book's work in itself, and not a book that I feel much like writing. The best that I can do here is to sketch a preliminary defense of the methodological commitments implicit in the kind of psychological theorizing with which I shall be mainly concerned. Insofar as these commitments differ from what many philosophers have been willing to accept, even a sketch of their defense may prove to be revealing.

Among the many passages in Ryle's *Concept of Mind* (1949) that repay close attention, there is one (around p. 33) in which the cards are more than usually on the table. Ryle is discussing the question: 'What makes a clown's clowning intelligent (witty, clever, ingenious, etc.)?' The doctrine he is disapproving goes as follows: What makes the clowning intelligent is the fact that it is the consequence of certain mental operations (computations, calculations) privy to the clown and causally responsible for the production of the clown's behavior. Had these operations been other than they were, then (the doctrine claims) either the clowning would have been witless or at least it would have been witty clowning of some different kind. In short, the clown's clowning was clever in the way that it was because the mental operations upon which the clowning was causally contingent had whatever character they did have. And, though Ryle doesn't say so, it is presumably implied by this doctrine that a psychologist interested in explaining the success of the clown's performance would ipso facto be in the business of saying what those operations were and how, precisely, they were related to the overt pratfalls that the crowd saw.

Strictly speaking, this is not a single theory but a batch of closely connected ones. In particular, one can distinguish at least three claims about the character of the events upon which the clown's behavior is said to be causally contingent:

1. That some of them are mental events;
2. That some (or all) of the mental events are privy to the clown in at least the sense that they are normally unobserved by someone who observes the clown's performance, and, perhaps, also in the stronger sense that they are in principle unobservable by anyone except the clown;
3. That it is the fact that the behavior was caused by such events that makes it the kind of behavior it is; that intelligent behavior *is* intelligent because it has the kind of etiology it has.

I want to distinguish these doctrines because a psychologist might accept the sorts of theories that Ryle doesn't like without wanting to commit himself to the full implications of what Ryle calls 'Cartesianism'. For example, Ryle assumes (as most psychologists who take a Realistic view of the designata of mental terms in psychological theories would not) that a mentalist must be a dualist; in particular, that mentalism and materialism are mutually exclusive. I have argued elsewhere that confusing mentalism with dualism is the original sin of the Wittgensteinian tradition (cf. Fodor, 1968, especially Chap. 2). Suffice it to remark here that one result of this confusion is the tendency to see the options of dualism and behaviorism as exhaustive in the philosophy of mind.

Similarly, it seems to me, one might accept some such view as that of item 3 without embracing a doctrinaire reading of item 2. It may be that some of the mental processes that are causally responsible for the clown's behavior are de facto unobservable by the crowd. It may be, for that matter, that some of these processes are de facto unobservable by the clown. But there would seem to be nothing in the project of explaining behavior by reference to mental processes which requires a commitment to epistemological privacy in the traditional sense of that notion. Indeed, for better or for worse, a materialist *cannot* accept such a commitment since his view is that mental events are species of physical events, and physical events are publicly observable at least in principle.[1, 2]

It is notorious that, even granting these caveats, Ryle doesn't think this kind of account could possibly be true. For this theory says that what makes the clown's clowning clever is the fact that it is the effect of a certain kind

---

[1] The purist will note that this last point depends on the (reasonable) assumption that the context 'is publicly observable at least in principle' is transparent to substitutivity of identicals.

[2] It might be replied that if we allow the possibility that mental events might be physical events, that some mental events might be unconscious, and that no mental event is essentially private, we will have so attenuated the term 'mental' as to deprive it of all force. It is, of course, true that the very notion of a mental event is often specified in ways that presuppose dualism and/or a strong doctrine of epistemological privacy. What is unclear, however, is what we want a definition of 'mental event' *for* in the first place.

Surely not, in any event, in order that it should be possible to do psychology in a methodologically respectable way. *Pre*-theoretically we identify mental events by reference to clear cases. *Post*-theoretically it is sufficient to identify them as the ones which fall under psychological laws. This characterization is, of course, question-begging since it rests upon an unexplained distinction between psychological laws and all the others. The present point, however, is that we are in no better position vis-à-vis such notions as chemical event (or meteorological event, or geological event . . . , etc.), a state of affairs which does not prejudice the rational pursuit of chemistry. A chemical event is one that falls under chemical laws; chemical laws are those which follow from (ideally completed) chemical theories; chemical theories are theories in chemistry; and chemistry, like all other special sciences, is individualated large post facto and by reference to its typical problems and predicates. (For example, chemistry is that science which concerns itself with such matters as the combinatorial properties of elements, the analysis and synthesis of compounds, etc.) Why, precisely, is this not good enough?

of cause. But what, in Ryle's view, actually *does* make the clowning clever is something quite else: For example, the fact that it happens out where the audience can see it; the fact that the things that the clown does are not the things that the audience expected him to do; the fact that the man he hit with the pie was dressed in evening clothes, etc.

There are two points to notice. First, none of *these* facts are in any sense private to the clown. They are not even de facto private in the sense of being facts about things going on in the clown's nervous system. On the contrary, what makes the clown's clowning clever is precisely the *public* aspects of his performance; precisely the things that the audience *can* see. The second point is that what makes the clowning clever is not the character of the *causes* of the clown's behavior, but rather the character of the behavior itself. It counts for the pratfall being clever that it occurred when it wasn't expected, but its occurring when it wasn't expected surely wasn't one of its causes on any conceivable construal of 'cause'. In short, what makes the clowning clever is not some event distinct from, and causally responsible for, the behavior that the clown produces. A fortiori, it is not a mental event prior to the pratfall. Surely, then, if the mentalist program involves the identification and characterization of such an event, that program is doomed from the start.

Alas for the psychology of clever clowning. We had assumed that psychologists would identify the (mental) causes upon which clever clowning is contingent and *thereby* answer the question: 'What makes the clowning clever?' Now all that appears to be left of the enterprise is the alliterations. Nor does Ryle restrict his use of this pattern of argument to undermining the psychology of clowns. Precisely similar moves are made to show that the psychology of perception is a muddle since what makes something (e.g.) the recognition of a robin or a tune is not the occurrence of some or other mental event, but rather the fact that what was claimed to be a robin was in fact a robin, and what was taken to be a rendition of "Lillibullero" was one. It is, in fact, hard to think of an area of cognitive psychology in which this sort of argument would not apply or where Ryle does not apply it. Indeed, it is perhaps Ryle's *central* point that 'Cartesian' (i.e., mentalistic) psychological theories treat what is really a *logical* relation between aspects of a single event as though it were a causal relation between pairs of distinct events. It is this tendency to give mechanistic answers to conceptual questions which, according to Ryle, leads the mentalist to orgies of regrettable hypostasis: i.e., to attempting to explain behavior by reference to underlying psychological mechanisms.[3]

---

3 'Criterion' isn't one of Ryle's words: Nevertheless, the line of argument just reviewed relates Ryle's work closely to the criteriological tradition in post-Wittgensteinian philosophy of mind. Roughly, what in Ryle's terms "makes" *a* be *F* is *a's* possession of those properties which are criterial for the application of '*F*' to *x*s.

If this *is* a mistake I am in trouble. For it will be the pervasive assumption of my discussion that such explanations, however often they may prove to be empirically unsound, are, in principle, methodologically impeccable. What I propose to do throughout this book is to take such explanations absolutely seriously and try to sketch at least the outlines of the general picture of mental life to which they lead. So something will have to be done to meet Ryle's argument. Let's, to begin with, vary the example.

Consider the question: 'What makes Wheaties the breakfast of champions?' (Wheaties, in case anyone hasn't heard, is, or are, a sort of packaged cereal. The details are very inessential.) There are, it will be noticed, at least two kinds of answers that one might give.[4] A sketch of one answer, which belongs to what I shall call the 'causal story' might be: 'What make Wheaties the breakfast of champions are the health-giving vitamins and minerals that it contains'; or 'It's the carbohydrates in Wheaties, which give one the energy one needs for hard days on the high hurdle'; or 'It's the special springiness of all the little molecules in Wheaties, which gives Wheaties eaters their unusually high coefficient or restitution', etc.

It's not important to my point that any of these specimen answers should be true. What *is* essential is that some causal story or other must be true if Wheaties really *are* the breakfast of champions as they are claimed to be. Answers propose causal stories insofar as they seek to specify properties of Wheaties which may be causally implicated in the processes that make champions of Wheaties eaters. Very roughly, such answers suggest provisional values of P in the explanation schema: 'P causes $((x$ eats Wheaties) brings about $(x$ becomes a champion)) for significantly many values of x'. I assume that, if Wheaties *do* make champions of those who eat them, then there must be at least one value of P which makes this schema true. Since that assumption is simply the denial of the miracle theory of Wheaties, it ought not be in dispute.

---

[4] I am reading 'What makes Wheaties the breakfast of champions?' as asking 'What about Wheaties makes champions of (some, many, so many) Wheaties eaters?' rather than 'What about Wheaties makes (some, many, so many) champions eat them?' The latter question invites the reasons that champions give for eating Wheaties; and though these *may* include reference to properties Wheaties have by virtue of which its eaters become champions, they need not do so. Thus, a plausible answer to the second question which is *not* plausibly an answer to the first might be: 'They taste good'.

I am uncertain which of these questions the Wheaties people have in mind when they ask 'What makes Wheaties the breakfast of champions?' rhetorically, as, I believe, they are wont to do. Much of their advertising consists of publicizing statements by champions to the effect that they (the champions) do, in fact, eat Wheaties. If, as may be the case, such statements are offered as arguments for the truth of the presupposition of the question on its *first* reading (viz., that there *is* something about Wheaties that makes champions of those who eat them), then it would appear that General Mills has either misused the method of differences or committed the fallacy of affirmation of the consequent.

Philosophy can be made out of anything. Or less.

I suggested that there is another kind of answer that 'What makes Wheaties the breakfast of champions?' may appropriately receive. I will say that answers of this second kind belong to the 'conceptual story'. In the present case, we can tell the conceptual story with some precision: What makes Wheaties the breakfast of champions is the fact that it is eaten (for breakfast) by nonnegligible numbers of champions. This is, I take it, a conceptually necessary and sufficient condition for *anything* to be the breakfast of champions;[5] as such, it pretty much exhausts the conceptual story about Wheaties.

The point to notice is that answers that belong to the conceptual story typically do not belong to the causal story and vice versa.[6] In particular, its being eaten by nonnegligible numbers of champions does not *cause* Wheaties to be the breakfast of champions; no more than its occurring unexpectedly causes the clown's pratfall to be witty. Rather, what we have in both cases are instances of (more or less rigorous) conceptual connections. Being eaten by nonnegligible numbers of champions and being unexpected belong, respectively, to the analyses of 'being the breakfast of champions' and 'being witty', with the exception that, in the former case, we have something that approaches a logically necessary and sufficient condition and, in the latter case, we very clearly do not.[7]

The notion of conceptual connection is notoriously a philosophical miasma; all the more so if one holds (as Wittgensteinians usually do) that there are species of conceptual connections which cannot, even in principle,

---

[5] This is not quite right. Being eaten for breakfast by nonnegligible numbers of champions is a conceptually necessary and sufficient condition for something being *a* breakfast of champions (cf. Russell, 1905). Henceforth I shall resist this sort of pedantry whenever I can bring myself to do so.

[6] The exceptions are interesting. They involve cases where the conceptual conditions for something being a thing of a certain kind include the requirement that it have, or be, a certain kind of cause. I suppose, for example, that it is a conceptual truth that nothing counts as a drunken brawl unless the drunkness of the brawlers contributed causally to bringing about the brawling. See also: flu viruses, tears of rage, suicides, nervous stammers, etc. Indeed, one can imagine an analysis of 'the breakfast of champions' which would make it one of these cases too; viz, an analysis which says that it is logically necessary that the breakfast of champions is (not only what champions eat for breakfast but also) what champions eat for breakfast that is causally responsible for their being champions. But enough!

[7] It is, by the way, no accident that the latter analysis is incomplete. The usual situation is that the logically necessary and sufficient conditions for the ascription of a mental state to an organism refer not just to environmental variables but to other mental states of that organism. (For example, to *know* that *P* is to *believe* that *P* and to satisfy certain further conditions; to be *greedy* is to be disposed *to feel pleasure* at getting, or at the prospect of getting, more than one's share, etc.) The faith that there *must* be a way out of this network of interdependent mental terms—that one will surely get to pure behavioral ascriptions if only one pursues the analysis far enough—is, so far as I know, unsupported by either argument or example.

be explicated in terms of the notions of logically necessary and/or sufficient conditions. The present point, however, is that on *any* reasonable construal of conceptual connectedness, Wheaties prove that *both* the causal *and* the conceptual story can be simultaneously true, distinct answers to questions of the form: 'What makes (an) *x* (an) *F*?' To put it succinctly, the dietitian who appears on television to explain that Wheaties is the breakfast of champions because it contains vitamins is not refuted by the philosopher who observes (though not, usually, on television) that Wheaties is the breakfast of champions because champions eat it for breakfast. The dietitian, in saying what he says, does not suppose that his remarks express, or can replace, the relevant conceptual truths. The philosopher, in saying what *he* says, ought not suppose that his remarks express, or can replace, the relevant causal explanations.

In general, suppose that *C* is a conceptually sufficient condition for having the property *P,* and suppose that some individual *a* does, in brute fact, satisfy *C,* so that '*Pa*' is a contingent statement true of *a*. Then: (a) it is normally pertinent to ask for a causal/mechanistic explanation of the fact that '*Pa*' *is* true; (b) such an explanation will normally constitute a (candidate) answer to the question: 'What makes *a* exhibit the property *P*?'; (c) referring to the fact that *a* satisfies *C* will normally *not* constitute a causal/mechanistic explanation of the fact that *a* exhibits the property *P*; although, (d) references to the fact that *a* satisfies *C* may constitute a certain (different) kind of answer to 'What makes '*Pa*' true?' I take it that, barring the looseness of the notion of a conceptual connection (and, for that matter, the looseness of the notion of a causal explanation) this pattern applies in the special case where *C* is the property of being unexpected, *a* is a pratfall, and '*Pa*' is the statement that *a* was witty.

To put this point as generally as I know how, even if the behaviorists were right in supposing that logically necessary and sufficient conditions for behavior being of a certain kind can be given (just) in terms of stimulus and response variables, that fact would not in the least prejudice the mentalist's claim that the *causation* of behavior is determined by, and explicable in terms of, the organism's internal states. So far as I know, the philosophical school of 'logical' behaviorism offers not a shadow of an argument for believing that this claim is false. And the failure of behavioristic psychology to provide even a first approximation to a plausible theory of cognition suggests that the mentalist's claim may very well be true.

The arguments we have been considering are directed against a kind of reductionism which seeks to show, somehow or other, that the mental events that psychological explanations appeal to cannot be causal antecedents of the behavioral events that psychological theories seek to account for; a fortiori that statements which attribute the intelligence of a performance to the quality of the agent's cerebrations can't be etiological. The recurrent theme in this sort of reductionism is the allegation of a conceptual connection between the behavioral and the mental predicates in typical instances of psychological explanations. It is from the existence of this connection that the second-class ontological status of mental events is inferred.

It should be clear by now that I don't think that this sort of argument will go through. I shall therefore assume, in what follows, that psychologists are typically in the business of supplying theories about the events that causally mediate the production of behavior and that cognitive psychologists are typically in the business of supplying theories about the events that causally mediate the production of intelligent behavior. There is, of course, no guarantee that this game can be played. It is quite conceivable that the kinds of concepts in terms of which current psychological theories are elaborated *will* turn out, in the long run, to be unsuitable for the explanation of behavior. It is, for that matter, quite conceivable that the mental processes which mediate the production of behavior are just too complicated for anyone to understand. One never can show, a priori, that a program of empirical research will certainly prove fruitful. My point has been only that the logical behaviorists have provided no a priori reason to suppose that the mentalist program in psychology will not.

Still, if mental events aren't to be reduced to behavioral events, what *are* we to say about their ontological status? I think it is very likely that all of the organismic causes of behavior are physiological, hence that mental events have true descriptions in the vocabulary of an ideally completed physiology. But I do not think that it is interesting that I think this. In particular, I don't suppose that it even begins to follow from this sort of materialism that any branch of physiology does or could supply the appropriate vocabulary for the construction of psychological theories. The likelihood that psychological events are physiological events does not entail the reducibility of psychology to physiology, ever so many philosophers and physiologists to the contrary notwithstanding. To see why this is so requires a fairly extensive discussion of the whole idea of interscience reduction, a notion which has done as much to obscure the methodology of psychology as any other except, perhaps, the verifiability criterion of meaning.

PHYSIOLOGICAL REDUCTIONISM

A typical thesis of positivistic philosophy of science is that all true theories in the special sciences should reduce to physical theories 'in the long run'. This is intended to be an empirical thesis, and part of the evidence which supports it is provided by such scientific successes as the molecular theory of heat and the physical explanation of the chemical bond. But the philosophical popularity of the reductionist program cannot be explained by reference to these achievements alone. The development of science has witnessed the proliferation of specialized disciplines at least as often as it has witnessed their elimination, so the widespread enthusiasm for the view that there will eventually be only physics can hardly be a mere induction over past reductionist successes.

I think that many philosophers who accept reductionism do so primarily because they wish to endorse the generality of physics vis-à-vis the special sciences: roughly, the view that all events which fall under the laws of any science are physical events and hence fall under the laws of physics.[8] For such philosophers, saying that physics is basic science and saying that theories in the special sciences must reduce to physical theories have seemed to be two ways of saying the same thing, so that the latter doctrine has come to be a standard construal of the former.

In what follows, I shall argue that this is a considerable confusion. What has traditionally been called 'the unity of science' is a much stronger, and much less plausible, thesis than the generality of physics. If this is true it is important. Though reductionism is an empirical doctrine, it is intended to play a regulative role in scientific practice. Reducibility to physics is taken to be a *constraint* upon the acceptability of theories in the special sciences, with the curious consequence that the more the special sciences succeed, the more they ought to disappear. Methodological problems about psychology, in particular, arise in just this way: The assumption that the subject matter of psychology is part of the subject matter of physics is taken to imply that psychological theories must reduce to physical theories, and it is this latter principle that makes the trouble. I want to avoid the trouble by challenging the inference.

Reductionism is the view that all the special sciences reduce to physics. The sense of 'reduce to' is, however, proprietary. It can be characterized as follows.[9]

Let formula (1) be a law of the special science S.

(1) $S_1x \rightarrow S_2y$

Formula (1) is intended to be read as something like 'all events which consist of x's being S_1 bring about events which consist of y's being S_2'. I

---

[8] For expository convenience, I shall usually assume that sciences are about events in at least the sense that it is the occurrence of events that makes the laws of a science true. Nothing, however, hangs on this assumption.

[9] The version of reductionism I shall be concerned with is a stronger one than many philosophers of science hold, a point worth emphasizing since my argument will be precisely that it is too strong to get away with. Still, I think that what I shall be attacking is what many people have in mind when they refer to the unity of science, and I suspect (though I shan't try to prove it) that many of the liberalized versions of reductionism suffer from the same basic defect as what I shall take to be the classical form of the doctrine.

assume that a science is individuated largely by reference to its typical predicates (see footnote 2 above), hence that if S is a special science 'S_1' and 'S_2' are not predicates of basic physics. (I also assume that the 'all' which quantifies laws of the special sciences needs to be taken with a grain of salt. Such laws are typically *not* exceptionless. This is a point to which I shall return at length.) A necessary and sufficient condition for the reduction of formula (1) to a law of physics is that the formulae (2) and (3) should be laws, and a necessary and sufficient condition for the reduction

(2a) $S_1x \rightleftharpoons P_1x$
(2b) $S_2y \rightleftharpoons P_2y$
(3) $P_1x \rightarrow P_2y$

of S to physics is that all its laws should be so reduced.[10]

'P_1' and 'P_2' are supposed to be predicates of physics, and formula (3) is supposed to be a physical law. Formulae like (2) are often called 'bridge' laws. Their characteristic feature is that they contain predicates of both the reduced and the reducing science. Bridge laws like formula (2) are thus contrasted with 'proper' laws like formulae (1) and (3). The upshot of the remarks so far is that the reduction of a science requires that any formula which appears as the antecedent or consequent of one of its proper laws must appear as the reduced formula in some bridge law or other.[11]

Several points about the connective '$\rightarrow$' are now in order. First, whatever properties that connective may have, it is universally agreed that it must be transitive. This is important because it is usually assumed that the reduction of some of the special sciences proceeds via bridge laws which connect their predicates with those of intermediate reducing theories. Thus, psychology is presumed to reduce to physics via, say, neurology, biochemistry, and other local stops. The present point is that this makes no difference to the logic of the situation so long as the transitivity of '$\rightarrow$' is assumed. Bridge laws which connect the predicates of S to those of S^* will satisfy the constraints upon the reduction of S to physics so long as there are other bridge laws which, directly or indirectly, connect the predicates of S^* to physical predicates.

There are, however, quite serious open questions about the interpreta-

---

[10] There is an implicit assumption that a science simply *is* a formulation of a set of laws. I think that this assumption is implausible, but it is usually made when the unity of science is discussed, and it is neutral so far as the main argument of this chapter is concerned.

[11] I shall sometimes refer to 'the predicate which constitutes the antecedent or consequent of a law'. This is shorthand for 'the predicate such that the antecedent or consequent of a law consists of that predicate, together with its bound variables and the quantifiers which bind them'. (Truth functions of elementary predicates are, of course, themselves predicates in this usage.)

tion of '→' in bridge laws. What turns on these questions is the extent to which reductionism is taken to be a physicalist thesis.

To begin with, if we read '→' as 'brings about' or 'causes' in proper laws, we will have to have some other connective for bridge laws, since bringing about and causing are presumably *a*symmetric, while bridge laws express symmetric relations. Moreover, unless bridge laws hold by virtue of the *identity* of the events which satisfy their antecedents with those that satisfy their consequents, reductionism will guarantee only a weak version of physicalism, and this would fail to express the underlying ontological bias of the reductionist program.

If bridge laws are not identity statements, then formulae like (2) claim at most that, by law, x's satisfaction of a P predicate and x's satisfaction of an S predicate are causally correlated. It follows from this that it is nomologically necessary that S and P predicates apply to the same things (i.e., that S predicates apply to a subset of the things that P predicates apply to). But, of course, this is compatible with a nonphysicalist ontology since it is compatible with the possibilty that x's satsfying S should not itself be a physical event. On this interpretation, the truth of reductionism does *not* guarantee the generality of physics vis-à-vis the special sciences since there are some events (satisfactions of S predicates) which fall in the domains of a special science (S) but not in the domain of physics. (One could imagine, for example, a doctrine according to which physical and psychological predicates are both held to apply to organisms, but where it is denied that the event which consists of an organism's satisfying a psychological predicate is, in any sense, a physical event. The upshot would be a kind of psychophysical dualism of a non-Cartesian variety; a dualism of events and/or properties rather than substances.)

Given these sorts of considerations, many philosophers have held that bridge laws like formula (2) ought to be taken to express contingent event identities, so that one would read formula (2a) in some such fashion as 'every event which consists of an x's satisfying S_1 is identical to some event which consists of that x's satisfying P_1 and vice versa'. On this reading, the truth of reductionism would entail that every event that falls under any scientific law is a physical event, thereby simultaneously expressing the ontological bias of reductionism and guaranteeing the generality of physics vis-à-vis the special sciences.

If the bridge laws express event identities, and if every event that falls under the proper laws of a special science falls under a bridge law, we get classical reductionism, a doctrine that entails the truth of what I shall call 'token physicalism'. Token physicalism is simply the claim that all the events that the sciences talk about are physical events. There are three things to notice about token physicalism.

First, it is weaker than what is usually called 'materialism'. Materialism claims *both* that token physicalism is true *and* that every event falls under the laws of some science or other. One could therefore be a token physicalist without being a materialist, though I don't see why anyone would bother.

Second, token physicalism is weaker than what might be called 'type physicalism', the doctrine, roughly, that every *property* mentioned in the laws of any science is a physical property. Token physicalism does not entail type physicalism, if only because the contingent identity of a pair of events presumably does not guarantee the identity of the properties whose instantiation constitutes the events; not even when the event identity is nomologically necessary. On the other hand, if an event is simply the instantiation of a property, then type physicalism does entail token physicalism; two events will be identical when they consist of the instantiation of the same property by the same individual at the same time.

Third, token physicalism is weaker than reductionism. Since this point is, in a certain sense, the burden of the argument to follow, I shan't labor it here. But, as a first approximation, reductionism is the conjunction of token physicalism with the assumption that there are natural kind predicates in an ideally completed physics which correspond to each natural kind predicate in any ideally completed special science. It will be one of my morals that reductionism cannot be inferred from the assumption that token physicalism is true. Reductionism is a sufficient, but not a necessary, condition for token physicalism.

To summarize: I shall be reading reductionism as entailing token physicalism since, if bridge laws state nomologically necessary contingent event identities, a reduction of psychology to neurology would require that any event which consists of the instantiation of a psychological property is identical with some event which consists of the instantiation of a neurological property. Both reductionism and token physicalism entail the generality of physics, since both hold that any event which falls within the universe of discourse of a special science will also fall within the universe of discourse of physics. Moreover, it is a consequence of both doctrines that any prediction which follows from the laws of a special science (and a statement of initial conditions) will follow equally from a theory which consists only of physics and the bridge laws (together with the statement of initial conditions). Finally, it is assumed by both reductionism and token physicalism that physics is the *only* basic science; *viz,* that it is the only science that is general in the senses just specified.

·I now want to argue that reductionism is too strong a constraint upon the unity of science, but that, for any reasonable purposes, the weaker doctrine will do.

Every science implies a taxonomy of the events in its universe of discourse. In particular, every science employs a descriptive vocabulary of theoretical and observation predicates, such that events fall under the laws of the science by virtue of satisfying those predicates. Patently, not every true description of an event is a description in such a vocabulary. For example, there are a large number of events which consist of things having been transported to a distance of less than three miles from the Eiffel Tower. I take it, however, that there is no science which contains 'is transported to a distance of less than three miles from the Eiffel Tower' as part of its descriptive vocabulary. Equivalently, I take it that there is no natural law which applies to events in virtue of their instantiating the property *is transported to a distance of less than three miles from the Eiffel Tower* (though I suppose it is just conceivable that there is some law that applies to events in virtue of their instantiating some distinct but coextensive property). By way of abbreviating these facts, I shall say that the property *is transported* . . . does not determine a (*natural*) *kind,* and that predicates which express that property are not (natural) kind predicates.

If I knew what a law is, and if I believed that scientific theories consist just of bodies of laws, then I could say that '*P*' is a kind predicate relative to S iff S contains proper laws of the form '$P_x \rightarrow \ldots y$' or '$\ldots y \rightarrow P_x$': roughly, the kind predicates of a science are the ones whose terms are the bound variables in its proper laws. I am inclined to say this even in my present state of ignorance, accepting the consequence that it makes the murky notion of a kind viciously dependent on the equally murky notions of *law* and *theory*. There is no firm footing here. If we disagree about what a kind is, we will probably also disagree about what a law is, and for the same reasons. I don't know how to break out of this circle, but I think that there are some interesting things to say about which circle we are in.

For example, we can now characterize the respect in which reductionism is too strong a construal of the doctrine of the unity of science. If reductionism is true, then *every* kind is, or is coextensive with, a physical kind. (Every kind *is* a physical kind if bridge statements express nomologically necessary property identities, and every kind is coextensive with a physical kind if bridge statements express nomologically necessary event identities.) This follows immediately from the reductionist premise that every predicate which appears as the antecedent or consequent of a law of a special science must appear as one of the reduced predicates in some bridge law, together with the assumption that the kind predicates are the ones whose terms are the bound variables in proper laws. If, in short, some physical law is related to each law of a special science in the way that formula (3) is related to formula (1), then every kind predicate of a special science is related to a kind predicate of physics in the way that formula (2) relates 'S_1' and 'S_2' to 'P_1' and 'P_2' respectively.

I now want to suggest some reasons for believing that this consequence is intolerable. These are not supposed to be knock-down reasons; they couldn't be, given that the question of whether reductionism is too strong is finally an *empirical* question. (The world could turn out to be such that every kind corresponds to a physical kind, just as it could turn out to be such that the property *is transported to a distance of less than three miles from the Eiffel Tower* determines a kind in, say, hydrodynamics. It's just that, as things stand, it seems very unlikely that the world *will* turn out to be either of these ways.)

The reason it is unlikely that every kind corresponds to a physical kind is just that (a) interesting generalizations (e.g., counterfactual supporting generalizations) can often be made about events whose physical descriptions have nothing in common; (b) it is often the case that *whether* the physical descriptions of the events subsumed by such generalizations have anything in common is, in an obvious sense, entirely irrelevant to the truth of the generalizations, or to their interestingness, or to their degree of confirmation, or, indeed, to any of their epistemologically important properties; and (c) the special sciences are very much in the business of formulating generalizations of this kind.

I take it that these remarks are obvious to the point of self-certification; they leap to the eye as soon as one makes the (apparently radical) move of taking the existence of the special sciences at all seriously. Suppose, for example, that Gresham's 'law' really is true. (If one doesn't like Gresham's law, then any true and counterfactual supporting generalization of any conceivable future economics will probably do as well.) Gresham's law says something about what will happen in monetary exchanges under certain conditions. I am willing to believe that physics is general *in the sense that it implies that any event which consists of a monetary exchange* (hence any event which falls under Gresham's law) *has a true description in the vocabulary of physics and in virtue of which it falls under the laws of physics.* But banal considerations suggest that a physical description which covers all such events must be wildly disjunctive. Some monetary exchanges involve strings of wampum. Some involve dollar bills. And some involve signing one's name to a check. What are the chances that a disjunction of physical predicates which covers all these events (i.e., a disjunctive predicate which can form the right hand side of a bridge law of the form '*x* is a monetary exchange $\rightleftharpoons$ . . .') expresses a physical kind? In particular, what are the chances that such a predicate forms the antecedent or consequent of some proper law of physics? The point is that monetary exchanges have interesting things in common; Gresham's law, if true, says what one of these interesting things is. But what is interesting about monetary exchanges is surely not their commonalities under *physical* description. A kind like a monetary exchange *could* turn out to be coextensive with a physical kind; but if it did, that would be an accident on a cosmic scale.

In fact, the situation for reductionism is still worse than the discussion thus far suggests. For reductionism claims not only that all kinds are coextensive with physical kinds, but that the coextensions are nomologically necessary: bridge laws are *laws*. So, if Gresham's law is true, it follows that there is a (bridge) law of nature such that '*x* is a monetary exchange $\rightleftharpoons$ *x* is P' is true for every value of x, and such that P is a term for a physical kind. But, surely, there is no such law. If there were, then P would have to cover not only all the systems of monetary exchange that there *are*, but also all the systems of monetary exchange that there *could be*; a law must succeed with the counterfactuals. What physical predicate is a candidate for P in 'x is a nomologically possible monetary exchange iff P_x'?

To summarize: An immortal econophysicist might, when the whole show is over, find a predicate in physics that was, in brute fact, coextensive with 'is a monetary exchange'. If physics is general—if the ontological biases of reductionism are true—then there must *be* such a predicate. But (a) to paraphrase a remark Professor Donald Davidson made in a slightly different context, nothing but brute enumeration could convince us of this brute coextensivity, and (b) there would seem to be no chance at all that the physical predicate employed in stating the coextensivity would be a physical kind term, and (c) there is still less chance that the coextension would be lawful (i.e., that it would hold not only for the nomologically possible world that turned out to be real, but for any nomologically possible world at all).[12]

---

[12] Oppenheim and Putnam (1958) argue that the social sciences probably *can* be reduced to physics assuming that the reduction proceeds via (individual) psychology. Thus, they remark, "in economics, if very weak assumptions are satisfied, it is possible to represent the way in which an individual orders his choices by means of an individual preference function. In terms of these functions, the economist attempts to explain group phenomena, such as the market, to account for collective consumer behavior, to solve the problems of welfare economics, etc." (p. 17). They seem not to have noticed, however, that even if such explanations can be carried through, they would not yield the kind of *predicate-by-predicate* reduction of economics to psychology that Oppenheim and Putnam's own account of the unity of science requires.

Suppose that the laws of economics hold because people have the attitudes, motives, goals, needs, strategies, etc., that they do. Then the fact that economics is the way it is can be explained by reference to the fact that people are the way that they are. But it doesn't begin to follow that the typical predicates of economics can be reduced to the typical predicates of psychology. Since bridge laws entail biconditionals, P_1 reduces to P_2 only if P_1 and P_2 are at least coextensive. But while the typical predicates of economics subsume (e.g.) monetary systems, cash flows, commodities, labor pools, amounts of capital invested, etc., the typical predicates of psychology subsume stimuli, responses, and mental states. Given the proprietary sense of 'reduction' at issue, to reduce economics to psychology would therefore involve a very great deal more than showing that the economic behavior of groups is determined by the psychology of the individuals that constitute them. In particular, it would involve showing that such notions as *commodity, labor pool,* etc., can be reconstructed in the vocabulary of stimuli, responses and mental states and that, moreover, the predicates which affect the reconstruction express psychological kinds (viz., occur in the proper laws of psychology). I think it's fair to say that there is no reason at all to suppose that such reconstructions can be provided; prima facie there is every reason to think that they cannot.

I take it that the preceding discussion strongly suggests that economics is not reducible to physics in the special sense of reduction involved in claims for the unity of science. There is, I suspect, nothing peculiar about economics in this respect; the reasons why economics is unlikely to reduce to physics are paralleled by those which suggest that psychology is unlikely to reduce to neurology.

If psychology is reducible to neurology, then for every psychological kind predicate there is a coextensive neurological kind predicate, and the generalization which states this coextension is a law. Clearly, many psychologists believe something of the sort. There are departments of psychobiology or psychology and brain science in universities throughout the world whose very existence is an institutionalized gamble that such lawful coextensions can be found. Yet, as has been frequently remarked in recent discussions of materialism, there are good grounds for hedging these bets. There are no firm data for any but the grossest correspondence between types of psychological states and types of neurological states, and it is entirely possible that the nervous system of higher organisms characteristically achieves a given psychological end by a wide variety of neurological means. It is also possible that given neurological structures subserve many different psychological functions at different times, depending upon the character of the activities in which the organism is engaged.[13] In either event, the attempt to pair neurological structures with psychological functions could expect only limited success. Physiological psychologists of the stature of Karl Lashley have held this sort of view.

The present point is that the reductionist program in psychology is clearly *not* to be defended on ontological grounds. Even if (token) psychological events are (token) neurological events, it does not follow that the kind predicates of psychology are coextensive with the kind predicates of any other discipline (including physics). That is, the assumption that every psychological event is a physical event does not guarantee that physics (or, a fortiori, any other discipline more general than psychology) can provide an appropriate vocabulary for psychological theories. I emphasize this point because I am convinced that the make-or-break commitment of many physiological psychologists to the reductionist program stems precisely from having confused that program with (token) physicalism.

What I have been doubting is that there are neurological kinds coextensive with psychological kinds. What seems increasingly clear is that, even if there are such coextensions, they cannot be lawful. For it seems increas-

---

13 This would be the case if higher organisms really are interestingly analogous to general purpose computers. Such machines exhibit no detailed structure-to-function correspondence over time; rather, the function subserved by a given structure may change from instant to instant depending upon the character of the program and of the computation being performed.

ingly likely that there are nomologically possible systems other than organisms (viz., automata) which satisfy the kind predicates of psychology but which satisfy no neurological predicates at all. Now, as Putnam has emphasized (1960a, b), if there are any such systems, then there must be vast numbers, since equivalent automata can, in principle, be made out of practically anything. If this observation is correct, then there can be no serious hope that the class of automata whose psychology is effectively identical to that of some organism can be described by *physical* kind predicates (though, of course, if token physicalism is true, that class can be picked out by some physical predicate or other). The upshot is that the classical formulation of the unity of science is at the mercy of progress in the field of computer simulation. This is, of course, simply to say that that formulation was too strong. The unity of science was intended to be an empirical hypothesis, defeasible by possible scientific findings. But no one had it in mind that it should be defeated by Newell, Shaw, and Simon.

I have thus far argued that psychological reductionism (the doctrine that every psychological natural kind is, or is coextensive with, a neurological natural kind) is not equivalent to, and cannot be inferred from, token physicalism (the doctrine that every psychological event is a neurological event). It may, however, be argued that one might as well take the doctrines to be equivalent since the only possible *evidence* one could have for token physicalism would also be evidence for reductionism: viz., that such evidence would have to consist in the discovery of type-to-type psychophysical correlations.

A moment's consideration shows, however, that this argument is not well taken. If type-to-type psychophysical correlations would be evidence for token physicalism, so would correlations of other specifiable kinds.

We have type-to-type correlations where, for every n-tuple of events that are of the same psychological kind, there is a correlated n-tuple of events that are of the same neurological kind.[14] Imagine a world in which such correlations are *not* forthcoming. What is found, instead, is that for every n-tuple of type identical psychological events, there is a spatiotemporally correlated n-tuple of type *distinct* neurological events. That is, every psychological event is paired with some neurological event or other, but psychological events of the same kind are sometimes paired with neurological events of different kinds. My present point is that such pairings would provide as much support for token physicalism as type-to-type pairings do *so long as we are able to show that the type distinct neurological events paired with a given kind of psychological event are identical in respect of whatever properties are relevant to type identification in psychology.* Suppose, for purposes of explication, that psychological events are type identi-

[14] To rule out degenerate cases, we assume that n is large enough to yield correlations that are significant in the statistical sense.

fied by reference to their behavioral consequences.[15] Then what is required of all the neurological events paired with a class of type homogeneous psychological events is only that they be identical in respect of their behavioral consequences. To put it briefly, type identical events do not, of course, have *all* their properties in common, and type distinct events must nevertheless be identical in *some* of their properties. The empirical confirmation of token physicalism does not depend on showing that the neurological counterparts of type identical psychological events are themselves type identical. What needs to be shown is just that they are identical in respect of those properties which determine what kind of *psychological* event a given event is.

Could we have evidence that an otherwise heterogeneous set of neurological events have those kinds of properties in common? Of course we could. The neurological theory might itself explain why an *n*-tuple of neurologically type distinct events are identical in their behavioral consequences, or, indeed, in respect of any of indefinitely many other such relational properties. And, if the neurological theory failed to do so, some science more basic than neurology might succeed.

My point in all this is, once again, not that correlations between type homogeneous psychological states and type heterogeneous neurological states would prove that token physicalism is true. It is only that such correlations might give us as much reason to be token physicalists as type-to-type correlations would. If this is correct, then epistemological arguments from token physicalism to reductionism must be wrong.

It seems to me (to put the point quite generally) that the classical construal of the unity of science has really badly misconstrued the *goal* of scientific reduction. The point of reduction is *not* primarily to find some natural kind predicate of physics coextensive with each kind predicate of a special science. It is, rather, to explicate the physical mechanisms whereby events conform to the laws of the special sciences. I have been arguing that there is no logical or epistemological reason why success in the second of these projects should require success in the first, and that the two are likely to come apart *in fact* wherever the physical mechanisms whereby events conform to a law of the special sciences are heterogeneous.

I take it that the discussion thus far shows that reductionism is probably too strong a construal of the unity of science; on the one hand, it is incompatible with probable results in the special sciences, and, on the other, it is more than we need to assume if what we primarily want, from an ontological point of view, is just to be good token physicalists. In what follows, I shall try to sketch a liberalized version of the relation between physics and

[15] I don't think there is any chance at all that this is true. What is more likely is that type identification for psychological states can be carried out in terms of the 'total states' of an abstract automaton which models the organism whose states they are. For discussion, see Block and Fodor (1972).

the special sciences which seems to me to be just strong enough in these respects. I shall then give a couple of independent reasons for supposing that the revised doctrine may be the right one.

The problem all along has been that there is an open empirical possibility that what corresponds to the kind predicates of a reduced science may be a heterogeneous and unsystematic disjunction of predicates in the reducing science. We do not want the unity of science to be prejudiced by this possibility. Suppose, then, that we allow that bridge statements may be of this form,

$$(4) \quad Sx \rightleftharpoons P_1x \lor P_2x \lor \ldots \lor P_nx$$

where $P_1 \lor P_2 \lor \ldots \lor P_n$ is *not* a kind predicate in the reducing science. I take it that this is tantamount to allowing that at least some 'bridge laws' may, in fact, not turn out to be laws, since I take it that a necessary condition on a universal generalization being lawlike is that the predicates which constitute its antecedent and consequent should be kind predicates. I am thus assuming that it is enough, for purposes of the unity of science, that every law of the special sciences should be reducible to physics by bridge statements which express true empirical generalizations. Bearing in mind that bridge statements are to be construed as species of identity statements, formula (4) will be read as something like 'every event which consists of x's satisfying S is identical with some event which consists of x's satisfying some or other predicate belonging to the disjunction $P_1 \lor P_2 \lor \ldots \lor P_n$'.

Now, in cases of reduction where what corresponds to formula (2) is not a law, what corresponds to formula (3) will not be either, and for the

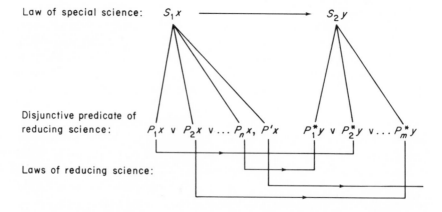

Figure I-1 Schematic representation of the proposed relation between the reduced and the reducing science on a revised account of the unity of science. If any S_1 events are of the type P', they will be exceptions to the law $S_1x \rightarrow S_2y$. See text.

same reason: viz., the predicates appearing in the antecedent and consequent will, by hypothesis, not be kind predicates. Rather, what we will have is something that looks like Figure I-1. That is, the antecedent and consequent of the reduced law will each be connected with a disjunction of predicates in the reducing science. Suppose, for the moment, that the reduced law is exceptionless, viz., that no S_1 events satisfy P'. Then there will be laws of the reducing science which connect the satisfaction of *each* member of the disjunction associated with the antecedent of the reduced law with the satisfaction of some member of the disjunction associated with the consequent of the reduced law. That is, if $S_1x \rightarrow S_2y$ is exceptionless, then there must be some proper law of the reducing science which either states or entails that $P_1x \rightarrow P^*$ for some P^*, and similarly for P_2x through P_nx. Since there must be such laws, and since each of them is a 'proper' law in the sense in which we have been using that term, it follows that each disjunct of P_1 v P_2 v . . . v P_n is a kind predicate, as is each disjunct of P^*_1 v P^*_2 v . . . v P^*_n.

This, however, is where push comes to shove. For it might be argued that if each disjunct of the P disjunction is lawfully connected to some disjunct of the P^* disjunction, then it follows that formula (5) is itself a law.

(5) P_1x v P_2x v . . . v $P_nx \rightarrow P^*_1y$ v P^*_2y v . . . v P^*_ny

The point would be that the schema in Figure I-1 implies $P_1x \rightarrow P^*_2y$, $P_2x \rightarrow P^*_my$, etc., and the argument from a premise of the form $(P \supset R)$ *and* $(Q \supset S)$ to a conclusion of the form $(P$ v $Q) \supset (R$ v $S)$ is valid.

What I am inclined to say about this is that it just shows that 'it's a law that _____' defines a nontruth functional context (or, equivalently for these purposes, that not all truth functions of kind predicates are themselves kind predicates); in particular, that one may not argue from: 'it's a law that P brings about R' and 'it's a law that Q brings about S' to 'it's a law that P or Q brings about R or S'. (Though, of course, the argument from those premises to 'P or Q brings about R or S' *simpliciter* is fine.) I think, for example, that it is a law that the irradiation of green plants by sunlight causes carbohydrate synthesis, and I think that it is a law that friction causes heat, but I do not think that it is a law that (either the irradiation of green plants by sunlight or friction) causes (either carbohydrate synthesis or heat). Correspondingly, I doubt that 'is either carbohydrate synthesis or heat' is plausibly taken to be a kind predicate.

It is not strictly mandatory that one should agree with all this, but one denies it at a price. In particular, if one allows the full range of truth-functional arguments inside the context 'it's a law that _____', then one gives up the possibility of identifying the kind predicates of a science with the ones which constitute the antecedents or consequents of its proper laws. (Thus formula (5) would be a proper law of physics which fails to satisfy that condition.) One thus inherits the need for an alternative construal of the notion of a kind, and I don't know what that alternative would be like.

The upshot seems to be this. If we do not require that bridge statements must be laws, then either some of the generalizations to which the laws of special sciences reduce are not themselves lawlike, or some laws are not formulable in terms of kinds. Whichever way one takes formula (5) the important point is that the relation between sciences proposed by Figure I-1 is weaker than what standard reductionism requires. In particular, it does not imply a correspondence between the kind predicates of the reduced and the reducing science. Yet it does imply physicalism given the same assumption that makes standard reductionism physicalistic: viz., that bridge statements express token event identities. But these are precisely the properties that we wanted a revised account of the unity of science to exhibit.

I now want to give two further reasons for thinking that this construal of the unity of science is right. First, it allows us to see how the laws of the special sciences could reasonably have exceptions, and, second, it allows us us to see why there are special sciences at all. These points in turn.

Consider, again, the model of reduction implicit in formulae (2) and (3). I assume that the laws of basic science are strictly exceptionless, and I assume that it is common knowledge that the laws of the special sciences are not. But now we have a dilemma to face. Since ' $\rightarrow$ ' expresses a relation (or relations) which must be transitive, formula (1) can have exceptions only if the bridge laws do. But if the bridge laws have exceptions, reductionism loses its ontological bite, since we can no longer say that every event which consists of the satisfaction of an S-predicate consists of the satisfaction of a P-predicate. In short, given the reductionist model, we cannot consistently assume that the bridge laws and the basic laws are exceptionless while assuming that the special laws are not. But we cannot accept the violation of the bridge laws unless we are willing to vitiate the ontological claim that is the main point of the reductionist program.

We can get out of this (*salve* the reductionist model) in one of two ways. We can give up the claim that the special laws have exceptions or we can give up the claim that the basic laws are exceptionless. I suggest that both alternatives are undesirable—the first because it flies in the face of fact. There is just no chance at all that the true, counterfactual supporting generalizations of, say, psychology, will turn out to hold in strictly each and every condition where their antecedents are satisfied. Even when the spirit is willing the flesh is often weak. There are always going to be behavioral lapses which are physiologically explicable but which are uninteresting from the point of view of psychological theory. But the second alternative is not much better. It may, after all, turn out that the laws of basic science have exceptions. But the question arises whether one wants the unity of science to depend on the assumption that they do.

On the account summarized in Figure I-1, however, everything works out satisfactorily. A nomologically sufficient condition for an exception to $S_1x \rightarrow S_2y$ is that the bridge statements should identify some occurrence of the satisfaction of S_1 with an occurrence of the satisfaction of a P-predicate which is not itself lawfully connected to the satisfaction of any P^*-predicate (i.e., suppose S_1 is connected to P' such that there is no law which connects P' to any predicate which bridge statements associate with S_2. Then any instantiation of S_1 which is contingently identical to an instantiation of P' will be an event which constitutes an exception to $S_1x \rightarrow S_2y$). Notice that, in this case, we need assume no exceptions to the laws of the *reducing* science since, by hypothesis, formula (5) is not a law.

In fact, strictly speaking, formula (5) has no status in the reduction at all. It is simply what one gets when one universally quantifies a formula whose antecedent is the physical disjunction corresponding to S_1 and whose consequent is the physical disjunction corresponding to S_2. As such, it will be true when $S_1x \rightarrow S_2y$ is exceptionless and false otherwise. What does the work of expressing the physical mechanisms whereby n-tuples of events conform, or fail to conform, to $S_1x \rightarrow S_2y$ is not formula (5) but the laws which severally relate elements of the disjunction P_1 v P_2 v . . . v P_n to elements of the disjunction P^*_1 v P^*_2 v . . . v P^*_m. Where there *is* a law which relates an event that satisfies one of the P disjuncts to an event which satisfies one of the P^* disjuncts, the pair of events so related conforms to $S_1x \rightarrow S_2y$. When an event which satisfies a P-predicate is not related by law to an event which satisfies a P^*-predicate, that event will constitute an exception to $S_1x \rightarrow S_2y$. The point is that none of the laws which effect these several connections need themselves have exceptions in order that $S_1x \rightarrow S_2y$ should do so.

To put this discussion less technically: We could, if we liked, *require* the taxonomies of the special sciences to correspond to the taxonomy of physics by insisting upon distinctions between the kinds postulated by the former whenever they turn out to correspond to distinct kinds in the latter. This would *make* the laws of the special sciences exceptionless if the laws of basic science are. But it would also likely loose us precisely the generalizations which we want the special sciences to express. (If economics were to posit as many *kinds* of monetary systems as there are physical realizations of monetary systems, then the generalizations of economics *would* be exceptionless. But, presumably, only vacuously so, since there would be no generalizations left for economists to state. Gresham's law, for example, would have to be formulated as a vast, open disjunction about what happens in monetary system$_1$ or monetary system$_n$ under conditions which would themselves defy uniform characterization. We would not be able to say what happens in monetary systems *tout court* since, by hypothesis, 'is a monetary system' corresponds to no kind predicate of physics.)

In fact, what we do is precisely the reverse. We allow the generalizations of the special sciences to *have* exceptions, thus preserving the kinds to which the generalizations apply. But since we know that the *physical* descriptions of the members of these kinds may be quite heterogeneous, and since we know that the physical mechanisms which connect the satisfaction of the antecedents of such generalizations to the satisfaction of their consequents may be equally diverse, we expect both that there will be exceptions to the generalizations and that these will be 'explained away' at the level of the reducing science. This is one of the respects in which physics really is assumed to be bedrock science; exceptions to *its* generalizations (if there are any) had better be random, because there is nowhere 'further down' to go in explaining the mechanism whereby the exceptions occur.

This brings us to why there are special sciences at all. Reductionism, as we remarked at the outset, flies in the face of the facts about the scientific institution: the existence of a vast and interleaved conglomerate of special scientific disciplines which often appear to proceed with only the most casual acknowledgment of the constraint that their theories must turn out to be physics 'in the long run'. I mean that the acceptance of this constraint often plays little or no role in the practical validation of theories. Why is this so? Presumably, the reductionist answer must be *entirely* epistemological. If only physical particles weren't so small (if only brains were on the *out*side, where one can get a look at them), *then* we would do physics instead of paleontology (neurology instead of psychology, psychology instead of economics, and so on down). There is an epistemological reply: viz., that even if brains were out where they could be looked *at,* we wouldn't, as things now stand, know what to look *for.* We lack the appropriate theoretical apparatus for the psychological taxonomy of neurological events.

If it turns out that the functional decomposition of the nervous system corresponds precisely to its neurological (anatomical, biochemical, physical) decomposition, then there are only epistemological reasons for studying the former instead of the latter. But suppose that there is no such correspondence? Suppose the functional organization of the nervous system cross-cuts its neurological organization. Then the existence of psychology depends not on the fact that neurons are so depressingly small, but rather on the fact that neurology does not posit the kinds that psychology requires.

I am suggesting, roughly, that there are special sciences not because of the nature of our epistemic relation to the world, but because of the way the world is put together: not all the kinds (not all the classes of things and events about which there are important, counterfactual supporting generalizations to make) are, or correspond to, physical kinds. A way of stating the classical reductionist view is that things which belong to different physical kinds ipso facto can have none of their projectable descriptions in common[16]: that if *x* and *y* differ in those descriptions by virtue of which they

---

[16] For the notion of projectability, see Goodman (1965). All projectable predicates are kind predicates, though not, presumably, vice versa.

fall under the proper laws of physics, they must differ in those descriptions by virtue of which they fall under any laws at all. But why should we believe that this is so? Any pair of entities, however different their physical structure, must nevertheless converge in indefinitely many of their properties. Why should there not be, among those convergent properties, some whose lawful interrelations support the generalizations of the special sciences? Why, in short, should not the kind predicates of the special sciences *cross-classify* the physical natural kinds?[17]

Physics develops the taxonomy of its subject matter which best suits its purposes: the formulation of exceptionless laws which are basic in the several senses discussed above. But this is not the only taxonomy which may be required if the purposes of science in general are to be served: e.g., if we are to state such true, counterfactual supporting generalizations as there are to state. So there are special sciences, with their specialized taxonomies, in the business of stating some of these generalizations. If science is to be unified, then all such taxonomies must apply *to the same things*. If physics is to be basic science, then each of these things had better be a physical thing. But it is not further required that the taxonomies which the special sciences employ must themselves reduce to the taxonomy of physics. It is not required, and it is probably not true.

Try as they may, many philosophers find it hard to take literally the things that nonphilosophers say. Since verificationism became unfashionable, most philosophers have conceded—some have even insisted—that the claims of the laity are often true when they are construed correctly. But the correct construal is frequently far to seek, and almost always proves remarkably different from what the laity had thought it had in mind. Thus, for a while, philosophers taught that talking about tables and chairs is an elliptical and misleading way of referring to the states of one's visual field and warned that the foundations of inductive inference would surely crumble unless physical objects turned out to be 'constructs' out of phenomena logically homogeneous with afterimages. In the event, however, 'physical object talk' was found to require considerably less analysis than had been supposed. Tables and chairs proved to be not at all like afterimages, and the practice of inductive inference survived.

But while reductionism is now widely deplored in epistemology proper, it lingers in philosophical discussions of 'theoretical constructs' in the sciences.

---

[17] As, by the way, the predicates of natural languages quite certainly do. (For discussion, see Chomsky, 1965.)

To assert that the taxonomies employed by the special sciences cross-classify physical kinds is to deny that the special sciences, together with physics, constitute a hierarchy. To deny that the sciences constitute a hierarchy is to deny precisely what I take the classical doctrine of the unity of science to assert insofar as it asserts anything more than token physicalism.

Psychological theories, in particular, have struck many philosophers as apt for dehypostatization, and the warnings that the alternative to reduction is a ruinous skepticism have an all too familiar ring. It has, however, been the burden of these introductory remarks that the arguments for the behavioral or physiological reduction of psychological theories are not, after all, very persuasive. The results of taking psychological theories literally and seeing what they suggest that mental processes are like might, in fact, prove interesting. I propose, in what follows, to do just that.

1
FIRST
APPROXIMATIONS

I'm the only President you've got.
LYNDON B. JOHNSON

The main argument of this book runs as follows:

1. The only psychological models of cognitive processes that seem even remotely plausible represent such processes as computational.
2. Computation presupposes a medium of computation: a representational system.
3. Remotely plausible theories are better than no theories at all.
4. We are thus provisionally committed to attributing a representational system to organisms. 'Provisionally committed' means: committed insofar as we attribute cognitive processes to organisms and insofar as we take seriously such theories of these processes as are currently available.
5. It is a reasonable research *goal* to try to characterize the representational system to which we thus find ourselves provisionally committed.
6. It is a reasonable research *strategy* to try to infer this characterization from the details of such psychological theories as seem likely to prove true.
7. This strategy may actually work: It is possible to exhibit specimen inferences along the lines of item 6 which, if not precisely apodictic, have at least an air of prima facie plausibility.

The epistemic status of these points is pretty various. I take it, for example, that item 3 is a self-evident truth and therefore requires no justification beyond an appeal to right reason. I take it that item 4 follows from items 1–3. Items 5–7, on the other hand, need to be justified *in practice*. What must be shown is that it is, in fact, productive to conduct psychological research along the lines they recommend. Much of the material in later chapters of this book will be concerned to show precisely that. Hence, the discussion will become more intimately involved with empirical findings, and with their interpretations, as we go along.

27

This chapter, however is primarily concerned with items 1 and 2. I shall argue that, quite independent of one's assumptions about the *details* of psychological theories of cognition, their general structure presupposes underlying computational processes and a representational system in which such processes are carried out. It is often quite familiar facts which, in the first instance, constrain one's models of the mental life, and this chapter is mostly a meditation on a number of these. I shall, in short, discuss some kinds of theories which, I think, most cognitive psychologists would accept in outline, however much they might disagree about specifics. I want to show how, in every case, these theories presuppose the existence and exploitation of a representational system of some complexity in which mental processes are carried out. I commence with theories of choice.

I take it to be self-evident that organisms often believe the behavior they produce to be behavior of a certain kind and that it is often part of the explanation of the way that an organism behaves to advert to the beliefs it has about the kind of behavior it produces.[1] This being assumed, the following model seems overwhelmingly plausible as an account of how at least some behavior is decided on.

8. The agent finds himself in a certain situation (S).

9. The agent believes that a certain set of behavioral options ($B_1, B_2, \ldots B_n$) are available to him in S; i.e., given S, B_1 through B_n are the things the agent believes that he can do.

10. The probable consequence of performing each of B_1 through B_n are predicted; i.e., the agent computes a set of hypotheticals of roughly the form if B_i is performed in S, then, with a certain probability, C_i. Which such hypotheticals are computed and which probabilities are assigned will, of course, depend on what the organism knows or believes about situations like S. (It will also depend upon other variables which are, from the point of view of the present model, merely noisy: time pressure, the amount of computation space available to the organism, etc.)

11. A preference ordering is assigned to the consequences.

Strictly numerical or maybe is tree?

[1] I am not supposing that this is, in any technical sense, a *necessary* truth. But I do think it is the kind of proposition that it would be silly to try to confirm (or confute) by doing experiments. One can (just barely) imagine a situation in which it would be reasonable to abandon the practice of appealing to an organism's beliefs in attempts to account for its behavior: either because such appeals had been shown to be internally incoherent or because an alternative theoretical apparatus had been shown to provide better explanations. As things stand, however, no such incoherence has been demonstrated (the operationalist literature to the contrary notwithstanding) and no one has the slightest idea what an alternative theoretical option would be like (the behaviorist literature to the contrary notwithstanding). It is a methodological principle I shall adhere to scrupulously in what follows that if one has no alternative but to assume that P, then one has no alternative but to assume that P.

12. The organism's choice of behavior is determined as a function of the preferences and the probabilities assigned.

Two caveats. First, this is not a theory but a theory schema. No predictions about what particular organisms will choose to do on particular occasions are forthcoming until one supplies values for the variables; e.g., until one knows how S is described, which behavioral options are considered, what consequences the exploitation of the options are believed to lead to, what preference ordering the organism assigns to these consequences and what trade-off between probability and preferability the organism accepts. This is to say that, here as elsewhere, a serious theory of the way an organism behaves presupposes extensive information about what the organism knows and values. Items 8–12 do not purport to give such a theory, but only to identify some of the variables in terms of which one would have to be articulated.

Second, it is obvious that the model is highly idealized. We do not always contemplate each (or, indeed, any) of the behavioral options we believe to be available to us in a given situation. Nor do we always assess our options in the light of what we take to be their likely consequences. (Existentialists, I'm told, make a point of never doing so.) But these kinds of departures from the facts do not impugn the model. The most they show is that the behaviors we produce aren't always in rational correspondence with the beliefs we hold. It is sufficient for my point, however, that some agents are rational to some extent some of the time, and that when they are, and to the extent that they are, processes like the ones mentioned by items 8–12 mediate the relation between what the agent believes and what he does.[2]

Insofar as we accept that this model applies in a given case, we also accept the kinds of explanations that it licenses. For example, given the model, we may explain the fact that organism a produced behavior B by showing:

13. That a believed himself to be in situation S.

---

[2] It is not, of course, a sufficient condition for the rationality of behavior that processes like items 8–12 should be implicated in its production. For example, behaviors so mediated will generally be *ir*rational if the beliefs involved in item 10 are superstitious, or if the preferences involved in item 11 are perverse, or if the computations involved in items 9–12 are grossly unsound. Nor, so far as I can see, do items 8–12 propose *logically* necessary conditions upon the rationality of behavior. To revert to the idiom of the introduction, the conceptual story about what makes behavior rational presumably requires a certain kind of correspondence between behavior and belief but doesn't care about the character of the processes whereby that correspondence is effected; it is, I suppose, logically possible that angels are rational by reflex. The claim for items 8–12, then, is just that they—or something reasonably like them— are *empirically* necessary for bringing about a rational correspondence between the beliefs and the behaviors of sublunary creatures. The short way of saying this is that items 8–12 propose a (schematic) psychological theory.

14. That a believed that producing behavior of the type B_i in S would probably lead to consequence C_i.
15. That C_i was a (or the) highly valued consequence for a.
16. That a believed and intended B to be behavior of the B_i type.

The point to notice is that it is built into this pattern of explanation that agents sometimes take their behavior to be behavior of a certain kind; in the present case, it is part of the explanation of a's behavior that he believed it to be of the B_i kind, since it is behavior of that kind for which highly valued consequences are predicted. To put it briefly, the explanation fails to *be* a (full) explanation of a's behavior unless that behavior was B_i and a believed it to be so.

Items 13–16 might, of course, *contribute* to an explanation of behavior even where B is *not* produced and where the actual behavior is *not* taken by the agent to be B_i behavior. 'Will nobody pat my hiccup?' cried the eponymous Reverend Spooner. We assume that what goes in for B_i is a structural description of the sentence type 'Will nobody pick my hat up?' and that the disparity between the behavior produced and a token of that type is attributable to what the networks call a temporary mechanical failure. In such cases, our confidence that we know what behavior the agent intended often rests upon three beliefs:

17. That items 14 and 15 are true under the proposed substitution for B_i.
18. That items 14 and 15 would be false if we were instead to substitute a description of the type of which the observed behavior was in fact a token. (In the present example, it is plausibly assumed that Spooner would have set no positive utility upon the production of a token of the type 'Will nobody pat my hiccup?'; why on earth should he want to say *that*?)
19. That it is plausible to hypothesize mechanisms of the sort whose operations would account for the respects in which the observed and the intended behaviors differ. (In the present case, mechanisms of metathesis.)

It is notorious that if 'psychodynamic' explanations of behavior are true, the mechanisms envisaged by item 19 may themselves be of practically fathomless complexity. My present point, in any event, is that not only accounts of observed behavior, but also attributions of thwarted behavioral intentions, may intimately presuppose the applicability of some such explanatory schema as items 8–12.

I am laboring these very obvious remarks because I think that their immediate consequences are of profound significance for the construction of cognitive theories in general: viz., that this sort of explanation can go through only if we assume that agents have means for representing their behaviors to themselves; indeed, means for representing their behaviors as having certain properties and not having others. In the present case, it is essential to the explanation that the agent intends and believes the behavior he produced to be behavior of a certain kind (viz., of the kind associated with relatively highly valued consequences in S) and not of some other kind (viz., not of the kind associated with relatively low-valued consequences in S). Give this up, and one gives up the possibility of explaining the behavior of the agent by reference to his beliefs and preferences.

The moral I want to draw, then, is that certain kinds of very central patterns of psychological explanation presuppose the availability, to the behaving organism, of some sort of representational system. I have emphasized, for purposes of exposition, the significance of the organism's representation of its own behavior in the explanation of its considered actions. But, once made, the point is seen to be ubiquitous. It was, for example, implicit in the model that the organism has available means for representing not only its behavioral options but also: the probable consequence of acting on those options, a preference ordering defined over those consequences and, of course, the original situation in which it finds itself. To use this sort of model is, then, to presuppose that the agent has access to a representational system of very considerable richness. For, according to the model, deciding is a computational process; the act the agent performs is the consequence of computations defined over representations of possible actions. No representations, no computations. No computations, no model.

I might as well have said that the model presupposes a language. For, a little prodding will show that the representational system assumed by items 8–12 must share a number of the characteristic features of real languages. This is a point to which I shall return at considerable length in Chapters 2 and 3. Suffice it to point out here just two of the properties that the putative system of representations must have in common with languages properly so-called (e.g., with natural languages).

In the first place, an infinity of distinct representations must belong to the system. The argument here is precisely analogous to the argument for the nonfiniteness of natural languages: Just as, in the latter case, there is no upper bound to the complexity of a sentence that can be used to make a statement, so in the former case, there is no upper bound to the complexity of the representation that may be required to specify the behavioral options available to the agent, or the situation in which he finds himself, or the consequences of acting one way or another.

This is not, of course, to argue that the *practical* possibilities are *literally* infinite. Just as there is a longest-sentence-that-anyone-can-utter, so there must be a most-complex-situation-that-anyone-can-act-upon. The infinite capacity of the representational system is thus an idealization, but it is not an *arbitrary* idealization. In both cases, the essential point is the organism's ability to deal with *novel* stimulations. Thus, we infer the productivity of natural languages from the speaker/hearer's ability to produce/understand sentences on which he was not specifically trained. Precisely the same argument infers the productivity of the internal representational system from the agent's ability to calculate the behavioral options appropriate to a kind of situation he has never before encountered.

But productivity isn't the only important property common to natural languages and whatever system of representation is exploited in deciding what to do. It is evident, for example, that the notion that the agent can represent to himself salient aspects of the situations in which he finds himself presupposes that such familiar semantic properties as truth and reference are exhibited by formulae in the representational system.[3] We have been supposing that, underlying the capacity for reasoned action, there must be a capacity for the description of real and possible states of affairs. But the notions of description, truth, and reference are inseparable: Roughly, 'D' describes what 'a' refers to iff ('Da' is true iff a is D).

A similar line of thought shows that mechanisms for expressing intensional properties will have to be available to the representational system. In particular, calculated action presupposes decisions between possible (but) nonactual outcomes. So, the representational system recruited for the calculations must distinguish between possible, nonactual states of affairs. Whether one ought to do this by defining preference orderings over propositions (as traditional treatments of intensionality would suggest) or over possible worlds (in the manner of model-theoretic approaches to semantics) is a question I won't even attempt to deal with. My present point is just that *some* such mechanism must be available to the representational system, and for reasons quite parallel to those that lead us to think that some such mechanisms are available to natural languages.

I have assumed so far in this discussion that anyone reasonable will accept that something like items 8–12 is essential to a theory of the psychology of choice; what I have been doing is just spinning out some of the implications of that assumption. But, notoriously, the assumption isn't true. Behaviorists, for example, don't accept that deciding is a computational process, so behavioristic accounts of action can make do without postulating a system of internal representations. I don't propose to raise the general question of the adequacy of such accounts; it seems to me a dead issue. Suffice it to remark that, in light of our discussion, some of the standard criticisms can be deepened.

It is a point often made against behaviorists that they seek a prima facie implausible reduction of calculated actions to habits. The intended criticism is usually that insofar as actions are viewed simply as trained responses to environmental inputs the productivity of behavior is rendered unintelligible.

---

[3] I use the term 'formulae' without prejudice for whatever the vehicles of internal representation may turn out to be. At this point in the discussion it is left open that they might be images, or semaphore signals, or sentences of Japanese. Much of the discussion in succeeding chapters will concern what is known about the character of internal representations and what can be inferred about it from what is known of other things.

(For elaboration, see Chomsky, 1959.) But this is not the only thing wrong with construing calculated behaviors as species of conditioned responses. What everyone knows, but the behaviorist's methodology won't allow him to admit, is that at least some actions are choices from among a range of options contemplated by the agent. The behaviorist cannot admit this because he is committed to describing actions as the effects of environmental causes. Since only *actual* states of affairs can be causes, the-possibility-that-*P* cannot be among the determinants of a response. But nor, however, can *contemplations* of possibilities since, though they are presumably real events on any rational ontology, they are not *environmental* events in the behaviorist's proprietary sense of that notion. Looked at either way, the behaviorist is methodologically committed to denying what would seem to be self-evident: that we sometimes act the way we do because that seems the best way to act given what we take to be the options. In short, the behaviorist requires us to view considered behaviors as responses to actual inputs, when what we want to do is view them as responses to possible outcomes.

It is, conversely, one of the great advantages of computational theories of action that they allow us to acknowledge what everybody knows: that deciding what to do often involves considering what might turn out to be the case. To assume a representational system which can distinguish among (viz., assign different representations to) distinct possible states of affairs is precisely to permit oneself to view the behavior that is actually produced as a choice from among those options that the agent regards as 'live'. It is worth emphasizing that the behaviorist literature offers no grounds for rejecting this immensely plausible treatment except the reiterated assertion that it is, somehow, 'unscientific'. So far as I can tell, however, this amounts only to the (correct) observation that one cannot both say what it is plausible to say about actions and adhere to a behavioristic methodology. So much the worse for the methodology.

It will have occurred to the reader that what I am proposing to do is resurrect the traditional notion that there is a 'language of thought' and that characterizing that language is a good part of what a theory of the mind needs to do. This is a view to which, it seems to me, much of the current psychological work on cognition bears a curious and mildly schizoid relation. On the one hand, it seems to be implicit in almost every kind of explanation that cognitive psychologists accept since, as I remarked above, most such explanations treat behavior as the outcome of computation, and computation presupposes a medium in which to compute. But, on the other hand, the assumption of such a medium is relatively rarely made explicit, and the pressing question to which it leads—what properties does the system of internal representations have—is only occasionally taken as the object of sustained research.

I propose, as we go along, to consider a variety of types of evidence that may bear upon the answer to that question. Before doing so, however, I want to explore two more lines of argument which seem to lead, with a fair show of inevitability, to the postulation of a language of thought as a precondition for any sort of serious theory construction in cognitive psychology. My point will be that not only considered action, but also learning and perception, must surely be viewed as based upon computational processes; and, once again, no computation without representation.

Let us first consider the phenomenon that psychologists sometimes call 'concept learning'. I want to concentrate on concept learning not only because it provides a useful illustration of our main thesis (cognitive processes are computational processes and hence presuppose a representational system) but also because the analysis of concept learning bears on a variety of issues that will arise in later chapters.

To begin with, then, concept learning is one of those processes in which what the organism knows is altered as a consequence of its experiences; in particular, as a consequence of its interactions with the environment. But, of course, not *every* case of an environmentally determined alteration in knowledge would count as learning; *a fortiori,* not all such cases count as *concept* learning. So, for example, aphasia is often environmentally induced, but catching aphasia isn't a learning experience. Similarly, if we could somehow induce knowledge of Latin by swallowing blue pills, I suppose that that would be acquiring Latin without learning it. Similarly, imprinting (see Thorpe, 1963) alters what the organism knows as a consequence of its experiences, but is only marginally a learning process if it is a learning process at all. A general theory of concept learning is, at best, *not* a general theory of how experience affects knowledge.

There are, moreover, kinds of *learning* that very probably aren't kinds of concept learning.[4] Rote learning is a plausible example (e.g., the learning of a list of nonsense syllables. However, see Young, 1968). So is what one might call 'sensory learning' (learning what a steak tastes like, learning what middle C sounds like played on an oboe, and so forth). Very roughly, and just by way of marking out the area of our concern, what distinguishes rote learning and sensory learning from concept learning is that, in the latter cases, what is *remembered of* an experience typically exhausts what is *learned from* that experience. Whereas concept learning somehow 'goes beyond' the experiential data. But what does *that* mean?

I think that what concept learning situations have in common is fundamentally this: The experiences which occasion the learning in such situations (under their theoretically relevant descriptions) stand in a *confirma-*

---

[4] I regard this as an empirical issue; whether it's true depends on what, in fact, goes on in the various learnings processes. It *might* turn out that the mechanism of concept learning is the general learning mechanism, but it would be a surprise if that were true and I want explicitly not to be committed to the assumption that it is. We badly need—and have not got—an empirically defensible taxonomy of kinds of learning.

tion relation to what is learned (under *its* theoretically relevant description). A short way of saying this is that concept learning is essentially a process of hypothesis formation and confirmation.[5] The best way to see that this is so is to consider the experimental paradigm in terms of which the concept learning 'construct' is, as one used to say, 'operationally defined'.

In the typical experimental situation, the subject (human or infra-human) is faced with the task of determining the environmental conditions under which a designated response is appropriate, and learning is manifested by *S*'s increasing tendency, over time or trials, to produce the designated response when, and only when, those conditions obtain. The logic of the experimental paradigm requires, first, that there be an 'error signal' (e.g., reinforcement or punishment or both) which indicates whether the designated response has been appropriately performed and, second, that there be some 'criterial property' of the experimentally manipulated stimuli such that the character of the error signal is a function of the occurrence of the designated response together with the presence or absence of that property. Thus, in a simple experiment of this kind, *S* might be asked to sort stimulus cards into piles, where the figures on the cards exhibit any combination of the properties red and black with square and circular, but where the only correct (e.g., rewarded) sorting is the one which groups red circles with black squares. In such a case, the 'designated response' is sorting into the positive pile and the 'criterial property' is *red circle or black square.*

It is possible to use this sort of experimental setup to study the rate of learning as a function of any of a large number of variables: e.g., the character of the criterial property; *S*'s ability to report the property in terms of which he is sorting; the character of the error signal; the character of the relation (temporal, statistical, etc.) between occurrences of the error signal and instantiations of the criterial property; the character of the subject population (age, species, intelligence, motivation, or whatever); and so on. Much of the experimental psychology of learning in the last thirty years has been concerned with ringing changes on the values of these variables; the paradigm has been central to the work of psychologists who have as little else in common as, say, Skinner and Vygotsky.[6]

---

[5] This analysis of concept learning is in general agreement with such sources as Bruner, Goodnow, and Austin (1956), as is the emphasis upon the inferential character of the computations that underlie success in concept learning situations.

[6] Though Skinner would not, perhaps, like to see it put this way. Part of the radical behaviorist analysis of learning is the attempt to reduce concept learning to 'discrimination learning'; i.e., to insist that *what* the organism learns in the concept learning situation is *to produce the designated response.* It seems clear, however, that the reduction ought to go the other way around: The concept learning paradigm and the discrimination learning paradigm *are* the same, but in neither is the existence of a designated response more than a convenience to the experimenter; all it does is

My present point is that there is only one kind of theory that has ever been proposed for concept learning—indeed, there would seem to be only one kind of theory that is conceivable—and this theory is incoherent unless there is a language of thought. In this respect, the analysis of concept learning is like the analysis of considered choice; we cannot begin to make sense of the phenomena unless we are willing to view them as computational and we cannot begin to make sense of the view that they are computational unless we are willing to assume a representational system of considerable power in which the computations are carried out.

Notice, to begin with, that at any given trial t and in respect of any given property P, the organism's experience in the concept learning paradigm is appropriately represented as a data matrix in which the rows represent trials and the columns represent the performance of the designated response, the presence or absence of P, and the character of the error signal.[7] Thus:

---

provide a regimented procedure whereby S can indicate which sorting he believes to be the right one at a given stage in the learning process.

This is, I take it, not a methodological but an empirical claim. It is clear on several grounds that concept learning (in the sense of learning which categorization of the stimuli is the right one) can, and usually does, proceed in the absence of specific designated responses—indeed, in the absence of any response at all. Nature addicts learn, I'm told, to distinguish oaks from pine trees, and many of them probably do so without being explicitly taught what the distinguishing criteria are. This is true concept learning, but there is no distinctive response that even nature addicts tend to make when and only when they see an oak.

There is, in fact, plenty of experimental evidence on this point. Tolman (1932) showed that what a rat learns when it learns which turning is rewarded in a T-maze is *not* specific to the response system that it uses to make the turn. Brewer (to be published), in a recent survey of the literature on conditioning in human beings, argues persuasively that the designated response can usually be detached from the criterial stimuli simply by instructing the subject to detach it ('From now on, please do *not* sort the red circles with the black squares'). It is, in short, simply not the case that learning typically consists of establishing connections between specific classes of stimuli and specific classes of responses. What *is* the case is (a) that S can often use what he has learned to effect a correspondence between the occurrence of criterial stimulation and the production of a designated response; (b) that it is often experimentally convenient to require him to do so, thereby providing a simple way for E to determine which properties of the stimuli S believes to be criterial; and (c) that Ss will go along with this arrangement providing that they are adequately motivated to do so. Here as elsewhere, what the subject does is determined by his beliefs together with his preferences.

[7] One might, ideally, want a three-valued matrix since, on any given trial, the organism may not have observed, or may have observed and forgotten, whether the designated response was performed, whether P was present, or what the value of the error signal was. This is the sort of nicety which I shall quite generally ignore. I mention it only to emphasize that it is the organism's internal representation of its experiences (and not the objective facts about them) that is immediately implicated in the causation of its behavior.

TRIAL	DESIGNATED RESPONSE PERFORMED	PROPERTY P PRESENT	VALUE OF ERROR SIGNAL
1	yes	yes	minus
2	no	no	minus
3	yes	no	plus

Put this way, it seems clear that the problem the organism faces on trial t is that of choosing a value of P for which, in the ideal case, the last column of the matrix is positive when and only when the first two columns are, and which is such that the matrix will continue to exhibit that correspondence for any (reasonable) value of $t_n > t$. This is the sense in which what is learned in concept learning 'goes beyond' what is given in the experiential data. What the organism has to do in order to perform successfully is to extrapolate a generalization (all the positive stimuli are P-stimuli) on the basis of some instances that conform to the generalization (the first n positive stimuli were P-stimuli). The game is, in short, inductive extrapolation, and inductive extrapolation presupposes (a) a source of inductive hypotheses (in the present case, a range of candidate values of P) and (b) a confirmation metric such that the probability that the organism will accept (e.g., act upon) a given value of P at t is some reasonable function of the distribution of entries in the data matrix for trials prior to t.

There are, of course, many many ways of fleshing out the details of this kind of model. For example, there is plenty of reason to believe that the various values of P are typically tested in a determinate order; indeed, that the choice of P may be very subtly determined by the character of the P-values previously assessed and rejected and by the particular configuration of the data matrix for those values. But, however the details go, what seems entirely clear is that the behavior of the organism will depend upon the confirmation relation between the data and the hypothesis, so that accounts of its behavior will require information about how, in the course of learning, the data and the hypotheses are represented.

Why is this entirely clear? Fundamentally, because one of the distinguishing characteristics of concept learning is the *nonarbitrariness* of the relation between what is learned and the character of the experiences that occasion the learning. (Compare the case of acquiring Latin by taking pills.) That is, what a theory of concept learning has to explain is why it is experiences of xs which are F (and not, say, experiences of xs which are G) that leads the organism, eventually, to the belief that all the xs are F. We *can* explain this if we assume (a) that the organism *represents* the relevant experiences as experiences of xs which are F; (b) that one of the hypotheses that the organism entertains about its environment is the hypothesis that perhaps all xs are F; and (c) that the organism employs, in the fixation of its beliefs, a rule of confirmation which says (*very* roughly) that all the observed *x*s being *F* is, *ceteris paribus,* grounds for believing that all the *x*s are *F*. To put it mildly, it seems unlikely that any theory radically incompatible with items (a–c) could account for the non-arbitrariness of the relation between what is learned and the experiences that occasion the learning.[8]

In short, concept learning begs for analysis as involving the determination of a confirmation relation between observed and extrapolated reward contingencies, and this is already to commit oneself to a representational system in which the observations and the candidate extrapolations are displayed and the degree of confirmation is computed. There is, however, also a more subtle way in which inductive extrapolation presupposes a representational system, and this point bears considering.

Inductive extrapolation is a form of nondemonstrative inference. For present purposes this means that, at any given trial *t*, there will be indefinitely many nonequivalent values of *P* that are 'compatible' with the data matrix up to *t*. That is, there will be indefinitely many values of *P* such that, on all trials prior to *t*, the designated response is rewarded iff *P* is exhibited by the stimulus, but where each value of *P* 'predicts' a different pairing of responses and rewards on future trials. Clearly, if the organism is to extrapolate from its experiences, it will need some way of choosing between these indefinitely many values of *P*. Equally clearly, that choice cannot be made on the basis of the data available up to *t* since the choice that needs to be made is precisely among hypotheses all of which predict the *same* data up to *t*.

This is a familiar situation in discussions of inductive inference in

---

[8] I have purposely been stressing the analogies between the theory of inductive confirmation and the theory of the fixation of belief. But I do *not* intend to endorse the view (which examples like item (c) might suggest) that the confirmation of universal hypotheses in science is normally a process of simple generalization from instances. For that matter, I do not intend to endorse the view, embodied in the program of 'inductive logic', that confirmation is normally reconstructable as a 'formal' relation between hypotheses and data. On the contrary, it appears that the level of confirmation of a scientific hypothesis is frequently sensitive to a variety of *in*formal considerations concerning the overall economy, plausibility, persuasiveness and productivity of the theory in which the hypothesis is embedded, to say nothing of the existence of competing theories.

It may well be that the fixation of belief is also sensitive to these sorts of 'global' considerations. Even so, however, the prospects for a formal theory of belief seem to me considerably better than the prospects for an inductive logic. To formalize the relation of inductive confirmation, we should have to provide a theory which picks the *best* hypothesis (the hypothesis that *ought* to be believed), given the available evidence. Whereas, to formalize the fixation of belief, we need only develop a theory which, given the evidence, picks the hypothesis that the organism *does* believe. To the extent that this *cannot* be done, we cannot view learning as a computational process; and it is, for better or for worse, the working assumption of this book that computational accounts of organisms will not break down.

the philosophy of science. The classic argument is due to Goodman (1965), who pointed out that, for any fixed set of observations of green emeralds, both the hypothesis that all emeralds are green and the hypothesis that all emeralds are *grue* will be compatible with the data. (One way of defining a *grue*-predicate is: An emerald is *grue* iff it is ((in the data sample and green) or (not in the data sample and blue)). It is part of Goodman's point, however, that there are indefinitely many ways of constructing predicates which share the counterinductive properties that *grue* exhibits.) Since both hypotheses are compatible with the data, the principle that distinguishes between them must appeal to something other than observations of green emeralds.

The way out of this puzzle is to assume that candidate extrapolations of the data receive an a priori ordering under a *simplicity metric*, and that that metric prefers 'all xs are green' to 'all xs are *grue*' as the extrapolation of any body of data compatible with both.[9] In the present case this means that the decision that a given value of P is confirmed relative to a given data matrix must be determined not only by the distribution of entries in the matrix, but also by the relative simplicity of P. This conclusion seems to be irresistible, given the nondemonstrative character of the extrapolations involved in concept learning. It has, however, immediate consequences for the general claim that theories of concept learning are incoherent unless they presuppose that a representational system is available to the organism.

The point is that, so far as anyone can tell, simplicity metrics must be sensitive to the *form* of the hypotheses that they apply to, i.e., to their syntax and vocabulary.[10] That is, so far as anyone can tell, we can get an a priori ordering of hypotheses only if we take account of the way in which the hypotheses are expressed. We need such an ordering if we are to provide a coherent account of the order in which values of P are selected in the concept learning situation. But this means that a theory of concept

[9] I take it that this is common ground among philosophers of science. Where they disagree is on how to characterize the difference between predicates like *grue* (which the simplicity metric doesn't like) and predicates like green (which it does); and also, on how to justify adopting a simplicity metric which discriminates that way.

[10] Notions like entrenchment, for example, are defined over the *predicates* of a science. If 'green' is more entrenched than 'grue', that is presumably because there are laws expressed in terms of the former but no laws expressed in terms of the latter. (For discussion, see Goodman, 1965.) One could, of course, try to avoid this conclusion by defining simplicity, entrenchment, and related notions for *properties* (rather than for predicates). But even if that *could* be done it would seem to be a step in the wrong direction: Insofar as one wants psychological processes to turn out to be *computational* processes, one wants the rules of computation to apply formally to the objects in their domains. Once again: my goal in this book is not to *demonstrate* that psychological processes are computational, but to work out the consequences of assuming that they are.

learning will have to be sensitive to the way that the organism represents its hypotheses. But the notion of the organism representing its hypotheses in one way or another (e.g., in one or another vocabulary or syntax) just *is* the notion of the organism possessing a representational system.

In fact, this argument states the case too weakly. In the formalization of scientific inference a simplicity metric distinguishes between hypotheses that are compatible with the data but make different predictions for *un*observed cases. Our point, thus far, has been that the corresponding remarks presumably hold in the special case where the hypotheses are *P*-values and the data are the observed values of the error signal. There is, however, a respect in which the case of scientific inference differs from the extrapolations involved in concept learning. A simplicity metric used in the evaluation of scientific theories is presumably *not* required to distinguish between *equivalent* hypotheses. To put it the other way around, two hypotheses are identical, for the purposes of formalizing scientific inferences, if they predict the same extrapolations of the data matrix and are equally complex. Pairs of hypotheses that are identical in this sense, but differ in formulation, are said to be 'notational variants' of the same theory.

There is ample evidence, however, that the a priori ordering of *P*-values exploited in concept learning *does* distinguish between hypotheses that are, in this sense, notational variants of each other; i.e., the ordering of *P*-values imposes *stronger* constraints upon the form of a hypothesis than simplicity metrics do.

It is, for example, a standard finding that *S*s prefer affirmative conjunctive representations of the data matrix to negative or disjunctive representations. (See Bruner et al., 1956.) Thus, subjects in the concept learning task will typically find it easier to learn to sort all the red triangles together than to learn to sort together all things that *aren't* triangles or all the things that are either triangles or red. Yet, affirmative conjunctive hypotheses are interdefinable with negative disjunctive hypotheses; the subject who is choosing all and only red triangles as instances of positive stimuli is ipso facto choosing all and only things that are (not triangles or not red) as instances of the negative stimuli.[11] What makes the difference in the subject's performance is which of these choices he takes himself to be making; i.e., the way he represents the choices. *S*s who report an affirmative conjunctive hypothesis typically learn faster than those who don't.[12] This is

---

[11] The point is, of course, that 'choosing' is opaque in the first occurrence and transparent in the second. Perhaps it's not surprising that what is chosen opaquely is chosen under a representation.

[12] For example, Wason and Johnson-Laird (1972) describe an experiment in which *S*s were, in effect, presented with data matrices and required to articulate the appropriate extrapolations. The basic prediction, which was confirmed, was that "concepts which were essentially conjunctive in form would be easier to formulate than con-

thoroughly intelligible on the assumption that the same hypothesis can receive different internal representations and that the subject's a priori preferences are sensitive to such differences. But it doesn't seem to be intelligible on any other account.

We have been considering some of the ways in which viewing the concept learning task as essentially involving inductive extrapolation commits one to postulating a representational system in which the relevant inductions are carried through. I think it is worth emphasizing that no alternative view of concept learning has ever been proposed, though there are alternative vocabularies for formulating the view just discussed. For example, many psychologists use the notion of habit strength (or strength of association) where I have used the notion of degree of confirmation of a hypothesis. But once it has been recognized that any such construct must be defined over candidate extrapolations of a data matrix (and not over S-R pairings; see footnote 6) the residual issue is entirely terminological. A theory which determines how habit strength varies as a function of reinforcement (or which determines strength of association as a function of frequency of association, etc.) just *is* an inductive logic, where the confirmation function is articulated by whatever laws of reinforcement/ association are assumed.

Similarly, some psychologists would prefer to speak of a theory of attention where I have spoken of a theory which determines the order in which *P*-values are tested. But again the issue is just terminological. A theory which determines what the organism is attending to at *t* thereby predicts the stimulus parameter that is extrapolated at *t*. It must therefore be sensitive to whatever properties of the data matrix, and of the previously contemplated hypotheses, affect the order in which *P*-values are tested, and to whatever a priori ordering of *P*-values determines their relative complexity. Whether or not one *calls* this a theory of attention,

---

cepts which were essentially disjunctive in form, and that whenever a component was negated there would be a slight increase in difficulty" (p. 70). They note that the order of difficulty that they obtained by asking the subject to state the relevant generalization "conforms to the order obtained when subjects have to *learn* concepts in the conventional manner" (p. 72), i.e., in the concept learning task. The point to notice is that, since conjunction is interdefinable with negation and disjunction, no concept is, *strictly speaking*, essentially conjunctive or essentially disjunctive. Strictly speaking, concepts don't *have* forms, though representations of concepts do. What Wason and Johnson-Laird mean by a conjunctive concept is, as they are careful to point out, just one which can be expressed by a (relatively) economical formula *in the representational system that the subject is using* (in the present case, in English). What the experiment really shows, then, is that the employment of such a representation facilitates the subject's performance; hence that formulations of a hypothesis which are, in the sense described above, mere notational variants of one another, may nevertheless be differentially available as extrapolations of a data matrix.

the function of the construct is precisely to predict what extrapolations of the data matrix the organism will try and in what order it will try them.

Finally, there are psychologists who prefer to describe the organism as 'sampling' the properties of the stimulus rather than as constructing hypotheses about which such properties are criterial for sorting. But the notion of a property is proprietary in the former kind of theory. In the nonproprietary sense of 'property', every stimulus has an infinity of properties an infinite subset of which are never sampled. The properties that *are* sampled, on the other hand, are of necessity a selection from those that the organism is capable of internally representing. Given that, talking about sampling the properties of the stimulus and talking about projecting hypotheses about those properties are two ways of making the same point.

To summarize: So far as anyone knows, concept learning is essentially inductive extrapolation, so a theory of concept learning will have to exhibit the characteristic features of theories of induction. In particular, concept learning presupposes a format for representing the experiential data, a source of hypotheses for predicting future data, and a metric which determines the level of confirmation that a given body of data bestows upon a given hypothesis. No one, so far as I know, has ever doubted this, though I suppose many psychologists have failed to realize what it was that they weren't doubting. But to accept that learning which 'goes beyond the data' involves inductive inference is to commit oneself to a language in which the inductions are carried out, since (a) an inductive argument is warranted only insofar as the observation statements which constitute its premises confirm the hypothesis which constitutes its conclusion; (b) whether this confirmation relation holds between premises and conclusion depends, at least in part, upon the *form* of the premises and conclusion; and (c) the notion of 'form' is defined only for 'linguistic' objects; viz. for representations.

I shall close this chapter by pointing out that the same kinds of morals emerge when one begins to think about the structure of theories of perception.

To begin with, there is an obvious analogy between theories of concept learning of the kind I have just been discussing and classical theories of perception in the empiricist vein. According to the latter, perception is essentially a matter of problem solving, where the form of the problem is to predict the character of future sensory experience given the character of past and current sensations as data. Conceived this way, models of perception have the same general structure as models of concept learning: One needs a canonical form for the representation of the data, one needs a source of hypotheses for the extrapolation of the data, and one needs a confirmation metric to select among the hypotheses.

Since some of the empiricists took their project to be the formalization of perceptual *arguments*—viz., of those arguments whose cogency justifies our knowledge claims about objects of perception—they developed fairly explicit doctrines about the kinds of representations that mediate perceptual inferences. It is possible (and it is in the spirit of much of the empiricist tradition) to regard such doctrines as implying theories of the computational processes that underlie perceptual integration. It is notorious, however, that in a number of respects empiricist accounts of perceptual inferences make dubious psychology when so construed. For example, the premises of perceptual inferences were sometimes presumed to be represented in a 'sense datum' language whose formulae were supposed to have some extremely peculiar properties: E.g. that sense datum statements are somehow incorrigible, that all empirical statements have a unique decomposition into sense datum statements; that each sense datum statement is logically independent of any of the rest, and so on.

For many of the empiricists, the defining feature of this data language was supposed to be that its referring expressions could refer only to qualia; If sense datum statements were curious, that was because qualia were curiouser. Conversely, the language in which perceptual hypotheses are couched was identified with 'physical object language', thereby making the distinction between what is sensed and what is perceived coextensive with the distinction between qualia and things. Redescriptions of sensory fields in physical object terms could mediate the prediction of future sensations because, on this view, to accept a description of one's experiences in a physical object language is logically to commit oneself to (at least hypothetical) statements about experiences yet to come. Roughly, sense datum statements provide inductive support for physical object statements, and physical object statements entail statements about further sensations. One thus accepts an 'inductive risk' in inferring from sensations to perceptions, and the problem posed to the perceiver is that of behaving rationally in face of this risk. That is, given a description of experience couched in the sensation language, he must somehow choose that *re*description in physical object terms which the experiences best confirm. Only by doing so can he be rationally assured that most of the expectations about future or hypothetical experiences to which his perceptual judgements commit him are likely to be true.

If, in short, I describe my current experience in terms of color patches, textures, smells, sounds, and so forth, I do not commit myself to predictions about the character of my prior or future experiences. But if I describe it in terms of tables and chairs and their logical kin then I *am* so committed since nothing can be a table or chair unless it performs in a reasonably table-or-chair-wise fashion across time. So, if I claim that what I see is a table, I am (implicitly) going bond for its past and future behavior; in particular, I am issuing guarantees about the sensations it will, or would, provide. So the story goes.

It is widely known that this account of perception has taken a terrific drubbing at the hands of epistemologists and Gestalt psychologists. It is hard, these days, to imagine what it would be like for the formulae of a representational system to be privileged in the way that formulae in the sense datum language were supposed to be. Nor is it easy to imagine a way of characterizing qualia which would make it turn out that one's perceptual information is all mediated by the sensing of them. Nor does it seem pointful to deny that what one sees are typically *things*; not, in any event, if the alternative is that what one sees are typically color patches and their edges.

This line of criticism is too well known to bear repeating here. I think that it is clearly cogent. But I think, nevertheless, that the core of the empiricist theory of perception is inevitable. In particular, the following claims about the psychology of perception seem to me to be almost certainly true and entirely in the spirit of empiricist theorizing:

1. Perception typically involves hypothesis formation and confirmation.
2. The sensory data which confirm a given perceptual hypothesis are typically internally represented in a vocabulary that is impoverished compared to the vocabulary in which the hypotheses themselves are couched.

Before I say why I think these aspects of the empiricist treatment of perception are right, I want to say something brief about where I think the empiricists went wrong.

I am reading the typical empiricist theory of perception as doing double duty: as an account of the justification of perceptual beliefs and as a psychology of the integration of percepts. I think it is clear that many of the empiricists took their views this way. But it is also pretty clear that when a conflict arose between what the psychology required and what the epistemology appeared to, it was the demands of the latter that shaped the theory.

For example, the claim of incorrigibility for sense datum statements was not responsive to any particular psychological insight, but rather to the presumed need to isolate inductive risk at some epistemic level other than the one at which the data are specified. The idea was, roughly, that we could not know physical object statements to be true unless we were certain of the data for those statements, and we could not be *certain* of the data statements if it is possible that some of them are false. Certainty is, as it were, inherited upward from the data to the perceptual judgments they support. Similarly, experiences of qualia have to be conscious events because the statements which such experiences confirm are the premises for arguments whose conclusions are the physical object statements we explicitly believe. If such arguments are to be our justification for believing such statements, their premises had better be available for us to cite.

This is, very probably, mostly muddle. Justification is a far more pragmatic notion than the empiricist analysis suggests. In particular, there is no reason why the direction of all justificatory arguments should be upward from epistemologically unassailable premises. Why should not one

*Kripke's
Circularity Condition*

of my physical object statements be justified by appeal to another, and
that by appeal to a third, and so on? What justificatory argument requires
is not that some beliefs be unquestionable but at most that some of them
be (de facto) unquestioned. What *can't* be done is to justify all my beliefs
at once. Well, what can't be done can't be done.

But while I think that the notion of *the* direction of justification is
largely confused, the notion that there is a direction of information flow
in perception is almost certainly well taken, though the arguments are
empirical rather than conceptual.

To begin with, it seems clear that causal interactions between the
organism and its environment must contribute to the etiology of anything
one would want to call *perceptual* knowledge. Insofar as this is right, there
is a good deal of empirical information available about the character of
these interactions.

So far as anybody knows, any information that the organism gets
about its environment as a result of such interactions must be mediated by
the activity of one or another *sensory mechanism*. By a sensory mechanism,
I mean one which responds to *physical properties* of environmental events.
By a physical property I mean one designated by a natural kind term in
some (ideally completed) physical science (for the notion of a natural kind
term, see the second part of the introduction). What *mediated by* comes
to will take some explaining, but as a first approximation I mean that the
operation of a sensory mechanism in responding to a physical property of
an environmental event is an empirically necessary condition for the organism's perception of *any* property of that environmental event.

Suppose, for example, that we think of a sensory mechanism as
represented by a characteristic function, such that the value of the function
is 1 in any case where the mechanism is excited and 0 otherwise. Then,
so far as anyone knows, we can develop a theory which predicts the values
of that function across time only if we take into account the physical
properties of inputs to the mechanism. And we can predict the perceptual
analysis that the organism will assign a given environmental event only
if we know which physical properties of that event the sensory mechanisms
of the organism have responded to. (Thus, for example, to predict the
state of excitation of the human auditory system, we need information
about the spectrum analysis of impinging wave forms. And to predict the
sentence type to which an utterance token will be perceptually assigned,
we must know at least which auditory properties of the utterance have
been detected.)

I want to stress that this is an *empirical* fact even though it is not a
surprising fact. We can imagine an organism (say an angel or a clair-
voyant) whose perceptual knowledge is *not* mediated by the operation
of sensory mechanisms; only, so far as we know, there are no such organisms, or, if there are any, psychologists have yet to find them. For all the

known cases, perception is dependent upon the operation of mechanisms whose states of excitation can be predicted from physical descriptions of their input and not in any other way.

Viewed in terms of information flow, this means that a sensory mechanism operates to associate token physical excitations (as input) with token physical descriptions (as output); i.e., a sensory mechanism is a device which says 'yes' when excited by stimuli exhibiting certain specified values of physical parameters and 'no' otherwise.[13] In particular, it does not care about any property that environmental events *fail* to share so long as the events have the relevant physical properties in common, and it does not care about nonphysical properties that environmental events have in common so long as they fail to share the relevant physical properties. In this sense, the excitation of a sensory mechanism encodes the presence of a physical property. (If the auditory system is a mechanism whose states of excitation are specific to the values of frequency, amplitude, etc., of causally impinging environmental events, then one might as well think of the output of the system as an encoded description of the environment in terms of those values. Indeed, one had better think of it this way if one intends to represent the integration of auditory percepts as a *computational* process.) But if this is true, and if it is also true that whatever perceptual information the organism has about its environment is mediated by the operation of its sensory mechanisms, it follows that perceptual analyses must somehow be responsive to the information about values of physical parameters of environmental events that the sensory mechanisms provide.[14]

[13] For purposes of exposition, I am ignoring the (serious) empirical possibility that some or all sensory mechanisms have output values between 0 and 1. Problems about the 'digitalness' of the various stages of cognitive processing are at issue here; but, though these problems are interesting and important, they don't affect the larger issues. Suffice is to say that the question is not just whether the outputs of sensory mechanisms are continuous under physical description, but rather whether intermediate values of excitation carry information that is used in later stages of processing. I don't know what the answer to this question is, and I don't mean to preclude the possibility that the answer is different for different sensory modalities.

[14] It bears emphasizing that the present account of sensory systems, like most of the psychological theorizing in this chapter, is highly idealized. Thus, "from the physical point of view the sensory receptors are transducers, that is, they convert the particular form of energy to which each is attuned into the electrical energy of the nerve impulse." (Loewenstein, 1960). But, of course, it does not follow that the sensors are *perfect* transducers, viz., that their output is predictable *just* from a determination of the impinging physical energies. On the contrary, there is evidence that any or all of the following variables may contribute to such determinations.

i. Cells in sensory systems exhibit a characteristic cycle of inhibition and heightened sensitivity consequent upon each firing. The effects of impinging stimuli are thus not independent of the effects of prior stimulations unless the interstimulus interval is large compared to the time course of this cycle.

That, I suppose, *is* the problem of perception insofar as the problem of perception is a problem in psychology. For though the information provided by causal interactions between the environment and the organism is information about physical properties in the *first* instance, in the *last* instance it may (of course) be information about any property the organism can perceive the environment to have. To a first approximation, the outputs of sensory mechanisms are appropriately viewed as physical descriptions, but perceptual judgments need not be articulated in the vocabulary of such descriptions. Typically they *are* not: A paradigm perceptual judgment is, 'There's a robin on the lawn' or 'I see by the clock that it's time for tea'.

It is, I take it, an empirical question whether psychological processes are computational processes. But if they are, then what must go on in perception is that a description of the environment that is *not* couched in a vocabulary whose terms designate values of physical variables is somehow computed on the basis of a description that *is* couched in such a vocabulary. Presumably this is possible because the perceptual analysis of an event is determined not just by sensory information but also by such background knowledge as the organism brings to the task. The computational processes in perception are mainly those involved in the integration of these two kinds of information. I take it that that is what is left of the classical empiricist view that perception involves the (nondemonstrative) inference from descriptions couched in a relatively impoverished language to conclusions couched in a relatively unimpoverished one.

Almost nothing is left of the empiricist epistemology. For example,

---

ii. Cells on the sensory periphery may be so interconnected that the excitation of any of them inhibits the firing of the others. Such mutual 'lateral' inhibition of sensory elements is usually interpreted as a 'sharpening' mechanism; perhaps part of an overall system of analog-to-digital conversion. (See Ratliff, 1961.)

iii. At any distance 'back' from the periphery of the sensory system one is likely to find 'logic' elements whose firing may be thought of as coding Boolean functions of the primary transducer information. (See Letvin et al., 1961, Capranica, 1965.)

iv. There may be central 'centripetal' tuning of the response characteristics of the peripheral transducers, in which case the output of such transducers may vary according to the motivational, attentional, etc. state of the organism.

v. Cells in the sensory system exhibit 'sponaneous' activity; viz., firing which is *not* contingent upon stimulus inputs.

A sensory transducer may thus diverge, in all these respects, from the ideal mechanisms contemplated in the text; nor do I wish to claim that this list is complete. But for all that, the main point holds: Insofar as the environment *does* contribute to the etiology of sensory information, it is presumably only under physical description that the uniformities in its contribution are revealed. Equivalently for these purposes: Insofar as the activity of sensory mechanisms encodes information about the state of the environment, it is the physical state of the environment that is thus encoded.

the perceptually pertinent description of sensory information is not given in the theory-free language of qualia but rather in the theory-laden language of values of physical parameters. (This is a way of saying what I said above: that, so far as anyone knows, the only way of providing a reasonably compact account of the characteristic function for a sensory mechanism is by taking its inputs under physical description.) Hence, there is no reason to believe that the organism cannot be mistaken about what sensory descriptions apply in any given case. For that matter, there is no reason to believe that organisms are usually conscious of the sensory analyses that they impose.

This distinction—between the notion of a sensory mechanism as the source of a mosaic of conscious experiences out of which percepts are constructed (e.g., by associative processes) and the notion of the sensors as transducers of such environmental information as affects perceptual integration—is now standard in the psychological literature. It is stressed even by such psychologists as Gibson (1966), whose approach to perception is not, on the whole, sympathetic to the sort of computational views of psychology with which I am primarily concerned. For Gibson, perception involves the detection of invariant (typically relational) properties of impinging stimulus arrays. He apparently assumes that any percept can be identified with such an invariant if only the relevant property is sufficiently abstractly described.[15] But, though Gibson denies that percepts are constructed from conscious sensory data, he does apparently hold that the presence of the relevant stimulus invariant must be inferred from the information output by sensory transducers.

> . . . I will distinguish the input to the nervous system that evokes conscious sensation from the input that evokes perception. . . . For

[15] The status of the claim that there are stimulus invariants corresponding to precepts is unclear. On one way of reading it it would seem to be a necessary truth: Since 'perceive' is a success verb, there must be at least one invariant feature of all situations in which someone perceives a thing to be of type t; viz., the presence of a thing of type t. On the other hand, it is a very strong *empirical* claim that, for any type of thing that can be perceived, there exists a set of *physical* properties such that the detection of those properties is plausibly identified with the perception of a thing of that type. This latter requires that the distinction between things of type t and everything else *is a physical distinction,* and, as we saw in the introduction, that conclusion does *not* follow just from the premise that t-type objects are physical objects.

The issue is whether there are physical kinds corresponding to perceptual kinds and that, as we have been saying all along, is an empirical issue. My impression of the literature is that the correspondence fails more often than it holds; that perception cannot, in general, be thought of as the categorization of *physical* invariants, however abstractly such invariants may be described. (For a discussion of the empirical situation in the field of speech perception, cf. Fodor et al., 1974.)

it is surely a fact that *detecting* something can sometimes occur without the accompaniment of sense impressions. An example is the visual detection of one thing behind another. . . . But this does not mean that perception can occur without stimulation of receptors; it only means that organs of perception are sometimes stimulated in such a way that they are not specified in consciousness. Perception cannot be . . . without input; it can only be so if that means without awareness of the visual, auditory, or other quality of the input. An example of this is the 'obstacle sense' of the blind, which is felt as 'facial vision' but is actually auditory echo detection. The blind man 'senses' the wall in front of him without realizing what sense has been stimulated. In short there can be sensationless perception, but not informationless perception. (p. 2)

Thus, even for psychologists who think of perceptual distinctions as distinctions between (abstract) stimulus invariants, the problem of how such invariants are themselves detected needs to be solved; and it appears that solving it requires postulating the same sorts of inferences from inputs that empiricist theories assumed. The difference is mainly that contemporary psychologists do not assume that the computations, or the data over which they are defined, must be consciously accessible.[16]

It is worth emphasizing that the claim that the outputs of sensory mechanisms are, in general, not consciously accessible is supposed to be an empirical result rather than a truth of epistemology. There is, for example, quite good empirical evidence that an early representation of a speech sig-

[16] Gibson sometimes writes as though the problem of how the (presumed) stimulus invariants are detected could be avoided by distinguishing between the stimulus for the *sensory transducers* (viz., physical energies) and the stimulus for the *perceptual organs* (viz., abstract invariants). But this way trivialization lies. If one is allowed to use the notion of a stimulus so as to distinguish the input to the retina (light energy) from the input to the optic system (patterns of light energy which exhibit invariancies relevant, e.g., to the explanation of perceptual constancies), why not also talk about the stimulus for the *whole organism* (viz., perceptibles)? Thus, the answer to 'How do we perceive bottles?' would go: 'It is necessary and sufficient for the perception of a bottle that one detect the present of the stimulus invariant *bottle*'. The trouble with this answer (which, by the way, has a curiously Rylean sound to my ears) is, of course, that the problem of how one detects the relevant stimulus invariant is the *same* problem as how one perceives a bottle, so no ground has been gained overall.

What this shows, I think, is not that the psychological problem of perception is a muddle, but that *stating* the problem requires choosing (and motivating) a proprietary vocabulary for the representation of inputs. I have argued that the vocabulary of values of physical parameters *is* appropriate on the plausible assumption that sensory transducers detect values of physical parameters and that all perceptual knowledge is mediated by the activity of sensory transducers.

nal must specify its formant relations.[17] Yet speaker/hearers have no conscious access to formant structure and, for that matter, very little conscious access to any other acoustic property of speech. It is, in fact, very probably a general truth that, of the various redescriptions of the input that underlie perceptual analyses, the degree of conscious accessibility of a representation is pretty well predicted by the abstractness of its relation to what the sensors specify. This is the kind of point that such philosophers as Cassirer have had in mind when they remark that we 'hear through' an utterance of a sentence to its meaning; one is much better at reporting the syntactic type of which an utterance is a token than at reporting the acoustic properties of the token, and one is much better at reporting those syntactic features which affect meaning than those which don't. One might put it that one does not hear the formant relations in utterances of sentences even though one does hear the linguistic relations and the formant structure (*inter alia*) causally determines *which* linguistic relations one hears. Of course, which descriptions are consciously accessible is to some extent labile. Artists and phoneticians learn consciously to note properties of their sensory experience to which the layman is blind and deaf. This fact is by no means uninteresting; some of its consequences for the theory of internal representation will be pursued in Chapter 4.

Where we have gotten to is that the etiology of perceptual analyses involves a series of redescriptions of the environment, and that the initial description in this series specifies perceptually relevant physical properties of the environment. Perception must involve hypothesis formation and confirmation because the organism must somehow manage to infer the appropriate task-relevant description of the environment *from* its physical description together with whatever background information about the structure of the environment it has available. Notoriously, this inference is non-demonstrative: There is typically no *conceptual* connection between a perceptual category and its sensory indicants; an indefinite number of perceptual analyses will, in principle, be compatible with any given specification of a sensory input.[18] On this account, then, perceptual integrations are most plausibly viewed as species of inferences-to-the-best-explanation, the computational problem in perceptual integration being that of choosing the best hypothesis about the distal source of proximal stimulations.

There is, in short, an enormous problem about how to relate the conditions for applying physical descriptions to the conditions for applying

[17] I have been assuming that the representations of an environmental event that are assigned in the course of perceptual analysis are computed serially. Actually, a weaker assumption will do: viz., that at least *some* information about physical parameters normally 'gets in' before any higher-level representations are computed. I don't suppose this is a claim that any psychologist would wish to deny.

[18] Hence the possibility of perceptual illusions. For a discussion of perception that runs along the lines I have endorsed, see Gregory (1966) or Teuber (1960).

such descriptions as 'time for tea'. My present point is that the computational capacities of the organism must constitute a solution to such problems insofar as its perceptual judgments are (a) mediated by sensory information, and (b) true.

It is time to draw the moral, which will by now sound familiar. If one accepts, even in rough outline, the kind of approach to perception just surveyed, then one is committed to the view that perceptual processes involve computing a series of redescriptions of impinging environmental stimuli. But this is to acknowledge that perception presupposes a representational system; indeed, a representational system rich enough to distinguish between the members of sets of properties all of which are exhibited by the same event. If, for example, e is a token of a sentence type, and if understanding/perceptually analyzing e requires determining which sentence type it is a token of (see the first part of Chapter 3), then on the current view of understanding/perceptually analyzing, a series of representations of e will have to be computed. And this series will have to include, and distinguish between, representations which specify the acoustic, phonological, morphological, and syntactic properties of the token. It will have to include all these representations because, so far as anybody knows, each is essential for determining the type/token relation for utterances of sentences. It will have to distinguish among them because, so far as anyone knows, properties of sentences that are defined over any one of these kinds of representation will, ipso facto, be undefined for any of the others.

We are back to our old point that psychological processes are typically computational and computation presupposes a medium for representing the structures over which the computational operations are defined. Instead of further reiterating this point, however, I shall close this part of the discussion by making explicit two assumptions that the argument depends upon.

I have claimed that the only available models for deciding, concept learning, and perceiving all treat these phenomena as computational and hence presuppose that the organism has access to a language in which the computations are carried through. But, of course, this argument requires taking the models literally as at least schemata for explanations of the phenomena. In particular, it requires assuming that if such a model attributes a state to an organism, then insofar as we accept the model we are ontologically committed to the state. Now many philosophers do not like to play the game this way. They are willing to accept computational accounts of cognitive processes if only for lack of viable theoretical alternatives. But the models are accepted only as *façons de parler*, some reductionist program having previously been endorsed.

As I remarked in the introduction, I cannot prove that it is impossible to get the force of computational psychological theories in some framework which treats mental states as (e.g.) behavioral dispositions. But I think it is fair to say that no one has ever given any reason to believe that it is possible, and the program seems increasingly hopeless as empirical research reveals how complex the mental structures of organisms, and the interactions of such structures, really are. I have assumed that one oughtn't to eat the cake unless one is prepared to bite the bullet. If our psychological theories commit us to a language of thought, we had better take the commitment seriously and find out what the language of thought is like.

My second point is that, while I have argued for a language of thought, what I have really shown is at best that there is a language of computation; for thinking is something that *organisms* do. But the sorts of data processes I have been discussing, though they may well go on in the nervous systems of organisms, are presumably not, in the most direct sense, attributable to the organisms themselves.

There is, obviously, a horribly difficult problem about what determines what a person (as distinct from his body, or parts of his body) did. Many philosophers care terrifically about drawing this distinction, and so they should: It can be crucial in such contexts as the assessment of legal or moral responsibility. It can also be crucial where the goal is phenomenology: i.e., the systematic characterization of the *conscious* states of the organism.[19] But whatever relevance the distinction between states of the organism and states of its nervous system may have for *some* purposes, there is no particular reason to suppose that it is relevant to the purposes of cognitive psychology.

What cognitive psychologists typically try to do is to characterize the etiology of behavior in terms of a series of transformations of information. See the second part of Chapter 2, where this notion will be spelled out at length; but, roughly speaking, information is said to be available to the organism when the neural event which encodes it is one of the causal determinants of the behavior of the organism. 'Behavior' is itself construed broadly (and intuitively) to include, say, thinking and dreaming but not accelerating when you fall down the stairs.

If one has these ends in view, it turns out (again on empirical rather than conceptual grounds) that the ordinary distinction between what the

---

[19] It is, of course, quite unclear whether the latter undertaking can be carried through in any very revealing way. That will depend upon whether there *are* generalizations which hold (just) for conscious mental states, and that depends in turn on whether the conscious states of an organism have more in common with one another than with the *un*conscious states of the nervous system of the organism. It is, in this sense, an open question whether conscious psychological states provide a natural domain for a theory, just as it is an open question whether, say, all the objects in Minnesota provide a natural domain for a theory. One can't have theories of everything under every description, and which descriptions of which things can be generalized is not usually a question that can be settled a priori. I should have thought that, since Freud, the burden of proof has shifted to those who maintain that the conscious states (of human beings) do form a theoretical domain.

organism does, knows, thinks, and dreams, and what happens to and in its nervous system, does not seem to be frightfully important. The natural kinds, for purposes of theory construction, appear to include some things that the organism does, some things that happen in the nervous system of the organism, and some things that happen in its environment. It is simply no good for philosophers to urge that, since this sort of theory does not draw the usual distinctions, the theory *must* be a muddle. It cannot be an objection to a theory that there are some distinctions it does not make; if it were, it would be an objection to every theory. (Aristotelians thought that it was an argument *against* the Galelean mechanics that it did not distinguish between sublunary and heavenly bodies; i.e., that its generalizations were defined for both. This line of argument is now widely held to have been ill-advised.)

In short, the states of the organism postulated in theories of cognition would not count as states of the organism for purposes of, say, a theory of legal or moral responsibility. But so what? What matters is that they should count as states of the organism for *some* useful purpose. In particular, what matters is that they should count as states of the organism for purposes of constructing psychological theories that are true.

To put this point the other way around, if psychological theories fail to draw the usual distinctions between some of the things that happen to organisms and some of the things that organisms do, that does *not* imply that psychologists are committed to denying that there are such distinctions or that they should be drawn for some purposes or other. Nor does it imply that psychologists are (somehow, and whatever precisely this may mean) committed to 'redrawing the logical geography' of our ordinary mental concepts. What *is* implied (and all that is implied) is just that the distinction between actions and happenings isn't a *psychological* distinction. Lots of very fine distinctions, after all, are not.[20]

---

[20] These remarks connect, in obvious ways, with the ones that concluded the introduction: The various intellectual disciplines typically cross-classify one another's subject matter.

2
PRIVATE LANGUAGE, PUBLIC LANGUAGES

The inner is not the outer.
  SØREN KIERKEGAARD

WHY THERE HAS TO BE
A PRIVATE LANGUAGE

The discussion thus far might be summarized as follows: One of the essential variables in any theory of higher cognitive processes that we can now imagine is the character of the representation that the organism assigns to features of its environment and to its response options. This is, of course, a very traditional remark to make. Gestalt psychologists, for example, used to emphasize the salience of the *proximal* stimulus in the causation of behavior. Their point was that if you want to know how the organism will respond to an environmental event, you must first find out what properties it takes the event to have.[1] They might, with equal propriety, have emphasized the salience of the proximal *response;* if you want to know why the organism behaved the way it did, you must first find out what description it intended its behavior to satisfy; what it took itself to be doing. Chapter 1 sought to make explicit one of the presuppositions of this line of argument: The 'proximal stimulus' is a proximal *representation* of the *distal* stimulus, and the 'proximal response' *stands for* an overt act. But representation presupposes a medium of representation, and there is no symbolization without symbols. In particular, there is no internal representation without an internal language.

---

[1] Not only because behavior is sometimes based on false beliefs (e.g., on misassignments of properties to the stimulus) but also because the behaviorally salient properties of the stimulus are a *selection* from the properties that belong to it: Of all the indefinitely many properties the stimulus *does* have, only those can be behaviorally salient which the organism *represents* the stimulus as having. That is why, in practice, it is usually only by attending to the behavior of the organism that we can tell what the (proximal) stimulus is.

I think, myself, that this conclusion is both true and extremely important. There are, however, ways of construing it which would make it true but not very important. For example, one might argue as follows:

> Of course there is a medium in which we think, and of course it is a language. In fact, it is a natural language: English for English speakers, French for French speakers, Hindi for Hindi speakers, and so on. The argument which seemed to lead to exciting and paradoxical conclusions thus leads only to one's own front door. Your 'traditional remarks' rest, in short, on a traditional confusion. You suppose that natural language is the medium in which we *express* our thoughts; in fact, it is the medium in which we *think* them.

This is a kind of view which has appealed to very many philosophers and psychologists. Indeed, it *is* appealing, for it allows the theorist both to admit the essential role of computation (and hence of representation) in the production of behavior and to resist the more scarifying implications of the notion of a language of thought. It is, for example, all right for hypothesis formation to be essential to learning, and for hypotheses to presuppose a language to couch them in, so long as the language presupposed is, e.g., English. For English is a representational system to whose existence we are committed independent of our views about cognitive psychology; ask any English speaker. We can, in short, allow that cognitive processes are defined over linguistic objects and we can do so without raising anybody's methodological hackles. All we need to do is assume that the linguistic objects that cognitive processes are defined over are drawn from one of the *public* languages.

The only thing that's wrong with this proposal is that it isn't possible to take it seriously: So far as I can see, the radical consequences of the internal language view will have to be lived with. The obvious (and, I should have thought, sufficient) refutation of the claim that natural languages are the medium of thought is that there are nonverbal organisms that think. I don't propose to quibble about what's to count as thinking, so I shall make the point in terms of the examples discussed in Chapter 1. All three of the processes that we examined there—considered action, concept learning, and perceptual integration—are familiar achievements of infrahuman organisms and preverbal children. The least that can be said, therefore, is what we have been saying all along: Computational models of such processes are the only ones we've got. Computational models presuppose representational systems. But the representational systems of preverbal and infrahuman organisms surely cannot be natural languages. So either we abandon such preverbal and infrahuman psychology as we have so far pieced together, or we admit that some thinking, at least, isn't done in English.

 Notice that although computation presupposes a representational language, it does *not* presuppose that that language must be one of the ones which function as vehicles of communication between speakers and hearers: e.g., that it must be a natural language. So, on the one hand, there is no internal reason for supposing that our psychology applies only to organisms that talk, and if we do decide to so restrict its application we shall have no model at all for learning, choosing, and perceiving in populations other than fluent human beings. On the other hand, to extend our psychology to infrahuman species is thereby to commit ourselves to cognitive processes mediated by representational systems other than natural languages.

I think many philosophers are unimpressed by these sorts of considerations because they are convinced that it is not a question of fact but, as it were, of linguistic policy whether such psychological predicates as have their paradigmatic applications to fluent human beings ought to be 'extended' to the merely infraverbal. I was once told by a very young philosopher that it is a matter for *decision* whether animals can (can be said to) hear. 'After all', he said, 'it's *our* word'.

But this sort of conventionalism won't do; the issue isn't whether we ought to be polite to animals. In particular, there are homogeneities between the mental capacities of infraverbal organisms and those of fluent human beings which, so far as anybody knows, are inexplicable except on the assumption that infraverbal psychology is relevantly homogeneous with our psychology.

To take just one example, we remarked in Chapter 1 that human subjects typically have more trouble mastering disjunctive concepts than they do with conjunctive or negative ones. But we remarked, too, that the notion of the form of a concept needs to be relativized to whatever system of representation the subject employs. For one thing, disjunction is interdefinable with conjunction and negation and, for another, which concepts are disjunctive depends upon which kind terms the vocabulary of the representational system acknowledges. *Color* isn't, I suppose, a disjunctive concept despite the fact that colors come in different colors. Whereas, 'red or blue' *is* a disjunctive concept; i.e., is disjunctively represented in English and, presumably, in whatever system of representation mediates the integration of our visual percepts.

The point is that these remarks apply wholesale to infraverbal concept learning. Animals, too, typically find (what *we* take to be) disjunctive concepts hard to master. We can account for this fact if we assume that the representational system that *they* employ is relevantly like the one that *we* employ (e.g., that an animal conditioned to respond positive to either-a-triangle-or-a-square represents the reinforcement contingencies disjunctively, just as the experimenter does).[2] Since no alternative account

---

[2] For an experimental demonstration that preverbal human infants have differential difficulties with disjunctive contingencies of reinforcement, see Fodor, Garrett and Brill, 1975.

suggests itself (since, so far as I know, no alternative account has ever been suggested) it would seem to be the behavioral facts, and not our linguistic policies, which require us to hypothesize the relevant homogeneities between our representational system and the ones infraverbal organisms use.[3]

As one might expect, these sorts of issues become critical when we consider the preverbal child learning a first language. The first point to make is that we have no notion at all of how a first language might be learned that does not come down to some version of learning by hypothesis formation and confirmation. This is not surprising since, as we remarked in Chapter 1, barring the cases where what is learned is something explicitly taught, we have no notion of how *any* kind of concept is learned except by hypothesis formation and confirmation. And learning a language L must at least involve learning such concepts as 'sentence of L'.

If, for example, Chomsky is right (see Chomsky, 1965; for detailed discussion of Chomsky's views of syntax acquisition, see Fodor et al., 1974), then learning a first language involves constructing grammars consonant with some innately specified system of language universals and testing those grammars against a corpus of observed utterances in some order fixed by an innate simplicity metric. And, of course, there must be a language in which the universals, the candidate grammars, and the observed utterances are represented. And, of course, this language cannot be a natural language since, by hypothesis, it is his first language that the child is learning.[4]

In fact, however, for these purposes it doesn't matter whether Chomsky is right, since the same sort of point can be made on the basis of much

---

[3] It is worth emphasizing that this example is in no way special. The widespread homogeneity of human and infrahuman mental processes has been the main theme of psychological theorizing since Darwin. The interesting, exciting, and exceptional cases are, in fact, the ones where interspecific differences emerge. Thus, for example, there are situations in which infrahuman organisms treat as homogeneous stimuli which *we* take to be disjunctive. It is very difficult to train *octopus* to discriminate diagonal lines which differ (only) in left-right orientation. The natural assumption is that the representational system the animal employs does not distinguish between (i.e., assigns identical representations to) mirror images. For ingenious elaboration, see Sutherland (1960).

[4] Chomsky's argument infers the innateness of linguistic information (and hence of the representational system in which it is couched) from the universality of language structure across historically unrelated communities and from the complexity of the information the child must master if he is to become fluent. Versions of this argument can be found in Katz (1966) and Vendler (1972). I think it is a good argument, though it leaves a number of questions pending. Until we know *which* features of language are universal, it gives us no way of telling which aspects of the child's representation of his native language are innate. And: *How* complex does learning have to be for the hypothesis of a task-specific innate contribution to be plausible?

The considerations I shall be developing seek to delineate aspects of the child's innate contribution to language learning in ways that avoid these sorts of difficulties. But I shall be assuming what Chomsky et al. have always assumed and what Vendler more modest assumptions about what goes on in language acquisition. I want to discuss this claim in quite considerable detail.

To begin with, I am going to take three things for granted: (1) that learning a first language is a matter of hypothesis formation and confirmation in the sense explored in Chapter 1; (2) that learning a first language involves at least learning the semantic properties of its predicates; (3) that S learns the semantic properties of P only if S learns some generalization which determines the extension of P (i.e., the set of things that P is true of).

These assumptions are unequally tendentious. Item 1 rests on the arguments reviewed in Chapter 1. I take it that item 2 will be granted by anyone who is willing to suppose that there is anything at all to the notion of semantic properties as psychologically real. Item 3, on the other hand, is serious; but I shan't argue for it, since, as will presently become apparent, it is assumed primarily for purposes of exposition. Suffice it to remark here that many philosophers have found it plausible that one understands a predicate only if one knows the conditions under which sentences that contain it would be true. But if this is so, and if, as we have supposed, language learning is a matter of testing and confirming hypotheses, then among the generalizations about a language that the learner must hypothesize and confirm are some which determine the extensions of the predicates of that language. A generalization that effects such a determination is, by stipulation, a *truth rule*. I shall henceforth abbreviate all this to "S learns P only if S learns a truth rule for P."[5]

---

has made explicit: There is an analogy between learning a second language on the basis of a first and learning a first language on the basis of an innate endowment. In either case, some previously available representational system must be exploited to formulate the generalizations that structure the system that is being learned. Out of nothing nothing comes.

[5] I shall, throughout, employ the following format for truth rules. Where P is a predicate in the language to be learned, T is a truth rule for P iff (a) it is of the same form as F, and (b) all of its *substitution instances are*

$$F: \ulcorner P_y \urcorner \text{ is true (in } L) \text{ iff } x \text{ is } G$$

true. The substitution instances of F are the formulae obtained by:

1. Replacing the angles by quotes. (In effect, variables in angles are taken to range over the expressions of the object language.)
2. Replacing 'P_y' by a sentence whose predicate is P and whose subject is a name or other referring expression.
3. Replacing 'x' by an expression which designates the individual referred to by the subject of the quoted sentence. (This condition yields a nonsyntactic notion of *substitution instance* since whether one formula bears that relation to another will depend, in part, on what their referring expressions refer to. This is, however, both convenient and harmless for our purposes.)

So, suppose that L is English and P is the predicate 'is a philosopher'. Then, a plausible truth role for P is $\ulcorner y$ *is a philosopher* $\urcorner$ *is true iff* x *is a philosopher*. Substitution instances of this truth rule would include '*Fred is a philosopher*' *is true iff Fred is a philosopher*; '*the man on the corner is a philosopher*' *is true iff the man on the corner*

Since I propose to work these assumptions very hard, I had better get my caveats in early. There are three. First, though it is, for my purposes, convenient to identify learning the semantic properties of P with learning a truth rule for P, nothing fundamental to the argument I want to give depends on doing so. Readers who object to the identification are free to substitute some other notion of semantic property or to take that notion as unanalyzed. Second, to say that someone has learned a truth rule for a predicate is not to say that he has learned a procedure for determining when the predicate applies, or even that there is such a procedure. Third, if there were anything to dispositional accounts of what is involved in understanding a predicate, we would have an alternative to the theory that learning a predicate involves learning a rule. So the whole discussion will proceed on the assumption that there is, in fact, nothing to be said for dispositional accounts of what is involved in understanding a predicate. I shall expand each of these points at some length before returning to the main argument.

1. Many philosophers think that truth conditions provide too weak a construal of what we learn when we learn a predicate; e.g., that what we learn must be what sentences containing the predicate entail and are entailed by, not what they materially imply and are materially implied by. I have, in fact, considerable sympathy with such views. But the point I want to stress is that the arguments that follow are entirely neutral so far as those views are concerned. That is, these arguments are neutral vis-à-vis the controversy between extensionalist and intensionalist semantics. If you are an extensionalist, then surely you believe that the semantic properties of a predicate determine its extension. If you are an intensionalist, then presumably you believe that the semantic properties of a predicate determine its *in*tension and that intensions determine extensions. Either way, then, you believe what I have wanted to assume.

Another way of putting it is this: Both intensionalists and extensionalists hold that semantic theories pair object language predicates with their metalinguistic counterparts. Extensionalists hold that the critical condition on the paired expressions is coextensivity. Intensionalists hold that the critical condition is logical equivalence or, perhaps, synonymy. But if either of these latter conditions is satisfied, then the former condition is satisfied too. So, once again, how the extensionalist/intensionalist question is resolved doesn't matter for the purposes I have in mind.

---

is a philosopher; and 'Fred is a philosopher' is true iff the man on the corner is a philosopher (assuming Fred is the man on the corner) . . . etc.

Of course, nothing requires that the expression which forms the right-hand side of a truth rule (or its instances) should be drawn from the same language as the sentence quoted on the left. On the contrary, we shall see that that assumption is quite *im*plausible when *learning* truth rules is assumed to be involved in learning a language. (For a useful introduction to the general program of analyzing meaning in terms of truth, see Davidson, 1967).

There are, however, philosophers who hold not only that the semantic properties of a predicate don't determine its *in*tension but that they don't determine its *ex*tension either. Such philosophers claim (very roughly) that what we know about the meanings of predicates determine at most their *putative* extensions, but that whether the putative extension of a predicate is in fact its *real* extension is, in the long run, at the mercy of empirical discoveries.

Thus, Putnam (to be published) argues that when we learn 'gold', 'cat', 'water', etc. we learn socially accepted stereotypes such that it is *reasonable to believe* of things that conform to the stereotypes that they satisfy the predicates. But what it is reasonable to believe need not prove, in the long run, to be true. Perhaps there was a time when only liquid water was known to *be* water. Perhaps it was then discovered that ice is water in a solid state. (Surely this is ontogenetically plausible even if it's a historical fairy tale.) To discover this would be to discover something about what the extension of 'water' *really* is (viz., that ice is in it). But if it *is* an empirical discovery that ice is water, then it is hard to see how the fact that 'water' applies to ice could have been determined, in any substantive sense, by what one learns when one learns what 'water' means. And if that is right, then it is hard to see how learning what 'water' means could involve learning something that determines the extension of 'water' in advance of such discoveries. In short, on this view, either the semantic properties of a word aren't what you learn when you learn the word, or the semantic properties of a word don't determine its extension.

I don't want to become involved in assessing these suggestions because, right or wrong, they are largely irrelevant to the main points that I shall make. I will argue, primarily, that you cannot learn a language whose terms express semantic properties not expressed by the terms of some language you are already able to use. In formulating this argument, it is convenient to assume that the semantic properties expressed by a predicate are those which determine its extension, since, whatever its faults may be, that assumption at least yields a sharp sense of identity of semantic properties (two predicates have the same semantic properties if they apply to the same set of things.) If, however, that assumption fails, then the same sort of argument can be constructed given any other notion of semantic property, so long as its semantic properties are what you learn when you learn a word. If, for example, what you learn when you learn P is (only) that it would be reasonable to believe that P applies iff S, then, according to my argument, in order to learn the language containing P you must already be able to use some (other) language which contains some (other) term such that it would be reasonable to believe that *it* applies iff it would be reasonable to believe that P applies. And so on, *mutatis mutandis,* for other construals of *semantic property.*

I shall, then, continue to do what it is convenient to do: take the extension of a predicate to be what its semantic properties primarily determine. But only on the understanding that alternative readings of 'semantic property' may be substituted ad lib.

2. To endorse the view that learning a predicate involves learning a generalization which determines its extension is not to subscribe to any species of verificationism, though the literature has exhibited an occasional tendency to confuse the two doctrines.

Consider the English predicate 'is a chair'. The present view is, roughly, that no one has mastered that predicate unless he has learned that it falls under some such generalization as $\ulcorner y$ is a chair$\urcorner$ is true iff Gx. (For a discussion of the notation, see footnote 5 above.) But, of course, it does not follow that someone who knows what 'is a chair' means is therefore in command of a general procedure for sorting stimuli into chairs and non-chairs. That *would* follow only on the added assumption that he has a general procedure for sorting stimuli into those which do, and those which do not, satisfy G. But that assumption is no part of the view that learning a language involves learning truth rules for its predicates.

If, e.g., it is true that 'chair' means 'portable seat for one', then it is plausible that no one has mastered 'is a chair' unless he has learned that it falls under the truth rule $\ulcorner y$ is a chair$\urcorner$ is true iff x is a portable seat for one'. But someone might well know this about 'is a chair' and still not be able to *tell* about some given object (or, for that matter, about any object) whether or not *it* is a chair. He would be in this situation if, e.g., his way of telling whether a thing is a chair is to find out whether it satisfies the right-hand side of the truth rule, and if he is unable to tell about *this* (or any) thing whether it is a portable seat for one.

I make these remarks in light of Wittgenstein's observation that many (perhaps all) ordinary language predicates are open-textured; e.g., that there are indefinitely many objects about which we cannot tell whether they are chairs; not just because the lighting is bad or some of the facts aren't in, but because 'is a chair' is, as it were, undefined for objects of those kinds, so that whether they are chairs isn't a question of fact at all (cf. the chair (sic) made of soap bubbles; the packing case that is used as a chair, etc.). This is all true and well taken, but the present point is that it doesn't prejudice the notion that learning truth rules is essential to language learning, or the point that truth rules are expressed by biconditional formulae. All it shows is that *if* the truth condition on 'is a chair' is expressed by 'is a portable seat for one', then 'portable seat for one' must be open-textured, undefined, etc., for just those cases where 'is a chair' is.

One can get into no end of trouble by confusing this point. For example, Dreyfus (1972), if I understand him correctly, appears to endorse the following argument against the possibility of machine models of human linguistic capacities: (a) Machine models would presumably employ rules to express the extensions of the predicates they use. (b) Such rules would presumably be biconditionals (e.g., truth rules). But (c) Wittgenstein has shown that the extension of natural language predicates cannot be expressed by such rules because such predicates are inherently fuzzy-edged. So (d) people can't be modeled by machines and (e) a fortiori, people can't *be* machines.

But Wittgenstein showed no such thing. The most that can be inferred from the existence of open texture is that if a formula expresses the truth conditions on *P,* then its truth value must be indeterminate wherever the truth value of *P* is indeterminate. To put it slightly differently, if a machine simulates a speaker's use of a predicate, then (the machine ought to be unable to determine whether the predicate applies) iff (the speaker is unable to determine whether the predicate applies). But there is nothing at all in the notion of machines as rule-following devices that suggests that that condition cannot be met. Correspondingly, there is nothing in the notion that people's use of language is rule governed which suggests that every predicate in a language must have a determinate applicability to every object of predication.

3. I have assumed not only that learning a predicate involves learning something which determines its extension, but also that 'learning something which determines the extension of *P*' should be analyzed as learning that *P* falls under a certain rule (viz., a truth rule). Now, someone could accept the first asumption while rejecting the second: e.g., by postulating some sort of behavioral analysis of '*S* knows the extension of *P*.' Equivalently for these purposes he could accept both assumptions and postulate a dispositional analysis of knowing a rule. Thus, if the truth rule for *P* is '⌜*Py*⌝ is true iff *Gx*', then to know the truth rule might be equated with having a disposition to say *P* just in cases where *G* applies. Similarly, learning the truth conditions on *P* would be a matter (not of hypothesizing and confirming that the corresponding truth rule applies, but just) of having one's response dispositions appropriately shaped.

A number of philosophers who ought to know better do, apparently, accept such views. Nevertheless, I shall not bother running through the standard objections since it seems to me that if *anything* is clear it is that understanding a word (predicate, sentence, language) isn't a matter of how one behaves or how one is disposed to behave. Behavior, and behavioral disposition, are determined by the interactions of a variety of psychological variables (what one believes, what one wants, what one remembers, what one is attending to, etc.). Hence, in general, any behavior whatever is compatible with understanding, or failing to understand, any predicate whatever. Pay me enough and I will stand on my head iff you say 'chair'. But I know what 'is a chair' means all the same.

So much for caveats. Now I want to draw the moral. Learning a language (including, of course, a first language) involves learning what the predicates of the language mean. Learning what the predicates of a language mean involves learning a determination of the extension of these predicates. Learning a determination of the extension of the predicates involves learning that they fall under certain rules (i.e., truth rules). But one cannot learn that *P* falls under *R* unless one has a language in which *P* and *R* can be represented. So one cannot learn a language unless one has a language. In particular, one cannot learn a first language unless one already has a system capable of representing the predicates in that language *and their extensions*. And, on pain of circularity, that system cannot be the language that is being learned. But first languages *are* learned. Hence, at least some cognitive operations are carried out in languages other than natural languages.

Wittgenstein, commenting upon some views of Augustine's, says:

> Augustine describes the learning of human languages as if the child came into a strange country and did not understand the language of the country;[6] that is, as if it already had a language, only not this one. Or again, as if the child could already *think,* only not yet speak. And 'think' would here mean something like 'talk to itself', (1953, para. 32).

Wittgensetin apparently takes it that such a view is transparently absurd. But the argument that I just sketched suggests, on the contrary, that Augustine was precisely and demonstrably right and that seeing that he was is prerequisite to any serious attempts to understand how first languages are learned.

I think, in fact, that this kind of argument can be extended in ways that have profound consequences for almost every area of the psychology of cognition. In the third part of this chapter, I shall provide some reasons for believing that this is true. At present, however, I have to start upon a rather lengthy digression. I want to deal with several interrelated kinds of objections which purport to show that, however plausible the individual steps in such an argument may seem, they *must* be wrong because the conclusions they lead to are incoherent. I shall take these objections seriously not only because, so far as I can tell, many philosophers hold that one or another of them is sound, but also because in the course of seeing what is wrong with them one can lay bare quite a lot of the philosophical foundations of computational approaches to psychology. I want to give an account of how appeals to internal representations function in psychological theories because I want to show that it's all right for such appeals to function in the ways they do.

---

[6] For example, Augustine represents the child as trying to figure out what the adults are referring to when they use the referring expressions of their language. Wittgenstein's point is that this picture could make sense only on the assumption that the child has access to a linguistic system in which the 'figuring out' is carried on.

HOW THERE COULD BE A
PRIVATE LANGUAGE

The first objection I want to consider is an allegation of infinite regress. It can be dealt with quickly (but for a more extensive discussion, see the exchange between Harman, 1969, and Chomsky, 1969).

Someone might say: 'According to you, one cannot learn a language unless one already knows a language. But now consider *that* language, the metalanguage in which representations of the extensions of object language predicates are formulated. Surely, learning *it* must involve prior knowledge of a meta-metalanguage in which its truth definitions are couched. And so on ad infinitum. Which is unsatisfactory'. There is, I think, a short and decisive answer. My view is that you can't learn a language unless you already *know* one. It isn't that you can't learn a language unless you've already *learned* one. The latter claim leads to infinite regress, but the former doesn't; not, at least by the route currently being explored. What the objection has in fact shown is that *either* my views are false *or* at least one of the languages one knows isn't learned. I don't find this dilemma embarrassing because the second option seems to me to be entirely plausible: the language of thought is known (e.g., is the medium for the computations underlying cognitive processes) but not learned. That is, it is innate. (Compare Atherton and Schwartz, 1974, which commits explicitly the bad argument just scouted.)

There is, however, another way of couching the infinite regress argument that is more subtle: 'You say that understanding a predicate involves representing the extension of that predicate in some language you already understand. But now consider understanding the predicates of the metalanguage. Doesn't that presuppose a representation of *its* truth conditions in some meta-metalanguage previously understood? And, once again, so on ad infinitum?' This argument differs from the first one in that the regress is run on 'understand' rather than on 'learn', and that difference counts. For, while I am not committed to the claim that the language of thought is *learned,* I am committed to the claim that it is, in a certain sense, understood: e.g., that it is available for use as the vehicle of cognitive processes. Nevertheless, this objection, like the other one, commits the fallacy of *ignoratio elenchi*: The position attacked is not the one defended.

What I said was that learning what a predicate means involved representing the extension of that predicate; not that understanding the predicate does. A sufficient condition for the latter might be just that one's use of the predicate is always in fact conformable to the truth rule. To see what's at issue here, consider the case of real computers.

Real computers characteristically use at least two different languages: an input/output language in which they communicate with their environment and a machine language in which they talk to themselves (i.e., in which they run their computations). 'Compilers' mediate between the two languages in effect by specifying biconditionals whose left-hand side is a formula in the input/output code and whose right-hand side is a formula in the machine code. Such biconditionals are, to all intents and purposes, representations of truth conditions for formulae in the input/output language, and the ability of the machine to use that language depends on the availability of those definitions. (All this is highly idealized, but it's close enough for present purposes.)[7] My point is that, though the machine must have a compiler if it is to use the input/output language, it doesn't *also* need a compiler for the machine language. What avoids an infinite regression of compilers is the fact that the machine is *built* to use the machine language. Roughly, the machine language differs from the input/output language in that its formulae correspond directly to computationally relevant physical states and operations of the machine: The physics of the machine thus guarantees that the sequences of states and operations it runs through in the course of its computations respect the semantic constraints on formulae in its internal language. What takes the place of a truth definition for the machine language is simply the engineering principles which guarantee this correspondence.

I shall presently return to this point in some detail. For the moment, suffice it to suggest that there are two ways in which it can come about that a device (including, presumably, a person) understands a predicate. In one case, the device has and employs a representation of the extension of the predicate, where the representation is itself given in some language that the device understands. In the second case, the device is so constructed that its use of the predicate (e.g., in computations) comport with the conditions that such a representation would specifiy. I want to say that the first is true of predicates in the natural languages people learn and the second of predicates in the internal language in which they think.

'But look', you might reply, 'you admit that there is at least one language whose predicates we understand without the internal representation of truth conditions. You admit that, for that language, the answer to: "How do we use its predicates correctly?" is that we just do; that we are just built that way. This saves you from infinite regress, but it suggests that even the

---

[7] Someone might point out that, if the compiler formulae are biconditional, they could be read as specifying truth conditions for formulae in the *machine language* with the input/output code providing the metalinguistic vehicles of representation. In fact, however, the appearance of symmetry is spurious even if the two languages are entirely intertranslatable. For while the machine uses the machine code formulae without appealing to the compiler, it has no access to formulae in the input/output language except via the translations that the compiler effects. There is thus a useful sense in which, so far as the machine is concerned, machine language formulae express the meanings of formulae in the input/output code but not vice versa. This point is related to one that will turn up in Chapter 3: Philosophers have been too inclined to assume that 'translation' theories of meaning are ineradicably infected with symmetry.

regress from the natural language to the inner langauge is otiose. You argue that we learn "is a chair" only if we learn that it falls under the truth rule ⌜y is a chair⌝ is true iff x is G) and then you say that the question of learning a truth role for G doesn't arise. Why not stop a step sooner and save yourself trouble? Why not say that the question of how we learn "is a chair" doesn't arise either? Explanation has to stop somewhere'.

The answer is that explanation has to stop somewhere but it doesn't have to—and it better not—stop *here*. The question of how we learn 'is a chair' *does* arise precisely because English *is* learned. The question of how G is learned does not arise precisely because, by hypothesis, the language in which G is a formula is innate. Once again, thinking about computers is likely to be illuminating.

The critical property of the machine language of computers is that its formulae can be paired directly with the computationally relevant physical states of the machine in such fashion that the operations the machine performs respect the semantic constraints on formulae in the machine code. Token machine states are, in this sense, interpretable as tokens of the formulae. Such a correspondence can *also* be effected between physical states of the machine and formulae of the input/output code, but only by first compiling these formulae: i.e., only by first translating them into the machine language. This expresses the sense in which machines *are* 'built to use' their machine language and are *not* 'built to use' their input/output codes. It also suggests an empirical theory: When you find a device using a language it was not built to use (e.g., a language that it has *learned*), assume that the way it does it is by translating the formulae of that language into formulae which correspond directly to its computationally relevant physical states. This would apply, in particular, to the formulae of the natural languages that speaker/hearers learn, and the correlative assumption would be that the truth rules for predicates in the natural language function as part of the translation procedure.

Admittedly this is just a *theory* about what happens when someone understands a sentence in a language he has learned. But at least it *is* a theory, and one which makes understanding a sentence analogous to computational processes whose character we roughly comprehend. On this view, what happens when a person understands a sentence must be a translation process basically analogous to what happens when a machine 'understands' (viz., compiles) a sentence in its programing language. I shall try to show, in Chapter 3, that there are broadly empirical grounds for taking this sort of model seriously. My present point, however, is just that it is at least *imaginable* that there should be devices which need truth definitions for the languages they speak but not for the language that they compute in. If *we* are such devices, then there is point to asserting that learning English involves learning that ⌜y is a chair⌝ is true iff x is G, even though one denies that learning that requires learning that ⌜y is G⌝, is true iff x is Ψ for any Ψ other than G or 'is a chair'.

I don't, in short, think that the view of language learning so far sketched leads to infinite regress. It does lead to a one-stage regress; viz., from the natural language to the internal code—and that one stage is empirically rather than conceptually motivated. That is, we can imagine an organism which is born speaking and born speaking whatever language its nervous system uses for computing. For such an organism, the question of how it learns its language would, *ex hypothesi,* not arise; and the view that its use of the language is controlled by an internal representation of the truth conditions upon the predicates of that language might well be otiose. All we would need to suppose is that the organism is so constructed that its use of the expressions in the language conforms to the conditions that a truth definition for the language would articulate. But we are not such organisms and, so far as I know, for us no alternative to the view that we learn rules which govern the semantic properties of the expressions in our language is tenable.

I turn now to a final kind of objection that might be raised against the conceptual coherence of the assumptions about language learning that I have been making. In the course of examining this objection, I shall try to make clear just how the appeal to internal representations works in psychological theories which assume that internal representations are the medium for cognitive processes. Having done so, I shall return to the main discussion and consider some of the general implications of the present view of language learning insofar as it bears on the question what internal representations must be like.

One way of describing my views is that organisms (or, in any event, organisms that behave) have not only such natural languages as they may happen to have, but also a private language in which they carry out the computations that underlie their behavior. I think this is a fair characterization of what I have been saying, but I recognize that some philosophers would take it to be a reductio ad absurdum argument. Wittgenstein is supposed to have proved that there can be no such thing as a private language (1953, around p. 258).

I don't propose to enter the miasma of exegetical dispute that surrounds the private language argument. What I shall do is provide a brief reconstruction and show that the argument, so construed, does no damage to the sorts of views I have been recommending. It remains open, of course, that the argument might prove damaging on some *other* reconstruction. But it is worth mentioning that, whatever Wittgenstein proved, it cannot have been that it is impossible that a language should be private in whatever sense the machine language of a computer is, for there *are* such things as computers, and whatever is actual is possible. I stress this because, as we go along, I shall continue to rely very heavily on the machine analogy both as an existence proof for devices which don't speak the language they compute in and as a potential empirical model for the relation between natural languages and the language of thought.

I take it that Wittgenstein is basically concerned to show that no definite sense attaches to the notion of a term in a private language being used coherently (as opposed, e.g., to being used at random). Wittgenstein has, in this respect, two ways of characterizing a private language: either as one whose terms refer to things that only its speaker can experience or as a language for the applicability of whose terms there exist no public criteria (or rules, or conventions). For Wittgenstein's purpose (which I take to be fundamentally that of attacking the idea of a sense datum language) these two formulations come to pretty much the same thing: If I am the only one who can know what a term like 'mild tickle' refers to, then, clearly, the conventions for applying that term cannot be public. For, by hypothesis, only I could tell when the conventions are satisfied; only I would know whether a certain event is of the kind that falls under the conventions.

But, on Wittgenstein's view, I wouldn't know either. Suppose I believe that a certain event (the occurrence of a sensation of mine) is of the kind properly described as my having a mild tickle. Then there are two possibilities: either there is something—some evidence—that would count to show that I am right in using the term to describe this kind of event or there is not. Suppose there is such evidence. Then, if I can appeal to it, why can't others? That is, if there is such evidence, it is presumably public property at least in principle. But if there are public reasons for believing that terms in my language apply, then by definition it isn't a private language.[8]

So, consider the other possibility: that there is *nothing* that would show that 'mild tickle' is properly applied to sensations like the one that I am having. If there is no such evidence, then there is no difference between getting the use of the term right and getting it wrong: no difference between obeying the conventions for the use of the term and failing to obey them. But a convention such that adhering to it and failing to adhere to it come to the same thing is no convention at all. And a term ungoverned by a convention is a term that may be used at random. And a term that may be used at random is no term at all. And a language without terms is no language at all. But if it isn't a language then, a fortiori, it isn't a private language.

Now, an internal representational system of the sort that I have hypothesized would be a private language by the second test even if not by the first. That is, it is certainly true that the applicability of terms in the putative language of thought is not determined by public conventions, though there is no particular reason to suppose that what such terms apply to must be private events; they might apply to numbers, or chairs, or predicates of English, or

8 'Mild tickle'—the English phrase—is, of course, a paradigm of a *public* language term; in particular, there are lots of ways in which I could tell if I were misapplying it, and these ways of telling are equally available to people who don't happen to be me. Imagine the case of a foreigner learning English where the question arises whether he hasn't gotten 'mild tickle' wrong. Imagine, for example, that it seems possible that he takes 'mild tickle' to mean what 'green afterimage' actually does mean. Wittgenstein's point is that there wouldn't be any philosophical problem for him (or for us) in finding out. What shows that there wouldn't be any *philosophical* problem is that there clearly wouldn't be any *practical* problem.

people with red hair, etc. In short, though nothing requires that the language of thought should be construed as a sense datum language, it may seem, nevertheless, to fall in the scope of Wittgenstein's argument and thus to be in peril of that argument being a good one. What shall we do about this?

To begin with, it seems clear that the private language argument isn't really directed against the sort of theory I have been endorsing. For there is no reason why a mentalist needs to assume that mental operations exhibit epistemic privacy in any very strong sense of that notion. Indeed, he had better not assume that if he wants his psychological theories to be compatible with a materialistic ontology; neurological events are public.

I suppose that Wittgenstein might argue that neurological evidence for the coherent use of internal language terms would be irrelevant even if it were available. We don't in fact use neurological criteria for determining that someone has mastered the use of a term when, e.g., we are teaching him a language. But this really would be doubly beside the point. First, the language of thought is presumably innate. Hence, though there is an obligation to make sense of the notion of its being used coherently, there is no obligation to show how it could be taught or learned. Second, the evidence that the language of thought *is* used coherently might be empirical without being neurological. It might, e.g., have the status of the best available explanation of the overall coherence of the organisms's mental life.

The next point is that the private language argument—at least as I have been construing it—isn't really any good. For, as many philosophers have pointed out, the most that the argument shows is that unless there are public procedures for *telling* whether a term is coherently applied, there will be no way of *knowing* whether it is coherently applied. But it doesn't follow that there wouldn't in fact *be* a difference between applying the term coherently and applying it at random. A fortiori, it doesn't follow that there isn't any *sense* to claiming that there is a difference between applying the term coherently and applying it at random. These consequences would, perhaps, follow on the verificationist principle that an assertion can't be sensible unless there is some way of telling whether it is true, but *surely* there is nothing to be said for that principle.

Notice (and this, for our purposes, is the crucial point) that the use of a language for computation does not require that one should be able to *determine* that its terms are consistently employed; it requires only that they should in fact *be* consistently employed. Someone might argue like this: 'Imagine a man doing sums, and suppose that he has no way of assuring himself that the number that he was using the numeral '2' to refer to five minutes ago was the same number that he is using the numeral '2' to refer to now. Then, surely, he *couldn't* use the numerals to effect his computations'. But, surely, he could. The soundness of inferences is not impugned by the *possibility* of equivocating, but only by instances of actual equivocation. Of course, if the poor man became convinced (say by reading bad philosophy) that he might in fact be using the numerals at random, his *faith* in his computations would be correspondingly shaken. If, however, there is a language of thought, it employment does not rest on faith. We use it the way we do not out of philosophical conviction but out of biological necessity.

Still, it is one thing to accuse Wittgenstein of verificationism; it is quite another to meet the challenge that the private language argument proposes. We must give some sense to the notion of terms in an internal representational system being used coherently and we must show how that sense is at least reasonably analogous to the sense in which the terms in public languages are coherently employable. If we can't do the former, then perhaps the notion of a language of thought is not itself coherent. If we can't do the latter, there's not much point to calling the language of thought a *language*.

Wittgenstein has, I think, a certain picture of what coherence of employment comes to for terms in a *public* language (e.g., English). Very roughly, the use of public language terms is controlled by the conventions of the speech community. These conventions relate the terms (in many different ways) to paradigm public situations. To use a term coherently is to use it in accordance with the governing conventions. To use it in accordance with the governing conventions is to use it when the paradigms are satisfied. In short, a term is coherently employed when its use is controlled (in the right sorts of ways) by the facts about the world.

Now, the first point to notice is that—quite aside from worries about public vs. private languages—this picture can't be right. For suppose my intentions are impeccable: Suppose, in the limiting case, that I intend to use a term in, and only in, those situations which are paradigmatic for that term. Still, my verbalizations are determined not just by my *intentions* but also by my *beliefs*. Hence, in particular, the degree of correspondence I can actually effect between my use of P and the occurrence of paradigm P-situations depends not only on my linguistic policies with respect to P but also on how good I am at determining which situations *are* P-situations. If my beliefs are very often badly wrong, then there may be little or no correspondence between what I say and the way the world is. But it may be true, for all that, that there is sense to the notion that the terms in my language are coherently employed. P may be the term that applies, paradigmatically, in P-situations even if I fail, and fail continually, to so apply it.

My point is that, even in the case of public languages, coherence doesn't require a stable relation between the way the terms are used and the way the world *is*: What it requires is a stable relation between the way the terms are used and *the way the speaker believes the world to be*.[9] That is,

---

[9] Communication between speaker and hearer requires, roughly, that the hearer should be able to infer *what the speaker believes* from what the speaker says (see Chapter 3). When the speaker's beliefs are *true*, the hearer will also be able to infer how the world is from what the speaker says. This latter may be what communication is *for*, but it isn't required for communication to occur.

what *does* seem to be essential to the coherent use of a language is the existence of a certain correspondence between the propositional attitudes and the linguistic practices of the speaker/hearer; in particular, between what he believes the facts are and what forms of words he takes to be true. So, then, to a first approximation, (Smith uses 'Jones is sick' to represent the state of affairs in which Jones is sick) iff (Smith assents to assertions made by employing the *form of words* 'Jones is sick' iff Smith believes that Jones is sick).[10] Similarly, (Bill uses 'Morris is a linguist' to represent the state of affairs in which Morris is a linguist) iff (Bill assents to assertions made by employing the form of words 'Morris is a linguist' iff Bill believes that Morris is a linguist). And, in general, (S uses $\ulcorner a$ is $P\urcorner$ to represent the state of affairs in which a is F) iff (S assents to assertions made by using the form of words $\ulcorner a$ is $F\urcorner$ iff x believes that a is F).[11]

It should be emphasized that this condition is entirely nontrivial. This can be seen by reflecting that it would *not* be satisfied, e.g., by someone who used $\ulcorner b$ is $G\urcorner$ to represent the state of affairs in which a is F. For such a one, it would be $\ulcorner b$ is $G\urcorner$ (and *not* $\ulcorner a$ is $F\urcorner$) that he assents to iff he believes that a is F.[12]

I am saying, roughly, that someone uses his language coherently when there is a certain correspondence between what he believes and the form of words he uses to express his beliefs. In the paradigm case—the use of terms in a natural language—this correspondence holds because the speaker knows and adheres to the conventions that govern the language. For, as we shall see in Chapter 3, such conventions fundamentally *are* the rules which pair propositional attitudes like beliefs with the forms of words that express those

---

[10] This includes, of course, assenting to his own assertions. I am not, by the way, assuming that assenting is a form of *behavior,* so the present analysis isn't intended to be reductive.

[11] This is, of course, not true. For one thing, x may have *many* ways of representing the state of affairs in which a is F and he may use different ones depending on which propositional attitude he bears to a's being F. Thus, one can imagine a language in which you represent a's being F one way if you *fear* that a is F, a different way if you *hope* that a is F, and a third way if you *believe* that a is F. For example, one could imagine languages in which the *form* of a sentence embedded to a complement verb varies depending on which propositional attitude the verb expresses. So far as I know, there aren't any such languages. *If* there aren't, that fact is striking.

I think this opens interesting lines of speculation, but I shan't pursue them in what follows. If the condition just suggested is reasonably close it's close enough for the purposes at hand.

[12] I am reading 'believes' as opaque in (S uses $\ulcorner a$ is $F\urcorner$ to represent the state of affairs in which a is F) iff (S assents to assertions made by using the form of words $\ulcorner a$ is $F\urcorner$ iff S believes that a is F). This of course yields a correspondingly opaque reading of 'represent', which seems to me the natural one. If, however, you think that S uses $\ulcorner P\urcorner$ to represent the state of affairs in which b is G follows from S uses $\ulcorner P\urcorner$ to represent the state of affairs in which a is F and the state of affairs in which a is $F =$ the state of affairs in which b is G, then read 'believe' transparently in the first formula.

attitudes. The kind of private language that Wittgenstein envisages departs from this paradigm insofar as the relation between linguistic forms and propositional attitudes is *not* mediated by public conventions. The challenge that the private language argument poses to the notion of a language of thought is, therefore this: Show how such a relation could be mediated by something *other* than public conventions. I want to do this now in some detail.

Every computational device is a complex system which changes physical state in some way determined by physical laws. It is feasible to think of such a system as a computer just insofar as it is possible to devise some mapping which pairs physical states of the device with formulae in a computing language in such fashion as to preserve desired semantic relations among the formulae. For example, we may assign physical states of the machine to sentences of the language in such a way that if $S_1 \ldots S_n$ are machine states, and if $F_1 \ldots F_{n-1}, F_n$ are the sentences paired with $S_1 \ldots S_{n-1}, S_n$, respectively, then the physical constitution of the machine is such that it will actually run through that sequence of states only if $F_1 \ldots F_{n-1}$ constitutes a proof of F_n. Patently, there are indefinitely many ways of pairing states of the machine with formulae in a language which will preserve this sort of relation, which is to say that the decipherment of the machine code exhibits indeterminacy of translation. Patently, there are indefinitely many ways of assigning formulae to machine states which do *not* preserve such relations among the formulae: only, in such assignments, we cannot interpret the machine's changes of state as proofs.

When we think of an organism as a computer, we attempt to assign formulae in the vocabulary of a psychological theory to physical states of the organism (e.g., to states of its nervous system). Ideally, the assignment should be carried through in such fashion that (some, at least) of the sequences of states that are causally implicated in the production of behavior can be interpreted as computations which have appropriate descriptions of the behavior as their 'last line'.[13] The idea is that, in the case of organisms as in the case of real computers, if we get the right way of assigning formulae

13 In the usual case a description of behavior is 'appropriate' insofar as it is the (or a) description that the organism intended the behavior to satisfy. There would, e.g., be no point to pairing the articulatory gestures of English speakers with sentences of English in such fashion that the acoustic form 'it's raining' gets assigned to the sentence 'someone is standing on my foot'. For, though such a pairing could certainly be defined—though we could adopt a scheme for translating one another's verbalizations such that, according to that scheme, what people are saying when they make the sound 'it's raining' is *that* their foot is being trod upon—to endorse this assignment would enormously complicate the part of the psychological theory which seeks to relate the verbalizations people produce to the intentions with which they produce them. At least the assumption that people who utter 'it's raining' are using the sentence 'it's raining' to say that it's raining allows for a simple and convincing explanation of the fact that such people are often to be found carrying umbrellas.

to the states it will be feasible to interpret the sequence of events that *causes* the output as a computational *derivation* of the output. In short, the organic events which we accept as implicated in the etiology of behavior will turn out to have two theoretically relevant descriptions if things turn out right: a physical description by virtue of which they fall under causal laws and a psychological description by virtue of which they constitute steps in the computation from the stimulus to the response. And so, of course, will the proximal representations of the stimulus and the response.[14, 15]

[14]Dennett (1969) is pretty brusque with this sort of view:

> It is possible, perhaps, that the brain has developed storage and transmission methods involving syntactically analysable events or structures, so that, for example, some patterns of molecules or impulses could be brain-word tokens, but even if there were some such 'language' or 'code' . . . there would also have to be mechanisms for 'reading' and 'understanding' this language. Without such mechanisms, the storage and transmission of sentence like things in the brain would be as futile as saying 'giddyap' to an automobile. These reading mechanisms, in turn, would have to be information processing systems, and what are we to say of *their* internal states and events? Do *they* have syntactically analysable parts? The regress must end eventually with some systems which store, transmit, and process information in non-syntactic form. (p. 87)

But, in fact, the regress never needs to start. The argument is fundamentally wrong-headed since it assumes a picture of the nervous system as issuing commands which must be 'read' and translated into actions (or, anyhow, into muscle contractions) by some *further* system that intervenes between the efferent nerves and the effectors. But this picture is no part of the theory. On the contrary, what is required is just that the *causal* properties of such physical events as are interpreted as messages in the internal code must be compatible with the *linguistic* properties that the interpretation assigns to those events. Thus, if events of the physical type P are to be interpreted as commands to effector system E, then it better be the case that, *ceteris paribus*, occurrences of P-events are causally sufficient for activating E. (*Ceteris paribus* means: barring mechanical breakdown and barring events interpretable as overriding countercommands to E.) If this condition *is* satisfied, it's hard to see where the need for an 'intelligent' device to 'read' P-events comes in. And, if it's *not* satisfied, it's hard to see what point there could possibly have been in interpreting P-events as commands to E in the first place.

[15] A—by now—chestnut of a question that is supposed to embarrass information flow psychologists goes like this: 'If you are willing to attribute regularities in the behavior of organisms to rules that they unconsciously follow, why don't you say (e.g.) that the planets 'follow' Kepler's laws in pursuit of their orbits about the sun?' The point, of course, is to suggest that the only *real* case of rule following is conscious rule following by articulate organisms. What other organisms do is (not *follow* rules but) merely act in accordance with them.

It should now be clear how this sort of question is to be dealt with. What distinguishes what organisms do from what the planets do is that a *representation of the rules they follow constitutes one of the causal determinants of their behavior.* So far as we know, however, this is not true of the planets: At no point in a causal account of their turnings does one advert to a structure which encodes Kepler's laws and causes them to turn. The planets *might* have worked that way, but the astronomers assure us that they do not. So the solar system is not a computational system, but you and I, for all we now know, may be.

The remarks thus far are supposed to hold independent of any particular assumptions about the content of psychological theories. Indeed, they hold of *any* physical system insofar as its changes of state are interpreted as computations. But it was the burden of the discussion in Chapter 1 that any psychological theory that has a prayer of being true will have to ascribe a special role to the computational states of organisms; viz., the way that information is stored, computed, accepted, rejected or otherwise processed by the organism explains its cognitive states and, particularly, its propositional attitudes. That is, the psychologist assumes that some organic processes satisfy descriptions like 'storing, accepting, rejecting, computing, etc., *P*' and that the organism learns, perceives, decides, remembers, believes, etc., whatever it does *because* it stores, accepts, rejects, or computes whatever it does.

I do not wish to discuss the probity of such assumptions at this point. As I have been saying all along, our options seem to be either to tolerate them or to do without theories in cognitive psychology altogether. Nor do I wish extensively to discuss *which* computational processes might appropriately be ascribed to organisms. But I think there are some widely (if inexplicitly) accepted conditions upon such ascriptions, and they take us very close to the heart of the methodological assumptions of modern cognitive psychology.

There are three of these: first, that the computational states ascribable to organisms can be directly explicated as relations between the organism and *formulae*: i.e., formulae in the internal code. So, e.g., insofar as one can (loosely) say that the organism stores the information that *P*, one must be able (*strictly*) to say that the organism is in a certain computational relation to the formula *P* (e.g., the relation of storing *P*). The second assumption is that the class of basic, theoretically relevant relations between the organism and formulae of the internal code (i.e., the class of relations that can be constitutive of the computational states and processes of the organism) is pretty small; in particular, that it is small compared to the class of theoretically relevant relations between the organism and propositions. Finally, and this is the important one, that for any propositional attitude of the organism (e.g., fearing, believing, wanting, intending, learning, perceiving, etc., that *P*) there will be a corresponding computational relation between the organism and some formula(e) of the internal code such that (*the organism has the propositional attitude iff the organism is in that relation*) is nomologically necessary.[16]

---

[16] It must be obvious that this third condition cannot be met as it stands; and, though I think it can be patched up in any of a variety of ways, I shan't attempt to choose between them here. The problem is that some propositional attitude terms are 'relational' in the sense that they apply to the organism (not just in virtue of its computational state, but) in virtue of the way the world is. That is, there are some propositional attitudes for which sufficient conditions *cannot* be given just in terms of internal data processes of the kinds we have been discussing. Consider, for example,

This is a long, but I hope helpful, way of saying that what one tries to do in cognitive psychology is to explain the propositional attitudes of the organism by reference to its (hypothetical) computational operations, and that the notion of a *computational* operation is being taken literally here; viz., as an operation defined for (internal) *formulae*. So, for example, assume that remembering P is one of the relations that a reasonable psychological theory might acknowledge between an organism and (the proposition) P. Suppose, too, that storing F is one of the computational relations that a reasonable psychological theory might acknowledge between an organism and the internal formula F. It would then be (at best) a contingent truth—precisely the kind of contingent truth that cognitive psychology seeks to formulate—that the organism remembers P if, and only if, the organism stores F.[17]

I should add one further point. I have been saying that theories in

---

knowing that a is F. Clearly, no organism knows that a is F unless it is the case that a is F. Equally clearly, whether a is F is not, in general, determined by a determination of the computational state of the organism. It follows that there can be no computational relation to a formula such that (an organism knows that a is F) iff (it stands in that relation to that formula). Similar remarks hold for (but not only for) the propositional attitudes designated by other factive verbs like 'regret', 'perceive', 'remember', etc.

There are, as I remarked above, several ways of fixing this, none of which seems to me to be obviously the best. For example, one might simply stipulate that the nonrelational propositional attitudes and only those are covered by the third condition, leaving it as a problem in analysis to determine which propositional attitudes the relational ones are. Or one might, as it were, 'construct' a nonrelational propositional attitude corresponding to each relational one by 'dropping' such conditions on the ascription of the latter as constrain nonpsychological states, events, or processes. So, to a first approximation, 'rationally believing' corresponds to 'knowing' in the sense that an organism rationally believes that a is F iff the organism satisfies all the conditions on knowing that a is F except the factivity condition. In a similar spirit, 'seeming to see' corresponds to seeing, 'seeming to hear' corresponds to hearing, etc. Of course, one isn't guaranteed that English contains a name for each of the nonrelational propositional attitudes, but I suppose that there can be no objection to the employment of neologisms in specifying the domain of a science. (Indeed, quite independent of the present difficulty, one could not expect more than a rough correspondence between the inventory of propositional attitudes that we pre-theoretically acknowledge and the ones which psychological theories prove eventually to be about. Sciences quite generally determine their subject matter as they go along.) For further discussion of the whole issue, see Fodor (1968).

[17] It is, in particular, not a tautology or some sort of stipulative definition of the technical term 'store', that organisms remember what, and only what, is stored by their nervous systems. In fact, it isn't even *true* that organisms remember what and only what their nervous systems store. For, on the one hand, much of what is remembered is reconstructed from stored fragments (cf. Bartlett, 1961; Bransford and Franks, 1971) and, on the other, much of what is stored often can't be remembered because it can't be retrieved (cf. the superiority of recognition memory to free recall). So the correspondence fails in both directions: Storage is probably essential

cognitive psychology seek to explain the propositional attitudes of organisms, and that they seek to do so in a certain way: viz., by providing, for each propositional attitude, nomologically necessary and sufficient conditions in terms of computational relations between the organism and formulae of the internal representational system. Now this may suggest the following ontological picture: There are, as it were, *two* things—the organisms's relation to propositions and the organisms's relation to formulae—and these two things are so arranged that the latter is causally responsible for the former (e.g., the organism's being in a certain relation to the formulae causes the organism to be in a certain relation to the propositions). I can imagine that someone might want to resist this picture on metaphysical grounds; viz., on the grounds that it takes propositions (or, anyhow, relations to propositions) as the bedrock on which psychology is founded.

The present point is that one *can* resist this picture while adhering to the account of psychological explanation I have been proposing. In particular, one might take the basic explanatory formulae as expressing (not causal relations between relations to formulae and relations to propositions but) contingent event identities. That is, one might think of cognitive theories as filling in explanation schema of, roughly, the form: *having the attitude R to proposition P is contingently identical to being in computational relation C to the formula (or sequence of formulae) F.* A cognitive theory, insofar as it was both true and general, would presumably explain the productivity of propositional attitudes by entailing infinitely many substitution instances of this schema: one for each of the propositional attitudes that the organism can entertain.

We have now arrived at what seems to me to be the heart of the specifically methodological issues about cognitive theories. For if we are willing to ascribe propositional attitudes to a system, then we can make sense of the claim that that system uses a language, and we can do this whether or not the system is a person and whether or not the use of the language is mediated by conventions, and whether or not the language used functions as a medium of communication. What is required (and all that seems to be required) is that there should be the right kind of correspondence between

---

to recall, but it is neither necessary nor sufficient. A fortiori recalling isn't 'criterial' for storing.

A cognitive theory tries to characterize the ways in which the propositional attitudes of an organism are contingent upon its data processes, where 'data processes' are sequences of operations upon formulae of the internal language. My present point is that this is often hard to do and is not to be achieved by stipulative definition. Indeed, it may not be so much as *possible* to achieve. We have no a priori guarantee that all the cognitive states of an organism *can* be explained by reference to the special subset which consists of relations between the organism and formulae of its internal representational system. All we know a priori is that such cognitive psychology as is currently available assumes that this is true.

the atittudes the system bears to propositions and the relations that it bears to formulae of the language. (If *S remembers that a is F iff S stores* ⌜*a is F*⌝ is nomologically necessary, then *S* uses ⌜a is F⌝ to represent *a*'s being *F*: or does so, at least, in such of its cognitive processes as are memory processes.) We remarked that, in the case of natural languages, the relevant correspondence between the speaker's relation to formulae and the attitudes he bears to propositions is mediated by his adherence to the conventions that govern the language. In the case of the internal code, it is presumably determined by the innate structure of the nervous system. But, so far as I can tell, that difference doesn't fundamentally affect the proposed account of representation. In both cases formulae of the system represent what they do because the relation between the use of the formulae and the propositional attitudes of the organism is what it is.

We are thus in a position to say, in some detail, what the analogy between 'private' and 'public' representation comes to. If ⌜a is F⌝ is a formula in a *public* language, then (*S* uses ⌜a is F⌝ to represent *a*'s being *F*) just in case (*S* believes that *a* is *F* just in case *S* assents to ⌜a is F⌝). Since what relates *S*'s believing that *a* is *F* to his assenting to ⌜a is F⌝ (what makes the embedded biconditional true) will, in the case of public languages, typically be *S*'s adherence to the conventions of the language, we can replace that condition with condition *C*.

(C) (*S* uses ⌜a is F⌝ to represent *a*'s being *F*) just in case ((*S* believes that *a* is *F* just in case *S* assents to ⌜a is F⌝) is conventional).

Now consider the case where ⌜a is F⌝ is a formula of the internal code. Then there will be a condition which holds for the formula and which differs from *C* only in that (a) 'assents to' is replaced by a sequence of one or more of the basic relations from which computational relations to internal formulae are constructed and (b) 'is conventional' is replaced by 'is nomologically necessary'.

We have, then, some sort of reply to what I took to be the basic challenge that the private language argument poses to the notion of an internal representational system: to provide an account of the representation relation for formulae of that system. It remains an open question whether internal representation, so construed, is sufficiently like natural language representation so that both can be called representation 'in the same sense'. But I find it hard to care much how this question should be answered. There is an analogy between the two kinds of representation. Since public languages are conventional and the language of thought is not, there is unlikely to be *more* than an analogy. If you are impressed by the analogy, you will want to say that the inner code is a language. If you are unimpressed by the analogy, you will want to say that the inner code is in some sense a representational system but that it is not a language. But in neither case will what you say affect what I take to be the question that is seriously at issue: whether the methodological assumptions of computational psychology are coherent. Nothing in the discussion so far has suggested that they are not. In particular, nothing has prejudiced the claim that learning, including first language learning, essentially involves the use of an *un*learned internal representational system. Since we have found no reason to believe that view to be confused, and since it is, as I have remarked repeatedly, the only one in the field, it seems a good idea to trace the implications of assuming that some such view is true. That's the job we now return to.

WHAT THE PRIVATE
LANGUAGE MUST BE LIKE

I have been trying to meet some of the more important philosophical objections that might be brought against taking literally the view that learning a (first) language involves formulating and confirming hypotheses about the semantic properties of its predicates. It seemed to me to be important to defend the conceptual coherence of that view since, on the one hand, it would appear to be empirically plausible and, on the other, if we accept it we are committed to assuming that organisms capable of learning a language must have prior access to some representational system in which such properties can be expressed. From here on I shall take all this as read. What I want to argue is that, having gone this far, we shall have to go a good deal further.

If we say that a *truth definition* for the natural language L is any theory which associates truth conditions with each of the infinitely many predicates of L, then the assumptions we have been defending can be abbreviated as: learning L involves (at least) learning its truth definition. Now, one way of formulating a truth definition (not the only way, but, so far as I can see, the differences don't affect the arguments we will consider) is this: We distinguish between a finite set of *elementary* predicates of L, for each of which the appropriate determination is actually *listed,* and an infinite set of *complex* predicates whose associated truth conditions are determined by some recursive procedure that the truth definition specifies. A variety of assumptions are usually made about the predicates so distinguished. First, every predicate of L is either elementary or compound and none is both. Second, every compound predicate is constructed from elementary predicates in some manner that the truth definition is required to make explicit. In particular, the truth conditions associated with any complex predicate are fixed given a specification of its syntactic structural description and of the elementary predicates it contains. This means that every predicate of L is either elementary or eliminable in favor of elementary predicates by a defining biconditional. In effect, then, a truth definition for a natural language contains a list of representations which determine the extensions of its elementary predicates and a set of rules for defining its complex predicates in terms of its elementary predicates.

Consider, then, a predicate P in the elementary vocabulary of L. To begin with, a truth theory for L will include a statement of the form of formula (1) such that (a) formula (1) is true and (b) $\ulcorner Gx \urcorner$ is a formula in the vocabulary of the metalanguage in which the truth definition is couched.

(1) $\ulcorner Py \urcorner$ is true iff Gx

It follows trivially that G must be coextensive with P; for, if it were not, the truth rule for P would not itself be true. Now, the view that we have been assuming is one which says that learning L is (or, anyhow, involves) learning a truth definition for L. Suppose that formula (1) is part of such a truth definition. Then learning L involves learning formula (1). In particular, learning L involves learning that $\ulcorner Px \urcorner$ *is true iff* x *is* G is true for all substitution instances. But notice that learning that could be learning P (learning what P means) only for an organism that already understands G. For, and this point is critical, <u>G in formula (1) is *used,* not mentioned.</u> Hence, if learning P is learning a formula of form (1), then an organism can learn P only if it is already able to use at least one predicate that is coextensive with P, viz., G.

Where we have gotten to is this: If learning a language is literally a matter of making and confirming hypotheses about the truth conditions associated with its predicates, then learning a language presupposes the ability to use expressions coextensive with each of the elementary predicates of the language being learned. But, as we have seen, the truth conditions associated with *any* predicate of L can be expressed in terms of the truth conditions associated with the elementary predicates of L.[18] The upshot would appear to be that one can learn L only if one already knows some language rich enough to express the extension of any predicate of L. To put it tendentiously, one can learn what the semantic properties of a term are only if one already knows a language which contains a term having the same semantic properties.

This is a pretty horrendous consequence for the view that learning a

[18] Indeed, it is precisely because this is true that truth definitions are plausible candidates for what-one-learns-when-one-learns-L. Truth definitions seek to answer the question: 'How can one understand the infinity of predicates of L on the basis of a finite representation of L?' The answer they give is: by performing a (finite) reduction of any complex predicate to one that is coextensive and constructed just from elementary predicates and expressions in the logical vocabulary. The analogous remarks hold, *mutatis mutandis,* for intensionalist semantic theories; viz., theories which holds that the critical semantic relation is (not equivalence but) mutual entailment or synonymy.

language is learning its truth definition to have; sufficiently so that it is worth pausing to ask how it could have been so widely missed. I think the answer is clear: While the view that semantic theories are, or entail, truth definitions has a long tradition in the philosophy of language, it is only recently that philosophers have come to think that *learning* a truth definition may be involved in learning a language. This difference makes all the difference. It is of central importance to keep clear on how the conceptual situation changes when we add to the conditions upon a truth definition the requirement that it should express what the speaker/hearer learns when he learns to talk.

Suppose we have a metalanguage M in which the truth conditions upon sentence of the object language L are couched. For any purposes *except* those of psychology, it is useful and harmless to assume that the elementary vocabulary of L is included in the vocabulary of M. It is useful because it guarantees us that, for each elementary predicate of L, there will be at least one coextensive predicate of M; viz., that predicate itself. It thus provides us with a sort of normal form for representing the extensions of the elementary predicates of L. Roughly, for any such predicate P, the canonical representation of those sentences whose predicate it is will be ⌜y is P⌝ is true iff x is P', where the very same predicate, viz., P, is mentioned on the left-hand side of the formula and used on the right.

It is harmless to include the elementary vocabulary of L in the vocabulary of M because the right-hand occurrence of P is transparent in the formula just cited. Given that such formulae remain true under the substitution of any predicate coextensive with P (and, a fortiori, under the substitution of any logically equivalent or synonymous predicate) we are guaranteed that *any* correct representation of the extension of P will be not worse than materially equivalent to the representation that the truth theory provides. In particular, whatever representation of the extension of P speakers of L may actually learn, we are assured that *it* will not be worse than materially equivalent to the cited formula.

But now suppose that we seek to embed a truth theory in an account of the psychology of speaker/hearers, such that the theory is required to entail an infinity of (true) formulae of the form F:

(F) An L-speaker understands 'P' iff (he has learned that ⌜y is P⌝ is true iff x is G) is true for all substitution instances.

The point to notice is that the occurrence of G in F (unlike the occurrence of G in the first formula) is *not* transparent. 'Y has learned that x is P' and P and Q are coextensive does not imply 'y has learned that x is Q.' In effect, then, a formula like F will be true only if G is a predicate in the language L-speakers actually use for representing the extensions of predicates in L. But, surely, P cannot be such a predicate if P is a predicate of L since, by hypothesis, L is the language to be learned. Trivially, one cannot use the predicates that one is learning in order to learn the predicates that one is using.

In short, what is useful and harmless in truth definitions *tout court* (having the same predicate occur mentioned on the left-hand side of a truth rule and used on the right-hand side) is the one thing that must *not* happen in those representations of truth conditions that are supposed also to represent what the speaker/hearer must learn about his language. That is, the one thing that G must *not* be in a formula like F is P. For F can be true only if 'G' denotes some predicate in a language S knows. And, by hypothesis, Ss who are learning L do not know any language in which the predicates of L occur.

We can now summarize the general point we have been making. Either it is false that learning L is learning its truth definition, or it is false that learning a truth definition for L involves projecting and confirming hypotheses about the truth conditions upon the predicates of L, or no one learns L unless he already knows some language different from L *but rich enough to express the extensions of the predicates of L*. I take it that, in the current state of theorizing about language and learning (and barring the caveats discussed in the first part of this chapter) only the third disjunct is tolerable. It follows immediately that not all the languages one knows are languages one has learned, and that at least one of the languages which one knows without learning is as powerful as any language that one can ever learn.

I admit that these conclusions really may seem scandalous. I should be inclined to view them as a reductio ad absurdum of the theory that learning a language is learning the semantic properties of its predicates, except that no serious alternative to that theory has ever been proposed.[19] Consonant with the general methodology of this study, I shall endure what I don't know how to cure. In particular, I shall continue to assume that learning a natural language is learning the rules which determine the extensions of its predicates and proceed to take seriously such consequences of that view as can be made apparent.

For example, certain otherwise quite reasonable sounding views of the relation between talking and thinking are immediately ruled out by the consideration that the internal language must be rich enough to express the extension of any natural language predicate that can be learned. Thus, it has seemed plausible to many theorists that there are certain thoughts that one would not be able to think but for the fact that one has learned a language. Such views are fairly explicit in the writings of Whorf (1956) and his followers, and they seem to be the point of such Wittgensteinian epigrams as

---

[19] Perhaps this would be a good point to reemphasize that the difference between intensionalist and extensionalist accounts of semantics is *not* implicated in the present argument. Intensionalist theories lead to precisely the same conclusions as I have just drawn, and do so by precisely the same route.

that a dog could not think: Perhaps it will rain tomorrow. I'll argue that, though there is a sense in which this may be true, there is another and equally important sense in which certainly is not.

To begin with, it may be felt that I have been less than fair to the view that natural language *is* the language of thought. It will be recalled that the main objection to this view was simply that it cannot be true for those computational processes involved in the acquisition of natural language itself. But, though it might be admitted that the *initial* computations involved in first language learning cannot themselves be run in the language being learned, it could nevertheless still be claimed that, a foothold in the language having once been gained, the child then proceeds by extrapolating his bootstraps: The fragment of the language first internalized is itself somehow essentially employed to learn the part that's left. This process eventually leads to the construction of a representational system more elaborate than the one the child started with, and this richer system mediates the having of thoughts the child could not otherwise have entertained.

Surely something that *looks* like this does sometimes happen. In the extreme case, one asks a dictionary about some word one doesn't understand, and the dictionary tells one, in one's own language, what the word means. That, at least, *must* count as using one part of one's language to learn another part. And if the adult can do it by the relatively explicit procedure of consulting a dictionary, why shouldn't the child do it by the relatively implicit procedure of consulting the corpus that adults produce? In particular, why shouldn't he use his observations of how some term applies to confirm hypotheses about the extension of that term? And why should not these hypotheses be couched in a fragment of the very language that the child is learning; i.e., in that part of the language which has been mastered to date?

This begins to seem a dilemma. On the one hand, it sometimes *does* help, in learning a language, to use the language that one is trying to learn. But, on the other hand, the line of argument that I have been pursuing appears to show that it *couldn't* help. For I have been saying that one can't learn P unless one learns something like "P_y" is true iff Gx', and that one can't learn *that* unless one is able to use G. But suppose G is a predicate (not of the internal language but) in the same language that contains P. Then G must itself have been learned and, *ex hypothesi,* learning G must have involved learning (for some predicate or other) that G applies iff *it* applies. The point is that this new predicate must either be a part of the internal language or 'traceable back' to a predicate in the internal language by iterations of the present argument. In neither case however does any predicate which belongs to the same language as P play an essential role in mediating the learning of P.

What makes the trouble is of course that the biconditional is *transitive.* Hence, if I can express the extension of G in terms of, say, H, and I can express the extension of P in terms of G, then I can express the extension of P in terms just of H (namely, ⌜y is P⌝) is true iff Hx. So, introducing G doesn't seem to have gained us any leverage. There doesn't seem to be any way in which the part of a natural language one knows could play an essential role in mediating the learning of the part of the language that one doesn't know. Paradox.

In fact, two closely related paradoxes. We want to make room for the possibility that there is *some* sense in which you can use one part of a language to learn other parts, and we want to make room for the possibility that there is *some* sense in which having a language might permit the thinking of thoughts one could not otherwise entertain. But the views we have so far been propounding seem not to admit of either possibility: Nothing can be expressed in a natural language that can't be expressed in the language of thought. For if something could, we couldn't learn the natural language formula that expresses it.[20]

Fortunately, both paradoxes are spurious and for essentially the same reasons. To begin with the learning case, what the argument thus far shows is this. Suppose F is a (proper) fragment of English such that a child has mastered F and only F at time t. Suppose that F' is the rest of English. Then the child can use the vocabulary and syntax of F to express the truth conditions for the predicates of F' only insofar as the semantic properties of F' terms is already expressible in F. What the child cannot do, in short, is use the fragment of the language that he knows to increase the expressive power of the concepts at his disposal. But he may be able to use it for *other* purposes, and doing so may, in brute empirical fact, be essential to the mastery of F'. The most obvious possibility is to use F for mnemonic purposes.

It is a commonplace in psychology that mnemonic devices may be essential to a memory-restricted system in coping with learning tasks. If, as it seems reasonable to suppose, relatively simple natural language expressions are often coextensive only with quite elaborate formulae in the internal code, it becomes easy to see how learning one part of a natural language could be an essential precondition for learning the rest: The first-learned bits might serve to abbreviate complicated internal formulae, thus allowing the child to reduce the demands on computing memory implicit in project-

---

[20] I know of only one place in the psychological literature where this issue has been raised. Bryant (1974) remarks: "the main trouble with the hypothesis that children begin to take in and use relations to help them solve problems because they learn the appropriate comparative terms like 'larger' is that it leaves unanswered the very awkward question of how they learned the meaning of these words in the first place." (p. 27) This argument generalizes, with a vengeance, to *any* proposal that the learning of a word is essential to mediate the learning of the concept that the word expresses.

ing, confirming, and storing hypotheses about the truth conditions on the later-learned items. This sort of thing is familiar from teaching the vocabulary of formal systems. Complex concepts are typically *not* introduced directly in terms of primitives, but rather by a series of interlinking definitions. The point of this practice is to set bounds on the complexity of the formulae that have to be coped with at any given stage in the learning process.[21]

Essentially similar considerations suggest how it might after all be the case that there are thoughts that only someone who speaks a language can think. True, for every predicate in the natural language it must be possible to express a coextensive predicate in the internal code. It does not follow that for every natural language predicate *that can be entertained* there is an *entertainable* predicate of the internal code. It is no news that single items in the vocabulary of a natural language may encode concepts of extreme sophistication and complexity. If terms of the natural language can become incorporated into the computational system by something like a process of abbreviatory definition, then it is quite conceivable that learning a natural language may increase the complexity of the thoughts that we can think. To believe this, it is only necessary to assume that the complexity of thinkable thoughts is determined (*inter alia*) by some mechanism whose capacities are sensitive to the form in which the thoughts are couched. As we remarked above, memory mechanisms are quite plausibly supposed to have this property.

So, I am not committed to asserting that an articulate organism has *no* cognitive advantage over an inarticulate one. Nor, for that matter, is there any need to deny the Whorfian point that the kinds of concepts one has may be profoundly determined by the character of the natural language that one speaks. Just as it is necessary to distinguish the concepts that can be expressed in the internal code from the concepts that can be entertained by a memory-restricted system that computes with the code, so, too, it is necessary to distinguish the concepts that *can* be entertained (*salve* the memory) from the ones that actually get employed. This latter class is obviously sensitive to the particular experiences of the code user, and there is no principled reason why the experiences involved in learning a natural language

---

[21] I am assuming—as many psychologists do—that cognitive processes exploit at least two kinds of storage: a 'permanent memory' which permits relatively slow access to essentially unlimited amounts of information and a 'computing memory' which permits relatively fast access to at most a quite small number of items. Presumably, in the case of the latter system, the ability to display a certain body of information may depend critically on the form in which the information is coded. For extensive discussions see Neisser (1967). Suffice it to remark here that one way in which parts of a natural language might mediate further language learning is by providing the format for such encoding.

should not have a specially deep effect in determining how the resources of the inner language are exploited.[22]

What, then, *is* being denied? Roughly, that one can learn a language whose expressive power is greater than that of a language that one already knows. Less roughly, that one can learn a language whose predicates express extensions not expressible by those of a previously available representational system. Still less roughly, that one can learn a language whose predicates express extensions not expressible by predicates of the representational system *whose employment mediates the learning*.

Now, while this is all compatible with there being a computational advantage associated with knowing a natural language, it is *in*compatible with this advantage being, as it were, principled. If what I have been saying is true, than all such computational advantages—all the facilitatory effects of language upon thought—will have to be explained away by reference to 'performance' parameters like memory, fixation of attention, etc. Another way to put this is: If an angel is a device with infinite memory and omnipresent attention—a device for which the performance/competence distinction is vacuous—then, on my view, there's no point in angels learning Latin; the conceptual system available to them by virtue of having done so can be no more powerful than the one they started out with.

It should now be clear why the fact that we can use part of a natural language to learn another part (e.g., by appealing to a monolingual dictionary) is no argument against the view that no one can learn a language more powerful than some language he already knows. One cannot use the defini-

---

[22] It should nevertheless be stressed that there is a fundamental disagreement between the kinds of views I have been proposing and those that linguistic relativists endorse. For such writers as Whorf, the psychological structure of the neonate is assumed to be diffuse and indeterminate. The fact about development that psychological theories are required to explain is thus the emergence of the adult's relatively orderly ontological commitments from the sensory chaos that is supposed to characterize the preverbal child's experience. This order has, to put it crudely, to come from somewhere, and the inventory of lexical and grammatical categories of whatever language the child learns would appear to be a reasonable candidate if a theorist is committed to the view that cognitive regularities must be reflexes of *environmental* regularities. On this account, the cognitive systems of adults ought to differ about as much as, and in about the ways that, the grammars and lexicons of their languages do and, so far as the theory is concerned, languages may differ without limit.

On the internal code story, however, all these assumptions are reversed. The child (indeed, the infraverbal organism of whatever species) is supposed to bring to the problem of organizing its experiences a complexly structured and endogenously determined representational system. Similarities of cognitive organization might thus be predicted even over wide ranges of environmental variation. In particular, the theorist is not committed to discovering environmental analogues to such structural biases as the adult ontology exhibits. He is thus prepared to be unsurprised by the prima facie intertranslatability of natural languages, the existence of linguistic universals, and the broad homologies between human and infrahuman psychology. (For further discussion, see Fodor et al., 1974.)

tion *D* to understand the word W unless (a) '*W* means *D*' is true and (b) one understands *D*. But if (a) is satisfied, D and W must be at least coextensive, and so if (b) is true, someone who learns W by learning that it means *D* must already understand at least one formula coextensive with W, viz., the one that *D* is couched in. In short, learning a word can be learning what a dictionary definition says about it *only for someone who understands the definition*. So appeals to dictionaries do not, after all, show that you can use your mastery of a part of a natural language to learn expressions you could not otherwise have mastered. All they show is what we already know: Once one is able to express an extension, one is in a position to learn that *W* expresses that extension.

We are now, at last, in a position to see why all this is important. To do so, we need only consider some implications for such areas of psychology as the theory of cognitive development.

There are, to begin with, lots of things that most adults can do and most children cannot. Many of these involve cognitive skills such as advanced problem solving, perceptual recognition of complex objects, and speaking a natural language. It is reasonable to suppose that an adequate cognitive psychology ought to postulate developmental processes whose operation mediates the attainment of these skills. Now, if I read it correctly, a good part of the psychology of cognitive development, especially as it has been influenced by Vygotsky, Bruner, and, above all, Piaget, has been concerned with defending three interrelated hypotheses about such processes.

1. The development of the child's cognitive capacities exhibits a reasonably orderly decomposition into *stages*.
2. These stages, though they are in the first instance characterized by reference to specific behavioral abilities that the child exhibits, are fundamentally expressions of the kinds of concepts it has available, with weaker conceptual systems corresponding to earlier stages.
3. Learning mediates the developmental progression from stage to stage.[23]

To put the claim in the kinds of terms we have just been using, the view under discussion is that the child's developing intellectual capacities reflect changes in competence rather than (mere) changes in performance. The older child can do more kinds of things than the younger child not, e.g., because he has more computational memory to work with, or because his attention span is longer, or because he has more extensive knowledge of

---

[23] 'Learning' does not, of course, necessarily imply *conditioning* or *association*. Rather, I am using the notion of concept learning explored in Chapter 1: An environmentally occasioned alteration in the system of the conceptual system counts as a concept learning experience only if *what* is learned (under its theoretically relevant description) stands in a confirmation relation to the events which cause it to be learned (under their theoretically relevant descriptions). That is, it's concept learning only if it involves the projection and testing of hypotheses.

matters of fact; rather the difference is intrinsic to the expressive power of the conceptual systems available at the various developmental stages.

Piaget is, perhaps, of all cognitive theorists the one who is most explicit in describing the child's development as involving the assimilation of a series of 'logics' of increasing representational power. To take an example almost at random, Piaget postulates a level of cognitive development intermediate between the 'sensori-motor' period (in which object constancy is first established[24]) and the 'concrete operational' period (in which the child first exhibits conservation of quantities).[25] At this intermediate stage,

> the order relations, for example, which on the sensori-motor plane were altogether immersed in the sensori-motor schema, now become dissociated and give rise to a specific activity of 'ranking' and 'ordering.' Similarly, the subordination schemes which were originally only implicit now become separated out and lead to a distinct classificatory activity, and the setting up of correspondence soon becomes quite systematic: one/many; one/one; copy to original, and so on. (Piaget, 1970, p. 64)

[24] Piaget apparently holds that the child's ontology is initially phenomenalistic: The concept of a world that is populated by objects which continue to exist even when they are displaced from the perceiver's sensory field is typical of the *post* sensori-motor child and (somehow) emerges from the integration and coordination of innately determined sensori-motor reflexes under the impact of environmental stimulations. Indeed, even this way of putting it probably does less than justice to the extent to which Piaget assumes that the perceptual universe of the infant is unstructured, for Piaget explicitly denies that the distinction between the perceiver and the objects of his perception is available at the sensori-motor stage. Insofar as the ontology postulated at this stage resembles anything philosophers have discussed, it is perhaps closest to neutral monism. For extensive elaboration, see Chapter 1 of *Construction of Reality in the Child* (1954). Suffice it to remark here that the primary empirical evidence cited for attributing phenomenalistic views to infants is their failure to search for hidden objects: e.g., for objects which have been removed from the visual field by the interpolation of an opaque screen.

[25] In the classical experiment on conservation of quantity, the child is shown two identical containers (A and B) which, he agrees, contain the same amount of liquid. The child then watches while the contents of one of the containers (say, B) is poured into a relatively tall, thin vessel (C). He is then asked, "Which has more, C or A?" The nonconserving child is defined by his willingness to judge that C has more than A (presumably on the grounds that the level of the liquid in C is higher than the level of the liquid in A). The fundamental explanation of nonconservation is supposed to be the absence, in the child's conceptual system, of inverses of relations. In particular, he fails to realize that the effects of the operation of pouring from B to C could be reversed by the paired operation of pouring from C to B. It has been argued, with some justice, that this explanation is question-begging (see Wallach, 1969). The present point is just that it provides a relatively clear example of how Piaget seeks to account for a specific cognitive incapacity by appeal to specific lacunae in the expressive power of the logic that the child is assumed to be using.

The point of present concern is Piaget's attempt to account for the pattern of abilities and disabilities alleged to be characteristic of this stage by reference to the formal properties of the conceptual system presumed to be available to the child:

> In observing this kind of behavior we undeniably meet with the advent of logic, but we should note that this logic is limited in two essential respects: such ordering or classifying or setting up of correspondences does not involve reversibility, so that we cannot as yet speak of 'operations' (since we have reserved that term for procedures which have an inverse), and because of this, there are as yet no principles of quantitative conservation. . . . So we should view this stage of intellectual development as a 'semi-logical' stage, in the quite literal sense of lacking one-half, namely, the inverse operations. (1970, pp. 64–65)

It is, indeed, the child's recruitment of a logic in which the inverse of an operation can be expressed that is said to account for the capacities characteristic of the succeeding stage:

> Between the ages of roughly seven and ten the child enters upon a third stage of intellectual development which involves the use of operations. . . . He now arranges things in series and understands that in lining them up, say, in order of increasing size he is at the same time arranging them in order of decreasing size; the transitivity of relations like bigger than, and so on, which previously went unrecognized or was noted as a mere matter of fact, is now something of which he is explicitly aware . . . the conservation principles which earlier were lacking are now established. . . . (Piaget, 1970, pp. 65–66).

and so on.

Now, all of this might be true. It might really turn out that the kinds of representational system that children use is, in a principled sense, weaker than the kind of system that adults use, and that a reasonable account of the stages of cognitive development could be elaborated by referring to increases in the expressive power of such systems. What I think one *cannot* have, however, is that concept learning provides the mechanisms for the stage-to-stage transitions. That is, if the child's cognitive development is fundamentally the development of increasingly powerful representational/conceptual systems, then cognitive development cannot be the consequence of concept learning.

The reasons should be familiar since they are essentially the ones that lead to the conclusion that one cannot learn a language whose predicates express extensions unexpressible in a previously available language; the difference between learning a predicate and learning a concept are inessential so far as that argument is concerned.

Suppose, e.g., that you are a stage one child trying to learn the concept C. Well, the least you have to do is to learn the conditions under which something is an instance of (falls under) C. So, presumably, you have to learn something of the form (x) $(x$ is C iff x is $F)$ where F is some concept that applies whenever C does. Clearly, however, a necessary condition on being able to learn *that* is that one's conceptual system should contain F. So now consider the case where C is, as it were, a stage *two* concept. If something is a stage two concept, then it must follow that it is not co-extensive with any stage *one* concept; otherwise, the difference between stages wouldn't be a difference in the expressive power of the conceptual systems that characterize the stages. But if the stage one child can't represent the extension of C in terms of some concept in the system available to him, he can't represent it at all since, by definition, his conceptual system just *is* the totality of representational devices that he can use for cognitive processing. And if he can't *represent* the extension of C, then he can't *learn* C since, by hypothesis, concept learning involves projecting and confirming biconditionals which determine the extension of the concept being learned. So, either the conditions on applying a stage two concept *can* be represented in terms of some stage one concept, in which case there is no obvious sense in which the stage two conceptual system is more powerful than the stage one conceptual system, or there are stage two concepts whose extension *cannot* be represented in the stage one vocabulary, in which case there is no way for the stage one child to learn them.

It is pretty clearly the second horn of this dilemma that Piaget is impaled upon. On his view, some concepts, like conservation of quantity, cannot be learned by the 'preoperational' child because characterizing the extension of the concepts presupposes algebraic operations not available in the preoperational logic. But if the child cannot so much as *represent* the conditions under which quantities are conserved, how in the world could he conceivably learn that those *are* the conditions under which quantities are conserved? Small wonder that Piaget gives so little by way of a detailed analysis of the processes of 'equilibration' which are supposed to effect stage-to-stage transitions. In fact, Piaget's account of equilibration is, so far as I can tell, *entirely* descriptive; there is simply no theory of the processes whereby equilibria are achieved.

Piaget apparently holds that the development of intelligence involves establishing a series of states of equilibrium between the child's demands upon the environment and the environment's demands upon the child: specifically, between the repertoire of response schemata the child imposes on the world and the objective features of the world upon which the schemata are required to operate. The basic idea is that the child's schemata become subtle and differentiated in response to objective environmental processes and the more subtle and differentiated the response schemata become, the more objective is the view of the environment implicit in the child's modes of adaptation.

> In its beginnings, assimilation is essentially the utilization of the external environment by the subject to nourish his hereditary or acquired schemata. It goes without saying that schemata such as those of sucking, sight, prehension, etc., constantly need to be accommodated to things, and that the necessities of this accommodation often thwart the assimilatory effort. But this accommodation remains so undifferentiated from the assimilatory processes that it does not give rise to any special active behavior pattern but merely consists in an adjustment of the pattern to the details of things assimilated. . . . On the other hand, in proportion as the schemata are multiplied and differentiated by their reciprocal assimilations as well as their progressive accommodation to the diversities of reality, the accommodation is dissociated from assimilation little by little and at the same time insures a gradual delimitation of the external environment and of the subject. . . . In exact proportion to the progress of intelligence in the direction of differentiation of schemata and their reciprocal assimilation, the universe proceeds from the integral and unconscious egocentrism of the beginnings to an increasing solidification and the objectivication. (1954, pp. 351–352)

The general character of this sort of account will be familiar to readers of Dewey, for whom, too, the function of intelligence is to effect an increasingly realistic correspondence between the actions of the organism and the objective features of the world on which it acts.

The present point is that, whatever one does or doesn't make of such views, what is conspicuously lacking in the Piagetian version is a theory that explains *how* the organism manages to differentiate its schemata *in the right direction*; i.e., in a direction that, in general, *increases* the correspondence between the picture of the environment that the schemata imply and the properties that the environment actually has. If I am right in what I said above, Piaget's views *preclude* his presenting such a theory since, on the one hand, he wants the characteristic difference between levels of equilibration (i.e., between stages of development) to consist in the expressive power of the "logics" they invoke, and, on the other, he wants the mechanism of equilibration to be learning. As we have seen, these two desiderata cannot be simultaneously satisfied.[26]

---

[26] Dewey, by the way, *does* have an explicit account of the processes whereby the beliefs of the child converge on an objective representation of its environment: viz., that they are processes of hypothesis formation and confirmation. This is a position that it is consistent for Dewey to hold precisely because, unlike Piaget, he is not committed to the view that relatively early developmental stages correspond to the employment of relatively impoverished logics.

I have thus far been reading Piaget as claiming that the underlying difference between different stages lies in the expressive power of the conceptual systems available. It is therefore worth remarking that the text sometimes invites[27] a different interpretation. On this alternative reading, the difference between stages lies not in the concepts that can be expressed but in the range of experiences *through which* the concepts can be employed. Usually the line is drawn between a stage at which the concepts are applied only to what is actually in the perceptual field and a succeeding stage at which they are extended to objects that are imagined but not perceived. The following passage is typical.

> ... the fifth stage marks considerable progress with regard to the construction of space; with the elaboration of objective groups of displacements which define the beginning of this period one may say, in effect, that the concept of experimental space is established. Everything that enters into direct perception (apart from actual errors, of course) can therefore be organized in a common space or in a homogeneous environment of displacements. Furthermore, the subject becomes aware of his own displacements and thus locates them in relation to others. But his intellectual elaboration of space perceptions does not yet transcend perception itself to give rise to true representation of displacements. On the one hand, the child does not take account of the displacements which occur outside the visual field. On the other, the subject does not represent to himself his own total movements, outside his direct perception of them. (1954, p. 203)

My own guess, for what it's worth, is that Piaget really does postulate two distinct kinds of differences between developmental stages; two respects in which stage changes can involve increasing the expressive power of one's conceptual system. In one case, stage changes correspond to the employment of increasingly powerful conceptual systems within a given domain. In the other, they correspond to the application of a given conceptual system to the organization of phenomena in new domains. My present point, however, is that the same sorts of arguments which show that learning cannot be the mechanism of the first kind of stage transition show equally that it cannot be the mechanism of transitions of the second kind, so long as we assume that stage transitions do increase the expressive power of one's conceptual system. For, presumably, learning that the concept C applies in the domain D is learning that there are individuals in D which do (or might) fall under C. But, by assumption, learning *that* is a matter of projecting and confirming a hypothesis, viz. the hypothesis that $(\exists x)$ (x is in D and (pos-

---

[27] If one can use the term without irony of a prose like Piaget's. Piaget exegesis is notoriously a mug's game. I hope that what I have been saying is true to the intentions of the texts, but it wouldn't surprise me much to find that it's not.

sibly or actually (Cx))). Trivially, however, one cannot project or confirm that hypothesis unless one is able to represent the state of affairs in which some individual in D satisfies C. So, again, learning does not increase the *expressive power* of one's system of concepts (construed as the set of states of affairs that one can represent) though, of course, it can and often does increase one's information about which states of affairs in fact obtain.

I think that this may all be beginning to seem a little glib: Such a lot is made to turn on such a *small* point. Let me, therefore, suggest a (non-Piagetian) example which makes clear the sort of bind that Piaget has gotten into.

Suppose I had a device programed with the formation rules, axioms, and inference rules of standard propositional logic. And suppose I got it into my head to use this device (somehow) as a model for the learning of first-order quantification logic. (I choose this example because there is a straightforward sense in which first-order quantificational logic is stronger than propositional logic: Every theorem of the former is a theorem of the latter but not vice versa.) How could I go about doing the job? Answer: I couldn't. For my device will not be able to learn quantificational logic unless it can at least learn the truth conditions on formulae like $(x) Fx$. But my little learning model cannot learn those conditions if it cannot represent then, and it cannot represent them precisely *because* propositional logic is weaker than quantificational logic. The best it could do would be to associate $(x) Fx$ with the indefinite conjunction Fa & Fb & Fc . . . , where the '. . .' tacitly abandons the project.

There are, of course, ways in which my device might get to understand the quantifiers and, among these, there are some which share with concept learning the fact that environmental variables are essentially involved. For example, dropping it or hitting it with a hammer might cause the right kind of fortuitous changes in its internal structure. Alternatively, physical processes at work in the device might eventually alter its wiring in the required ways even without the intervention of environmental inputs. But what *couldn't* happen, however, is that the device uses the available conceptual system to *learn* the more powerful one. That is, what couldn't happen is that it gets from stage one to stage two by anything that we would recognize as a *computational* procedure. In short, trauma might do it; so might maturation. Learning won't.[28]

---

[28] A less tendentious way of putting it is that the role of environmental inputs might be to *trigger* whatever internal reorganization is required for stage-to-stage transition. Imprinting (see Thorpe, 1963) appears to provide a good precedent for this sort of organism-environment interaction, since the role of the imprinted stimulus seems to be primarily that of releasing innately structured behavior patterns that the organism would not otherwise display. The present point is that this kind of exploitation of environmental inputs must be sharply distinguished from what happens in any variety of concept learning, since, as we remarked in Chapter 1, it is definitive of the

There are, of course, plenty of alternatives to the Piagetian story which allow us to preserve the putative insight that cognitive development decomposes into stages. For example, it might be possible to show that cognitive development is, after all, a matter of performance variables rather than shifts in the underlying conceptual competence. Bryant and Trabasso have recently demonstrated that the level at which a child performs on certain typical Piagetian tasks alters with alteration of the memory demands that the tasks impose.[29] It is an open question how many of the Piagetian findings may be explained in this sort of way.[30]

Or again, it is left open that the child's cognitive development really is conceptual development, but that the shift from a weaker to a stronger conceptual system is effected by maturational variables, analogous to an alteration of the physical structure of a real computer. (It needn't be denied that the environment may supply inputs that are essential—and even specific—to initiating or supporting such endogenously determined maturational reorganizations.) Mixed versions of these stories are also available. Some of the computational systems available to the child may be limited only or pri-

---

latter that the organism's knowledge of its environment is exploited to confirm (or disconfirm) generalizations about the extensions of concepts. In effect, triggering stimuli may have an *arbitrary* relation to the structures they release, but in concept learning environmental data must be in a relation of *confirmation* to the hypotheses that they select.

[29] Bryant and Trabasso (1971). In particular, he showed that 'preoperational' children can cope with inferences which turn on the transitivity of length so long as they are intensively trained on the premises of the inference before they are required to draw the conclusion. This suggests that the problem is not that the child's conceptual system cannot express the notion of transitivity, but rather that the computational memory available to the preoperational child is simply not big enough to hold the premises from which the conclusions of transitivity arguments follow. The child *is* able to draw the right conclusion if the premises are first established in a memory system large enough to hold them: viz., in 'permanent' memory.

[30] A useful *gedanken* experiment in developmental psychology is to try to imagine models which exhibit stagelike discontinuities in *behavior* as the result of incremental increases in such 'performance' parameters as the span of computational memory. It is trivially obvious that there are many such systems. Imagine, for example, a theorem-proving device for propositional logic whose only 'cut-rule' is n items long. Imagine that the bound on the computing memory of the machine is given in terms of the number of items in the formulae displayed, and that it increases over time, starting at some value less than $m + n$, where m is the shortest formula that the cut-rule applies to. (In effect, we are imagining that the available computational memory gets bigger as the device 'grows up'.) The output of such a device will exhibit a stagelike behavioral discontinuity in that there will be a value of t such that all the proofs it yields prior to t will contain only sequences of strings of increasing length whereas, after t, the length of strings may increase *or* decrease within a given proof. The interest of this otherwise entirely uninteresting device is that it provides a caution against assuming that behavioral discontinuities must invariably be attributed to the operation of nonincremental underlying processes.

marily by performance variables while others may, in fact, mature. Something like this is suggested by the consideration that the relatively limited computational power the child exhibits in explicit problem-solving situations of the kind Piaget explores apparently does not preclude his exercise of extremely powerful computational mechanisms for such specialized processes as motor integration, language learning, spatial orientation, and face recognition. A time-slice of the child's cognitive career might thus exhibit bundles of computational mechanisms each at a *different* stage of development and each placing its own kinds of demands upon the type and amounts of environmental inputs it is able to exploit. None of these theories about stages is precluded by the arguments we have been setting forth. What the arguments *do* show is just that if there are stages and if they are determined by the expressive power of the underlying conceptual system, then the mechanism of cognitive development cannot, in point of logic, be concept learning.

We may end this chapter by exposing a paradox. What has been argued is, in effect, this: If the mechanism of concept learning is the projection and confirmation of hypotheses (and what else *could* it be), then there is a sense in which there can be no such thing as learning a new concept. For, if the hypothesis-testing account is true, then the hypothesis whose acceptance is necessary and sufficient for learning C is that C is that concept which satisfies the individuating conditions on $\emptyset$ for some or other concept $\emptyset$. But, trivially, a concept that satisfies the conditions which individuate $\emptyset$ *is* the concept $\emptyset$. It follows that no process which consists of confirming such a hypothesis could be the learning of a *new* concept (viz., a concept distinct from $\emptyset$).[31] What must go on in the 'concept learning' task described in Chapter 1, for example, is not that a new concept is internalized, but simply that the subject learns

---

[31] This way of putting it is really no different from the ones I used above, though it may *sound* different. All I have done is to couch the argument in a form which makes explicit its neutrality on the intentionalist/extensionalist controversy about the individuation of concepts.

Suppose one takes an extensionalist view of concepts and suppose, as usual, that we identify learning concept C with learning that (x) Cx iff Fx; viz. that being F is necessary and sufficient for being C. Since C and F are coextensive concepts and since, by the extensionalist hypothesis, coextensive concepts are identical, the concept $C = $ the concept F. The same sort of argument will go through on an intentionalist account, except that the material biconditioned will have to be approximately strengthened to yield a criterion for learning C.

This paradox does not, by the way, arise for *predicates*; for to learn a predicate is not to learn which predicate it *is*, but which semantic properties it *expresses*. To put this less gnomically, if I learn that the *predicate* P applies to x iff $\emptyset x$, I learn a bit of thoroughly contingent information about the *linguistic form* 'P'. Predicates differ from concepts in that the conditions for individuating the former make reference to the syntax and vocabulary in which they are couched. Synonymous predicates are distinct although they express the same concept. Distinct predicates may, therefore, have identical semantic properties. But distinct concepts, presumably, cannot.

which of several locally coextensive concepts is criterial for the occurrence of reward. To put it succinctly, the concept-learning task cannot coherently be interpreted as a task in which concepts are learned. Since, barring rote memorization, 'concept learning' is the only sort of learning for which psychology offers us a model, it is probably fair to say that if there is such a process as learning a new concept, no one has the slightest idea of what it might be like.

If this *is* a paradox, however, it is just the one that we have had to face all along: The only coherent sense to be made of such learning models as are currently available is one which presupposes a very extreme nativism. And this may not be so bad as it seems, for there are several ameliorating considerations.

1. It may be that complex concepts (like, say, 'airplane') decompose into simpler concepts (like 'flying machine'). We shall see in the next chapter that this sort of view is quite fashionable in current semantic theories; indeed, some or other version of it has been around at least since Locke. But it may be true for all that, and if it is true it may help. Granted that no one can learn what an airplane is unless he already has the concepts from which that concept is composed together with whatever combinatorial operations on elementary concepts are necessary to put 'airplane' together. But, though we are required to be nativistic in that sense, we can perfectly well acknowledge that only such experiences as, e.g., being exposed to airplanes, trying to invent a way to fly, etc., could cause the relevant complex concept to be constructed. If, in short, there are elementary concepts in terms of which all the others can be specified, then only the former need to be assumed to be unlearned. 'Concept learning' can, to this extent, be reconstructed as a process in which novel complex concepts are composed out of their previously given elements. (For an illuminating discussion of this 'mental chemistry' approach to the psychology of concept learning, see Savin, 1973.)

2. The view presently being proposed doesn't require that the innate conceptual system must literally be present 'at birth', only that it not be learned. This may be cold comfort, but I think the fact is that it's cold out.

3. The environment may have a role to play in determining the character of one's conceptual repertoire quite distinct from its role in fixing the set of concepts that one's repertoire contains; viz., it provides *exemplars* of one's concepts. I stress this since it may well be that all there is to say about some concepts (e.g., 'red')[32] is that they are the concepts of something sufficiently similar to certain designated exemplars. To say this is to say that learning the concept 'red' is learning something like '(x) x is red iff x is sufficiently similar to E_i' where E_i names some such exemplar of the color as

---

[32] But also, perhaps, 'cow' and other kind-concepts. For philosophical elaboration, see Putnam (to be published) and Kripke (1972). For a psychological perspective on the relation between exemplars, stereotypes, and kind-concepts, see Heider (1971).

a poppy, a sunset, or a nose in winter. Patently, environmental inputs could make an essential contribution to *this* sort of concept learning: viz., by supplying the exemplar. The present point is that the process by which one becomes acquainted with the exemplar is not itself a process of hypothesis formation and testing; it is, rather, the process of opening one's eyes and looking.

How much does this consideration help? Well, it will mitigate the nativistic assumptions about *concepts* at the price of nativistic assumptions about similarity. (One cannot use *C is the concept of things sufficiently similar to E_i* to learn *C* unless one is already in a position to employ *is sufficiently similar to E_i*.) This could be a real gain if the relevant notion of similarity turns out to be simple and general. If, however, the ways in which things that fall under a concept are similar to the exemplars of that concept turn out to be about as various as the concepts themselves, then the appeal to similarity will provide no serious reduction of the nativistic assumptions of the theory of development. I think this is an open empirical issue, but I am not optimistic: first, because appeals to similarity to define the dimensions along which training transfers have thus far had a fairly dismal history in psychological theories of generalization; second, because it appears to be a brute fact that the ways in which things resemble one another don't much resemble one another. What is common to what cabbages have in common and what kings do?

I have been suggesting some ways in which one might hope to take the sting out of the fact that one can't learn a conceptual system richer than the conceptual system that one starts with, where learning is construed as a process of hypothesis formation and confirmation. Perhaps I'd better end this discussion by emphasizing that, even if we can contrive to make it hurt less, there *is* a sense in which hypothesis formation and testing cannot provide a source of new concepts, just as there is a sense in which it cannot provide for the learning of predicates except those coextensive with the ones that the hypotheses themselves deploy. This is, as it were, an intrinsic limitation of the model and, as such, it places severe constraints on the kinds of theories of language learning, or of conceptual development, with which the model is compatible. There is, I think, nothing that can be done about this except to learn to live with it. We argued in Chapter 1 that such cognitive theories as are currently available presuppose an internal language in which the computational processes they postulate are carried out. We must now add that the same models imply that that language is extremely rich (i.e., that it is capable of expressing any concept that the organism can learn or entertain) and that its representational power is, to all intents and purposes, innately determined. So be it.

3
THE STRUCTURE OF THE INTERNAL CODE: SOME LINGUISTIC EVIDENCE

I've got to use words when I talk to you.

T. S. ELIOT

Never try to give necessary and sufficient conditions for anything.
PROFESSOR L. LINSKY
(in conversation)

The main conclusions of the discussion so far are these:

1. The available models of cognitive processes characterize them as fundamentally computational and hence presuppose a representational system in which the computations are carried out.
2. This representational system cannot itself be a natural language, although:
3. The semantic properties of any learnable natural language predicate must be expressible in the representational system.

These reflections—if they are true—serve to establish a sort of lower bound upon the expressive power which the language of thought must be assumed to have. But they tell us very little about the detailed character of that system, and it is precisely such details that the working psychologist most wants to discover. In this chapter and the next, I shall survey some of the kinds of empirical evidence which may bear upon answering this question. The goal of the exercise, is however, pretty modest. I want to try to convince the reader that the internal language hypothesis is not, in the pejorative sense of the term, 'metaphysical': that there are factual considerations which constrain theories about the internal code. I shall therefore be content if it is accepted that the *kinds* of arguments I will rehearse are pertinent to the confirmation of such theories. Finding instances of these kinds that are certainly sound and can be shown to be so is, it seems to me, the proper object of a long, collaborative effort in several different research disciplines. We can't now imagine what views this enterprise may finally lead us to.

I have argued that the language of thought cannot be a natural language. Nevertheless, facts about the latter provide us with some of our best data for inferences about the former. In the first section of this chapter, I shall say something about why this is so. In later sections, I shall provide some examples of arguments from facts about natural languages to theories about the internal code.

It is no news that the publication, in 1957, of Chomsky's *Syntactic Structures* precipitated a series of fundamental changes in the way that scientists think about natural languages and about the psychological processes that mediate their employment. It is, indeed, probably because things have moved so fast in linguistics and psycholinguistics that relatively little attention has been paid the question of how models of language articulate with theories of cognition. One must, however, take this question seriously if one proposes to use the natural language data to constrain such theories. What follows is an attempt to see what, from the point of view of the psychologist, the new linguistics is about.

'Paradigm clashes', as everyone who goes to cocktail parties knows, are diffuse confrontations of world views. They do not turn on single issues and they are not resolved by crucial experiments. It is, nevertheless, often possible and useful to characterize fundamental assumptions on which paradigms disagree. If, in the present case, one wished to say in a sentence what it is that most psycholinguists accepted prior to the Chomskian revolution and have stopped accepting since, it would surely be the assumption that a theory of language is essentially a theory of the causation of verbalizations.

Utterances have, presumably, got causes and it is not at issue that a sufficiently elaborated psychology might, at least in principle, identify the causally necessary and/or sufficient conditions for the utterances that people produce. It does not follow, however, that the right way (or even a useful way) of taxonomizing the utterance forms in a language is by grouping together the ones whose production is contingent upon the same (or similar) eliciting stimuli. It is perhaps Chomsky's most important contribution to psycholinguistic theory to have noticed that that inference is a non sequitur.

Prior to Chomsky's work, very many Anglo-American psychologists seem to have supposed that utterances refer to the stimuli that elicit their production: hence, that a theory which groups together linguistic types whose tokens have like causes will, ipso facto, group together structures that exhibit at least one semantically interesting property: coreferentiality.[1]

---

[1] Coreferentiality was not the only linguistic property that was supposed to be characterizable in terms of shared conditions of elicitation. It was widely believed, for example, that the notion of two words belonging to the same syntactic class (noun, verb, article, or whatever) could be reconstructed on the assumption of overlap

Chomsky's (1959) polemic against Skinner is fundamentally an argument that:

1. The environmental variables operating upon the speaker are only one of the determinants of what he says; among the others are his utilities, his nonlinguistic beliefs, and his information about the conventions of his language.
2. Since verbal behavior is typically the product of complexly interacting variables, there is no particular reason to suppose that a taxonomy of linguistic structures according to their conditions of elicitation will preserve any of their theoretically interesting properties.
3. It is clear, a posteriori, that it will not preserve coreferentiality. The presence of the thing referred to among the stimuli that elicit an utterance is neither a necessary nor a sufficient condition for the elicitation. What's worse, insofar as there *is* a coincidence between eliciting stimuli and referents (as when a man says 'my nose' referring to his nose) it is almost certainly of no theoretical significance: the mechanisms upon which the referential use of language depend do not require such coincidence. (Pay me enough and I will undertake here and now to refer to anything you like, past or present, real or imaginary. And 'enough' wouldn't come to much.)

Chomsky's critique is, I think, extremely radical and entirely well founded. It is not just, as some commentators have suggested, that Chomsky is interested in one thing (language structure) and psychologists another (the environmental variables that enter into the causation of verbal behavior). Chomsky's point is that, as things now stand, there is no reason to believe that *any* part of psychology, *including* the causal analysis of verbal behavior, will find a use for a taxonomy of linguistic forms into classes whose members have their conditions of elicitation in common. If verbal behavior really *is* an interaction effect, one would *expect* such a taxonomy to be useless; the utterances a given stimulus elicits may be arbitrarily heterogeneous depending on the psychological state of the organism upon which the stimulus acts.

I stress this because the point of Chomsky's attack seems to have been pretty widely missed. For example, Judith Greene (1972) writes:

> . . . as has been pointed out by MacCorquodale (1970) in a valiant defense of Skinner, Chomsky leaves the competent speaker with nothing to say. As long as the *what* of a verbal response is not reduced to a Skinnerian 'ouch' to the prick of a pin, it makes perfect sense to ask under what stimulus conditions a speaker will make use of his knowledge of complex linguistic rules to produce a particular utterance.

---

among certain of their eliciting stimuli. For extensive discussion, see Chapter 2 of Fodor et al. (1974).

Otherwise, when Chomsky says that language behavior is undetermined even probabilistically, does he mean that it is never true to say that some utterances are more likely than others in a particular context? The failure of the Chomskyan and Skinnerian approaches to interact in meaningful discussions is because Chomsky sees no problem here while Skinner thinks he has already solved it. (pp. 192–193)

But the disagreement between Chomsky and Skinner is *not* about whether verbal behavior is caused (they *both* assume that it is, and they both do so on what are, I suppose, largely metaphysical grounds). Nor is Skinner's theory reducible to the remark that it would be nice to know something about the contribution of environmental variables to the causation of verbal behavior. Nor is Chomsky insensitive to the existence of a problem about *how* verbal behavior is caused. On the contrary, what Skinner (1957) tried to show is that learning a language is learning the stimulus conditions upon discriminated responses, hence that a theory of verbal behavior must treat verbalizations *as* responses (i.e., it must define its generalizations over classes of linguistic types whose tokens are elicited under similar or identical environmental conditions). What Chomsky argued is that learning a language is *not* learning S-R connections, hence that a taxonomy of verbal forms according to their eliciting stimuli is unlikely to provide insight into *any* aspect of the use of language.

Greene's basic mistake, like Skinner's, is simply to take for granted that the question 'What are the causal determinants of verbal behavior?' and the question 'What are the stimuli that elicit verbal behavior?' are interchangeable. They aren't. It is very likely that *all* the fundamental psychological states and mechanisms (memory, attention, motivation, belief, utility, etc.) are implicated in the causation of utterances. One cannot, therefore, infer from the premise that verbalizations are *caused* to the conclusion that verbalizations are *responses*.

If Chomsky is right in all this (and I don't think there is any serious doubt but that he is) then learning a language is not to be identified with (does not, in fact, involve) learning the stimulus conditions under which tokens of its types are to be produced. And, if that is right, it follows that 'What eliciting stimulus caused speaker *S* to produce utterance *U*?' is the wrong *kind* of question for a psychologist interested in the explanation of verbal behavior to try to answer. But then, what is the *right* kind of question? If theories of language aren't about the stimulus control of utterances, what *are* they about?

Since *Syntactic Structures,* the orthodox proposal has been that linguistic theories are characterizations of what speaker/hearers know about the structure of their language and that psycholinguistic theories are characterizations of the procedures whereby this information is deployed in the production and comprehension of speech. I am, for reasons I have discussed elsewhere (Garrett and Fodor, 1968; Fodor et al., 1974) less than wildly enthusiastic about this way of understanding the relation between linguistics and psycholinguistics. And I am quite certain that it has severe heuristic limitations as a way of illuminating the bearing of facts about language upon the general concerns of cognitive psychology. In what follows, I shall therefore propose a somewhat eccentric way of reading the linguistics and psycholinguistics that developed out of *Syntactic Structures*. I shall suggest, in particular, that this work is best viewed as contributing to the development of a theory of verbal communication.

The fundamental question that a theory of language seeks to answer is: How is it possible for speakers and hearers to communicate by the production of acoustic wave forms? To put this question more precisely: under certain conditions[2] the production by speaker S of an acoustic object U which is a token of a linguistic type belonging to the language L suffices to communicate a determinate message between S and any other suitably situated L-speaker. How is this fact to be explained?

It is, I think, quite clear what the general form of the answer to this question must be. Verbal communication is possible because, when U is a token of a linguistic type in a language that they both understand, the production/perception of U can effect a certain kind of correspondence between the mental states of the speaker and the hearer. The ultimate goal of a theory of language is to say what kind of correspondence this is and to characterize the computational processes involved in bringing it about. All this will stand some spelling out.

I assume that the essence of communication in a natural language is roughly this: Speakers produce wave forms that are intended to satisfy certain descriptions. When things go well—when the speaker says what he means to say and the hearer understands what was said in the way that the speaker meant that it should be understood—the wave form satisfies the description it was intended to satisfy and the hearer recognizes that it satisfies that description and that it was intended to do so. Commonsensically: Communication is successful only when the hearer infers the speaker's intentions from the character of the utterance he produced.

I am not attempting to provide a full-dress analysis of 'S_1 communicated C to S_2 by producing the utterance U'. My point is just to emphasize the essential role of the descriptions that the speaker intends his utterances to satisfy, and of the hearer's recognition that they *do* satisfy those descriptions, in effecting verbal communication.[3] The point is easiest to see if we think about written communication in a natural language.

[2] For example, that the utterance is audible, that the hearer is attending, and so forth. From now on I shall take these background conditions for granted.

[3] For an analysis of 'speaker's meaning' that does run along roughly these lines, see Grice (1957). A good deal of what I have to say about theories of language in the

THE STRUCTURE OF THE INTERNAL CODE:
SOME LINGUISTIC EVIDENCE

Anything I write in English has a true description in a metalanguage whose fundamental syntactic operation is concatenation and whose vocabulary consists of the letters a–z (inclusive) and certain punctuation marks (e.g., '(', ')', ',', '.' ' ', ' ' ', these being respectively, the names of left parenthesis, right parenthesis, comma, period, word juncture, and single quote).[4] So, if I write 'the dog', what I write has a true description in this language as: the letter t, followed by the letter h, followed by the letter e, followed by word juncture, followed by the letter d . . . , etc. Moreover, such descriptions are type-individuating in the following sense: Any such description fully specifies the type to which a given orthographic token belongs, so long as we are taking types to be letter sequences. (If we take types to be word sequences, then this sort of description does not succeed in individuating, since an ambiguous inscription like 'the bank' receives only one orthographic description though it is a token of two distinct types.)

My point is that though what I write when I write 'the dog' has a true orthographic description, what I intend to communicate when I write 'the dog' has none. In fact, there is a sense in which I cannot even use the orthographic language to refer to what I intend to refer to when I write 'the dog' since symbols in the orthographic language denote letters and punctuation marks, but what I intend to refer to when I write 'the dog' is neither a letter nor a punctuation mark but some contextually definite dog.

So, when I write 'the dog' I use an orthographic sequence to refer to something that is not the designatum of such a sequence. (The same point applies, of course, to spoken English, except that there the relevant metalanguage is phonetic rather than orthographic.) This is, however, no mys-

---

first part of this chapter is an attempt to suggest how they might be embedded in theories of communication which are Griceian in spirit though certainly not in detail.

It may be worth emphasizing that this sort of account has a quite natural interpretation as a *causal* theory of communication. For if, as I have supposed, the utterance of a wave form can bring about a certain correspondence between the mental states of the speaker and the hearer, this is presumably because, in the relevant cases, the utterance is causally sufficient to initiate the sequence of psychological processes in the hearer which eventuates in his coming to be in a mental state that corresponds to the one that the speaker is in. (Speaker/hearers are *embodied* computational systems, and any sequence of events which constitutes the encoding/decoding of an utterance will, presumably, have a true description as a sequence of causes and effects.) So, one might say, a necessary and sufficient condition for communication between speaker and hearer is that the mental states of the one should be in the right sort of causal relation to the mental states of the other. Similarly, a necessary and sufficient condition for linguistic communication in L is that its tokens should play the right sort of role in the causal chains which mediate the causal relations between the mental states of speaker/hearers of L. And a *theory* of communication in L is true iff it says what sort of role the right sort of role is.

[4] For the sake of simplicity, and in order to avoid irritating the reader beyond bearing, I omit inscriptional devices such as underlining, which are not concatenated with other symbols in the orthographic vocabulary.

tery; in fact, it is a triviality. For though what I write when I write 'the dog' has a true description as a sequence of letters, it *also* has a true description as a certain referring expression (viz., the expression which consists—solely —of the English word 'the', followed by juncture, followed by the English word 'dog'; viz., the expression 'the dog') and what tokens of that expression-type designate (when they designate anything) are dogs. It is, of course, precisely *because* 'the dog' has a true description as an expression-type whose tokens refer to dogs that English speakers who are bent on designating dogs often execute tokens of that type.

There are actually some morals to be drawn from these considerations. First, if we are to think of verbal communication as a process wherein the speaker produces utterances that are intended to satisfy certain descriptions and the hearer recovers the descriptions that the utterances were intended to satisfy, then we can constrain the characterization of the relevant descriptions in important ways. For example, the description which I intend the reader to recover when he reads my inscription 'the dog' is *not,* in the first instance, the orthographic description; rather, it is some such description as 'expression referring to a contextually definite dog'. If I did not have some such description in mind when I wrote 'the dog', and if my reader did not recognize that the inscription that I wrote satisfies that description, then I did not succeed in communicating a reference to the dog by writing 'the dog'.

Second, though the description I intended my inscription 'the dog' to satisfy is not, in the *first* instance, its description as an orthographic sequence, it better *in fact* satisfy that description, and it better be recognized to do so, if it is to serve as a vehicle for communicating a reference to the dog to readers *of English*. It is all very well for me to write 'le chein' intending, thereby, to produce a token of a type used for referring to contextually definite dogs. But if my reader knows not even that much French, he will be unable to recover the description I intended from the form of inscription I produced, and the ends of communication will therefore be defeated. If, in short, I intend to communicate *in English,* I had better see to it that what I write satisfies not only the appropriate description as a referring expression but *also* the appropritae descriptions as a sequence of English letters, words, etc. It is, after all, precisely because what I wrote *does* satisfy these descriptions that it can serve as a vehicle of communication between (suitably literate) English speakers.

To put it briefly, one of the things that I share with other members of my language community is a knowledge of the descriptions that a written form must satisfy if it is to serve to communicate references to the dog to people who belong to that community. In particular, I know what inferences from the form of my inscriptions to the state of my intentions literate English speakers *qua* literate English speakers can be expected to make when they encounter the tokens I produce. When I wrote 'the dog' and succeed in communicating a reference to a contextually definite dog by doing so, this sort of knowledge comes into play: I produce an inscription from which an English speaker *qua* English speaker can be expected to infer an intended reference to a dog and English speakers *qua* English speakers do infer the intended reference from the linguistic properties of the inscription I produce.

What I am saying (to come to the point at last) is that a natural language is properly viewed in the good old way: viz., as a system of conventions for the expression of communicative intentions. One might think of the conventions of the language as a sort of cookbook which tells us, for any C that can be communicated by an expression of the language, 'if you want to communicate C, produce an utterance (or inscription) which satisfies the descriptions $D_1, D_2 \ldots D_n$' where specimens Ds might be syntactic, morphological, and phonological representations of the utterance. The converse remarks hold for the hearer: To know the conventions of a language is at least to know that an utterance which satisfies $D_1, D_2 \ldots D_n$ also standardly satisfies the description 'produced with the intention to communicate C'.[5]

This all leads to a certain model of communicative exchanges between speakers and hearers which seems to me not just natural but inevitable. A speaker is, above all, someone with something he intends to communicate. For want of a better term, I shall call what he has in mind a message. If he is to communicate by using a language, his problem is to construct a wave form which is a token of the (or a) type standardly used for expressing that message in that language. When things go well, what he utters or writes *will* be a token of such a type; and, even when things go badly, what he writes or utters will be *intended* to be a token of such a type. That is, it will be intended to satisfy the description 'a token of the type standardly used to express the message M in language L'.

In the paradigm case, the speaker will be able to cope with his problem precisely because he *is* a speaker. To be a speaker of L is to know enough about L to be able to produce the linguistic form that L-speakers standardly use to communicate M, for variable M. Of course, this is very much idealized. There may be no way of communicating M in L, in which case the speaker may have to resort to another language, or to nonlinguistic

---

[5] 'Standardly' means something like: assuming that the speaker is using the language in accordance with the conventions. A speaker *can* use a form of words intending to communicate something other than what that form of words is standardly used to communicate. Only, if he does so, he does so at risk: He cannot assume that anyone knowing the language will ipso facto be able to construe his communicative intentions. (In fact, we usually do *not* assume this; rather, we assume that the hearer knows not only the linguistic conventions but also a great deal about what anyone rational is likely to *want* to say. This is the classic reason why it is so hard to construct formal procedures for the content analysis or translation of natural language texts. See, e.g., the discussion of this point by Bar-Hillel (1970).

forms of communication, or to forms of words that only approximate his communicative intentions. Again, there may be more than one way of communicating M in L. In fact, it is reasonable to assume that if there is one way there will be indefinitely many, and the speaker will have to choose among them. This means, in effect, that the speaker's intentions are underdescribed by saying that he intends to communicate M by uttering a token that belongs to L. What he actually does say will reflect a range of stylistic preferences which may impose constraints of any degree of subtlety upon the form of words he chooses. The point is, however, that in the paradigm cases:

1. The speaker produces a wave form.
2. The wave form he produces will instantiate a form of words standardly used for communicating M in L.
3. The fact that he produced that wave form (and not some other) will therefore be explicable, to a first approximation, by reference to the details of M and the conventions of L.[6]

The hearer has the same problem, only from the other end. Given a wave form, he must determine the message that the speaker intended to communicate by producing it. And again, in paradigm cases, what he knows about his language will be adequate to effect the determination. Of course, what he knows about his language may tell him more than what the speaker intended to communicate. For example, insofar as the speaker's utterance is a choice from among the stylistic options that L provides for expressing M, what the speaker says will communicate not only M but also his stylistic preferences to a hearer with a sensitive ear. There is, in short, a rather loose use of 'communicate' in which your words may communicate more than you intended: in which 'communicate' is used to mean 'reveal'. I shall, in future, avoid that usage, since it seems clearly inappropriate in the paradigm cases where the speaker produces a form of words standardly used to communicate M, intending thereby, to communicate M.

One can reveal a *penchant* for Gallicisms by italicizing words like 'penchant'. But one cannot, in that sense, *reveal* one's belief that it's about to rain by saying: 'It's about to rain'. There is no point in talking in a way that conflates these two kinds of cases, and there's not much plausibility to the view that the latter kinds of cases reduce to the former. Roughly, communicating is one of those activities where the organism's intentions in producing the behavior are among the *logical* determinants of the kind

[6] The model I have been discussing is idealized in the further sense that it assumes that the speaker's choice of a message to communicate is literally and entirely prior to his choice of a linguistic form in which to couch the communication. In cases of considered speech this is, of course, quite implausible; which is to say that whatever mechanisms mediate the translation from messages to wave forms must be controlled by the operation of feedback loops.

of behavior that is produced. Ignore this and you get the ethological notion of communication which, to all intents and purposes, embraces any and every exchange of information between organisms, however inadvertent; a notion so inflationary as to be incapable of bearing theoretical weight.

So, we have a model: A speaker is a mapping from messages onto wave forms, and a hearer is a mapping from wave forms onto messages. The character of each mapping is determined, *inter alia,* by the conventions of the language that the speaker and the hearer share. Verbal communication is possible because the speaker and hearer both know what the conventions are and how to use them: What the speaker knows allows him to pick the value of U which encodes a given value of M, and what the hearer knows allows him to pick the value of M which is encoded by a given value of U. The exercise of their knowledge thus effects a certain correspondence between the mental states of speaker and hearer: The speaker is enabled to construct utterances which *do* express the messages that he intends them to express; the hearer is enabled to construe the communicative intentions of the speaker. The speaker, in short, has a value of M in mind and the hearer can tell which value of M it is.[7]

It is frequently remarked that contemporary approaches to language are 'mentalistic'. What is usually meant by this is just that items in the theoretical vocabulary of linguistics and psycholinguistics are presumed to designate nonbehavioral states and processes. Any psychologist who is not a behaviorist is ipso facto a mentalist in this sense, and I should have thought that it was no longer possible seriously to doubt that useful theorizing about language will have to be in this sense mentalistic. The present approach to communication is, however, mentalistic in a stronger sense as well. For it is asserted not only that nonbehavioral processes mediate the communication relation between the speaker and his hearer, but also that communication actually *consists in* establishing a certain kind of correspondence between their mental states. It therefore seems to me to be comforting that this is what everybody has always thought that communication consists in.

---

[7] Another way of putting it is this: The hearer's problem is to decide which hypothesis about the speaker's intentions best explains his (the speaker's) verbal behavior. Under normal circumstances, the assumption that the speaker is following the rules of his language will provide for a general solution of problems of this kind. Thus, e.g., the best explanation of the verbal behavior of someone who says 'It's raining' will normally be that he intends to communicate the information that it's raining; the best explanation of the verbal behavior of someone who says 'I have only one nose' will normally be that he intends to communicate the information that he has only one nose, etc.

These remarks are intended to connect the present discussion with a tradition in the philosophy of mind according to which attributions of mental states to others are, in general, to be analyzed as inferences to the best explanation of their behavior: Attributions of communicative intentions constitute the special case where the behaviors to be explained are (e.g.) verbalizations. For discussion of the broader issues, see Putnam (1960b), Chihara and Fodor (1965), and Fodor (1968).

We have communicated when you have told me what you have in mind and I have understood what you have told me.

I commenced this discussion by saying that I wanted to show how the recent work on linguistics and psycholinguists can be viewed as contributing to a theory of communication: in effect, to illuminate the goals of that work by embedding it in such a theory. It seems important to do this because the theory of communication can itself be embedded, in a very natural way, in the sort of account of cognitive processes developed in Chapters 1 and 2. Insofar as this strategy works, we should be able to throw a good deal of light on the main topic of *this* chapter: the bearing of facts about natural languages and natural language processing upon theories about the character of the central code. The general idea is that facts about natural languages will constrain our theories of communication, and theories of communication will in turn constrain our theories about internal representations. I now propose to try to make' some progress in that direction. In particular, I want to show that there are a variety of different kinds of conditions that an adequate theory of *messages* would have to satisfy, and that this is to the point because messages are most plausibly construed as formulae in the language of thought.

The first point to notice is that what we have had to say about the nature of verbal communication so far does not entail any particular view of language structure beyond the truism that since linguistic tokens are acoustic objects, verbal communication must involve the production and interpretation of such objects. What connects the account of communication just given with current work on the structure of natural languages is the claim that a generative grammar of L specifies (some or all of) the descriptions that a token must satisfy if it is to conform to the linguistic conventions of L. To put the same point slightly differently, it specifies, for each $M,$ the descriptions (morphological, phonological, syntactic, etc.) that a token must satisfy if it is to belong to that sentence type which expresses M in L.[8] Since, according to the model of communication just proposed, an utterance will normally serve to communicate M in L only if the speaker assures (and the hearer recognizes) that the utterance does satisfy such descriptions, we can characterize the connection between the theory of communication and the theory of generative grammar by reference to two specific hypotheses:

1. The mapping from messages to wave forms and vice versa is indirect: Wave forms are paired with messages via the computation of a number of intervening representations.

2. Among these intervening representations there are several which correspond

---

[8] Chomsky sometimes puts it that a grammar of L specifies the correspondence between 'form and meaning' for the sentences of L. See especially the discussion in Chomsky (1965).

to the structural descriptions of sentences which generative grammars provide.

Taken together, hypotheses (1) and (2) amount to the claim that linguistic structural descriptions are 'psychologically real' and that they 'mediate' the communication process.

I shall not, at this point, review the evidence for this claim (but see Fodor et al., 1974, for extensive discussion). What I do want to do is to say enough about the notion of a structural description to make it clear what the claim is claiming.

Every generative grammar of a natural language acknowledges a certain fixed, finite set of *levels of description* at which the sentences of the language receive analyses. Traditionally (i.e., in the kinds of grammars inspired by Chomsky, 1957) at least the following levels are posited: phonetic, morphophonological, surface syntactic, and deep syntactic. Now, a level of description can itself be associated with a formal language. That is, each level of description can be identified with a certain (typically infinite) set of formulae whose elements are drawn from the vocabulary of the level and whose syntax is determined by the well-formedness rules of the level. The population of the phonetic level, for example, consists of an infinite set of sequences of concatenated phones. Analogously, the population of the surface syntactic level consists of an infinite set of single-rooted phrase structure trees, each containing a finite number of branching nodes with labels drawn from a proprietary vocabulary which includes 'noun phrase', 'noun', 'verb', 'adjective', etc. Similarly, *mutatis mutandis,* for each of the other levels of description.

It is a condition upon the adequacy of a generative grammar that each sentence in the language it describes must receive at least one representation (and at most a finite number of representations) at each of the levels of description that the grammar recognizes. That is, every sentence must be associated with a set of representations such that each formula in the set is well formed at some level of description and such that each level of description contributes at least one formula to the set. This set of formulae is the *structural description* of the sentence relative to the grammar.[9]

I remarked above that there are good grounds for accepting some or or other version of hypotheses (1) and (2). That is: The computations

---

[9] Since, so far as anyone knows, the linguistic levels are universal (i.e., since every empirically adequate grammar must acknowledge the same set of levels as every other) to claim that every sentence of every language has a structural description is tantamount to claiming that every sentence of every language has a phonetic spelling, a morphophonological analysis, a surface structure, a deep structure, etc. If, as I have assumed, structural descriptions are psychologically real and mediate the communication relation, then the universality of the descriptive levels implies a corresponding universality of the psychological processes involved in the production and perception of speech.

underlying verbal communication specify wave forms corresponding to given messages and messages corresponding to given wave forms. And, in the course of this processing, a series of intermediate representations are computed, at least some of which correspond closely to the ones that sentences receive at the various levels of description that generative grammars acknowledge. If this is so, it begins to suggest how facts about language structure and language processes can constrain theories which seek to specify the character of messages.

1. Nothing can be an adequate representation of a message unless it can serve as input to a device capable of computing the structural description of those sentences which express that message; 'structural description' is here taken in its technical linguistic sense.

2. Nothing can be an adequate representation of a message unless it can be produced as output by a device whose input is the structural description of a sentence which expresses the message.

The point is, of course, that we know a good deal about the form of structural descriptions and the information they contain, and we know something—though not much—about the kinds of information processing that goes on in encoding and decoding the acoustic objects that structural descriptions apply to. This sort of information bears on the nature of messages since, whatever else messages are, they must exhibit a systematic relation to structural descriptions and that relation must be computable by such information-handling procedures as speaker/hearers have available.

But, in fact, we can do better. We have argued that theories about messages are constrained to provide appropriate input/outputs for models of the speaker and hearer, and that this is a substantive constraint insofar as work in linguistics and psycholinguistics is able to provide such models. But if, as we have been assuming, messages specify the information communicated in verbal exchanges, then an account of the structure of messages will have simultaneously to satisfy a number of other conditions as well. To put it as generally as I can, the structures that we identify with messages will have to provide appropriate domains for *whatever* cognitive operations apply to the information that verbalizations communicate. Encoding/decoding to and from wave forms is one such operation, the one with which linguistics and psycholinguistics are primarily concerned. But it is quite clear that it isn't the only one.

To take an example almost at random, one of the things that we are able to do with linguistically carried information is to compare it with information that arrives through nonlinguistic channels. The things that speakers say are often confirmed, or disconfirmed, by the things that they see, hear, taste, touch, and smell, and, presumably, part of knowing the language is knowing that this is so. There must, in short, be computational procedures which allow one to use what one can see out the window to confirm the remark that it is raining, and such procedures somehow contrive to apply simultaneously to linguistically and visually carried information. An obvious way to achieve this would be to translate all perceptual inputs into a common code and then define the confirmation relation for formulae in that code: that would be a precise analog to what one attempts to achieve in the formalization of the confirmation relation for scientific theories.[10] It is compatible with this proposal that people often lose information about the input channel while retaining information about what was communicated along that channel. Did you first *read* or *hear* that the sum of triangle is 180 degrees? (For some discussion of this point,

[10] It is obvious that there is an intimate relation between psychological theories of the fixation of belief and philosophical theories of scientific confirmation, and not only for the reason discussed in Chapter 2, that both are concerned with the analysis of nondemonstrative inferences. Thus, in psychology, we think that the subject's willingness to believe a statement is determined, *inter alia,* by his current percepts. And, in philosophy, we think that the degree of confirmation of a scientific theory is determined, *inter alia,* by the character of the events which fall in the domain of that theory. The present point is that, in each case, we have a confirmation relation that holds, *prima facie,* between 'linguistic' objects (like statements and theories) and 'nonlinguistic' objects (like percepts and pointer readings). This poses a problem insofar as a theory of scientific inference, or of the fixation of beliefs, seeks to treat confirmation as a *formal* relation since it is, to put it mildly, hard to think of a notion of form which would make linguistic and nonlinguistic objects formally comparable.

The standard way of coping with this problem in the philosophy of science is simply to *assume* that both the hypotheses and the facts that confirm them have canonical representations in a proprietary language; confirmation is then defined as a formal relation between formulae in that language if it is formally definable at all. The present suggestion is that an analogous move is conceivable in the psychology of belief: A theory of the confirmation relation between, say, visual percepts and linguistic percepts might postulate (a) a neutral language in which both can be displayed, (b) a canonical form for such displays, and (c) computational principles which determine the degree of confirmation of the sentence as a function, *inter alia,* of formal relations between its canonical representation and the canonical representation of the visual input.

There is, in fact, empirical evidence that at least *some* visual information is 'translated' into discursive format prior to being used for the confirmation or disconfirmation of sentences. (See, e.g., Clark and Chase, 1972.) It is, however, important to emphasize that, even if the translation story should prove to be general, the problem of specifying procedures for the *direct* comparison of discursive and nondiscursive representations will have to be faced somewhere in a psychological theory of the fixation of belief. Roughly, either a *confirmation* relation will have to be defined for pairs consisting of visual percepts and discursive representations, or, if the translation story is true, then the *translation* relation will itself have to be defined for such pairs. I remarked above that philosophers of science typically just *assume* a canonical representation of the data pertinent to the confirmation of theories. They don't often raise the question of how the data get into the data language. But psychologists will have to solve the analogous question if they are after a full account of the computational procedures whereby the statements we hear are tested against what we perceive to be the facts.

see Fodor, 1972. For pertinent experimental data and a model see Rosenberg, 1974.)

But whether or not this is the way it's done, the present point is that it must be done *some* way and that doing it requires that messages fall within the domain of whatever principles define the confirmation relation. This requirement is conceptually independent from the requirement that messages should provide appropriate input/outputs for the devices that produce and analyze sentence tokens. One could imagine a kind of organism which is incapable of using what it sees to check on what it's told though, of course, having a language would do that sort of organism very much less good than it does us. ('Split-brain' patients appear, in some respects, to approximate such organisms; cf. Sperry, 1956.) The point is that by embedding the theory of communication within the theory of cognition, we increase the empirical demands on each: On the one hand, messages will have to be so represented as to fall within the domain of the theory of the fixation of belief, and, on the other, the principles that that theory appeals to will have to be so formulated as to apply to linguistically encodable objects. A psychology which satisfies this double constraint is ipso facto better confirmed than one which accounts only for the encoding of messages or only for the confirmation of such messages as we can encode.

Consider another example. We remarked in Chapter 2 that many philosophers now believe that learning a natural language involves (at least) learning a truth definition for the language. A truth definition is understood to be a theory which pairs each object-language sentence S_O with a metalinguistic sentence S_L such that '$\ulcorner S_O \urcorner$ is true iff S_L' is itself a true consequence of the semantic theory. Philosophers who accept this view presumably do so because they believe:

1. that understanding an utterance of a sentence involves, at very least, knowing what would make the utterance true;
2. that an empirically necessary condition for knowing what would make an utterance of a sentence true is computing a representation of the utterance which formally determines what it implies and what it is implied by;
3. that an adequate truth definition would associate S_O with S_L only if S_L does, in this sense, formally determine what S_O implies and is implied by.[11]

To put this point more economically, if you hold, *qua* semanticist, that a theory of meaning pairs natural language sentences with formulae that represent their truth conditions, then it is at least very natural to hold, *qua* psychologist, that understanding any given utterance of a sentence is a matter of computing a formula which represents *its* truth conditions. The upshot is

[11] To simplify the exposition, I'm being very cavalier about what's to count as the vehicle of truth and implication and about the type/token relation at large. What I'm saying could be said with much greater rigor, but it would take much longer.

that the structure whose recovery we identify with understanding an utterance of a sentence must be an object of the kind formally suited to fall under the rules of inference that (informally) apply to the sentence. But it is, by assumption, *messages* whose recovery constitutes understanding a sentence since, by assumption, it is messages which utterances of sentences communicate. So insofar as we take truth definitions seriously as theories of meaning, we know two things about messages: They must provide appropriate input/outputs for models of speaker/hearers, and they must provide appropriate domains for rules of inference.

The notion that a theory of meaning serves, in effect, to pair natural language sentences with some sort of canonical representation of their truth conditions is, of course, not new. It has been in the philosophical literature for as long as philosophers have distinguished between the surface form of sentences and their 'logical' form. Indeed, the precise point of this distinction has always been that the sentences of a natural language do not provide appropriate domains for the application of logical rules, but that some specifiable translations of such sentences would. To represent the logical form of a sentence is to represent the truth condition of the sentence explicitly, in a way that the sentence itself fails to do.

Our difference from this tradition is twofold. First, we are taking the notion of a canonical representation seriously as part of a *psychological* theory; the appropriate canonical representation of a sentence is the one that the speaker has in mind when he utters the sentence and the hearer recovers when he understands what the speaker said; i.e., it is that representation which makes explicit what utterances of the sentence are intended to communicate. Second, there is no particular reason why that representation should only be constrained to provide an appropriate domain for *logical* operations. There are, after all, psychological processes other than the drawing of inferences that linguistically communicated information enters into, and, insofar as canonical representations contribute to theory construction in psychology, they had better supply appropriate domains for those processes too.

It is, for a final example, pertinent that one of the things that we can do with linguistically carried information is forget it. It is pertinent because it seems certain that the various parts of a sentence are not forgotten at random. If I say to you 'the boy and the girl went to the store' and later ask you to tell me what I said (viz., uttered), you may forget the boy or the girl or where they went, but there is no chance that you will forget just the first phone from 'boy' and the words 'to the'. (Contrast what happens when you try to remember someone's name; here you *are* likely to get just the first letter or two right.) Now, we remarked in Chapter 2 that the heart of the computational approach to psychology is the attempt to explain the propositional attitudes of the organism by reference to relations that the organism bears to internal representations. This generalization holds, *inter alia,* for such propositional attitudes as forgetting that someone said such and such.

In particular, it may be possible to constrain the internal representation of what was said (or, for that matter, of any other percept) by the requirement that the bits that are forgotten together must have a unitary representation at the level of description for which storage and retrieval processes are defined. What psycholinguists call the 'coding hypothesis' was, in fact, a preliminary attempt to specify representations of sentences which satisfy this condition. (For discussion, see Fodor et al., 1974.) Patently, a representation of a sentence which provides a formal domain for memory processes, *and* expresses its meaning, *and* provides an appropriate input/output for a model of the speaker/hearer, etc., would have a pretty reasonable claim to be recognized as psychologically real.

Where we have gotten to is this. The theoretical concerns of linguistics and psycholinguistics can plausibly be located by reference to a theory which treats communication as the encoding and decoding of messages. Insofar as the structural descriptions that grammars postulate can be shown to be psychologically real, we may think of linguistics as characterizing the set of representations computed in the course of this encoding/decoding process. Analogously, it is plausible to think of (ideally completed) psycholinguistic theories as specifying the order in which such representations are computed and the information-handling processes which affect the computations. A theory of the structure of messages is thus constrained by a theory of natural languages in at least the sense that messages must provide appropriate input/outputs for these computational mechanisms.

But messages must also specify the information that linguistic communications communicate, and we have seen that this requirement brings a host of others in its train. We can summarize them by saying that if a message is that representation of a sentence which is recovered by someone who understands the sentence that conveys the message, then cognitive operations which are defined for the information that sentences convey must ipso facto be defined for messages. Either that is true or we must abandon the general project of identifying the cognitive processes of organisms with operations defined for representations. This is, of course, the consideration which relates what we have been saying about natural languages to what we said earlier about the language of thought. For formulae in the internal code just *are* those representations over which cognitive operations are defined; the whole point of assuming such representations in Chapter 1 and 2 was to provide domains for the kinds of data-handling processes that theories in cognitive psychology postulate. If, in short, facts about language and language processes constrain theories about messages, then they constrain theories about formulae in the language of thought. For if the kind of theory of communication I have been sketching is right, messages must *be* formulae in the language of thought; i.e., they must be formulae in whatever representational system provides the domains for such cognitive operations as apply (inter alia) to linguistically carried information.

Most of what follows in this chapter will be directed toward showing that facts about languages really do condition theories about messages in the way this account suggests that they should. Before I turn to that, however, here are a few further points about the view of communication I have presented that seem to me to be worth the digression. To begin with, we remarked in Chapter 2 that it is characteristic of the organization of general purpose digital computers that they do not communicate in the languages in which they compute and they do not compute in the languages in which they communicate. The usual situation is that information gets into and out of the computational code via the operation of compiling systems which are, in effect, translation algorithms for the programing languages that the machine 'understands'. The present point is that, if the view of communication I have been commending is true, then these remarks hold, in some detail, for the mechanisms whereby human beings exchange information via natural languages. To all intents and purposes, such mechanisms constitute 'compilers' which allow the speaker/hearer to translate from formulae in the computational code to wave forms and back again.[12] To paraphrase a very deep remark that Professor Alvin Liberman (personal communication) once made, it seems clear, if only on biological grounds, that the production/perception mechanisms for language mediate the relation between two systems which long predate them: The ear-mouth apparatus which actually transduces verbal signals, and the central nervous system which carries out whatever computational operations are defined over the information that verbalizations communicate. The present view is that this process of *mediation* is fundamentally a process of *translation*; viz.,

[12] The analogy between the psychological mechanisms involved in understanding a natural language and the compiling systems employed in getting information into and out of a digital computer has recently recommended itself to a number of theorists. (See particularly Miller and Johnson-Laird, to be published.) I am not supposing, however, as these authors apparently do, that the internal representation of a natural language sentence is typically a computational 'routine' (e.g., a routine for verifying the sentence). On the contrary, the internal representation of a sentence is simply its translation in the language of thought; what shows this is that it is perfectly possible to understand what someone says without having the least idea how the statement he made might be verified. A statement isn't normally a request (or a command, or even an invitation) to find out whether what it states is true. The failure to observe the distinction between the processes involved in understanding an utterance and the processes involved in confirming it has vitiated much of the work on machine simulation of sentence comprehension.

There is, in short, no particular plausibility to the view, embodied in what is sometimes called "procedural semantics," that natural language sentences are typically represented by imperatives in the internal code. That notion comes, first, from taking verificationism too seriously as a doctrine about meaning and, second, from taking the man/computer analogy too literally as a doctrine about psychology. Real computers do, in a sense, deal primarily in imperatives. Roughly, that is because their typical function is to perform the tasks that we set for them. But people have no 'typical function', and their interest in sentences is usually just to understand them.

translation between formulae in a language whose types describe wave forms and formulae in a language rich enough to represent the data on which cognitive processes operate. I suggested that linguistic and psycholinguistic theories, insofar as they contribute to accounts of communication, must specify the procedures whereby this translation is affected. One might however add, with equal propriety, that they must contribute to accounts of how much procedures are *internalized* in the course of language acquisition. Imagine a device which *learns* one of its compilers and, if the present view of communication is right, you will be imagining a device in some respects like us.

I said a device which learns *one* of its compilers, and this brings us to the second point. On the present view, there is a fairly striking analogy between natural languages and sensory modes. Pretty obviously, there are computational procedures which map a representation of the acoustic properties of a speech event onto a representation of the message it encodes. But, equally obviously, this is not the only system the organism has available for associating physical descriptions of environmental inputs with descriptions elaborated in terms of cognitively relevant variables.

Suppose that F is that formula of the internal code which corresponds to the English sentence 'There's an ink-blot on this page' (hereafter, 'S'). Then, presumably, understanding tokens of S involves assigning tokens of F as their internal representations, and believing that a certain token of S is true involves believing that the corresponding token of F is true.[13] A natural account of what is involved in believing that a token of F is true is simply that F is *taken* to be true in those computations in which it is involved; e.g., that it is treated as a nonlogical axiom in those computations.

So, one way that F can get to be among the formulae that are believed to be true is by being that formula which internally represents a sentence that is believed to be true. But there must be at least one other way; viz., one sees something that looks like this: and one believes what one sees (i.e., takes what one sees to be nonhallucinatory, veridical, etc.).

I am claiming that there must be some circumstances in which the psychological consequences of seeing an ink blot on the page are the same as the psychological consequences of reading that there is an ink blot on the page; if believing what one reads is a sufficient condition for taking F to be true, then so is believing what one sees. I take it that this must be the case because the ink blot confirms what the sentence says, and part of understanding the sentence is understanding that this is so. All this is instantly intelligible on the view that the computational state of a device which sees the blot and understands what it sees is identical with the computational

---

[13] Among the niceties that I am prepared to ignore at this point is the treatment of indexicals. If one were being serious, one would have to ensure that F determines a definite referent for 'this page'. A standard proposal is to take F as containing a schema for a many-place relation between a speaker, a location, a time, etc.; the arguments of this relation would thus differ for different tokens of S.

state of a device which reads the sentence and understands what it reads. But it wouldn't seem to be intelligible on any other view.

If, in short, the sentence comprehension system functions, eventually, to map transducer outputs onto formulae in the internal code, so, too, does the visual system. We have to assume this if we are to hold, on the one hand, that having a belief is a matter of being in a certain computational relation to a certain internal formula and, on the other, that the *very same* beliefs can be determined by hearing sentences and by seeing ink blots.[14] So, if we are to think of the mechanisms of sentences perception/production as constituting a sort of compiler, then we have the same reasons for thinking of sensory modes that way.

To return to the machine analogy: One of the reasons why multipurpose computers use compilers is precisely that using them allows them to be multipurpose. Useful information can get into the machine in as many different forms as the machine has distinct compilers since, by the point at which the information enters into computational processes, differences in input code have been neutralized by the operations that the compilers perform. After compiling, all the inputs are represented by formulae in the same internal language, hence they are all available, at least in principle, to whatever computational routines are defined over the internal representations. As Norman (1969, p. 164) remarks: "One of the most important properties of computers is that they make no distinction in their memory between instructions, numbers and letters. Thus any operation possible by the computer can be performed on anythings that is stored."

Once again, on the kind of view that I have been constructing, the analogy between people and machines is pretty exact. People, like machines, accept several different input codes, thereby ensuring a variety of routes along which cognitive processes can gain access to news about the outside world. As in machines, the trick is managed by having compilers for each

---

[14] It should be noticed that the issues I am raising here are different from, and largely independent of, the one discussed in footnote 10 above: whether, in the confirmation of sentences by visual percepts, the confirmation relation is defined for the visual data directly or only for their translations into *discursive* formulae in the internal code.

In effect, one can imagine two patterns of information flow, either of which might be involved in the visual confirmation of sentences. If the 'translation story' discussed in footnote 10 is true, then the sentence and the visual ink blot are both translated into tokens of the type F, and the confirmation of the sentence by the percept is accomplished by identity matching of these tokens. If the translation story is false, then the token of F that is associated with the sentence is directly compared with the visual input. In either case, the organism ends up in the same relation to tokens of F: viz., the relation of taking them to be true. In short, the beliefs that visual inputs warrant will have to be represented by the same formulae that represent the beliefs that linguistic inputs warrant since they are very often the same beliefs. This will be true whatever view you take of how sentences are confirmed by nonlinguistic percepts.

of the input modes. The recognition procedures for natural languages are one of these.

There are, of course, plenty of differences between people and (extant) machines for all that. One difference is that people have more kinds of sensors than any machine thus far devised; people can pair internal representations with more kinds of physical displays than machines can. There are, in fact, machines which can represent visually carried information in their central computing language. Within limits these machines can run their computations on such information and they can integrate it with inputs that come through more conventional channels (like punch cards). However, the visual inputs that currently available machines can compile are *very* rudimentary, and the information they decode from visual displays is pretty gross by the standards of the human visual system. And there are no machines which can, in this sense, smell, taste, or hear.

The second difference is, of course, that people can learn new compiling procedures; viz. by learning languages. They can do this precisely *because* the relation between sentence tokens and their internal representations (unlike the relation between visual arrays and *their* internal representations) is mediated by a system of conventions. But if the ability to learn such systems of conventions distinguishes man from *machines,* it is only fair to add that it distinguishes him from all other *organisms* as well (*pace* Sarah, Washoe, and the rest of their kind).[15]

One final reflection on the communication model which we have been considering. I remarked in Chapter 2 that a compiler which associates each formula in the input language *I* with some formula in the computing language *C* can usefully be thought of as providing a semantic theory for *I,* taking *C* as the metalanguage in which the semantic properties of the sentences of *I* are represented. In effect, the theory of meaning for formulae in *I* is simply the translation function which maps them onto formulae of *C.* On the present account then, it would be plausible to think of a theory of meaning for a *natural* language (like English) as a function which carries English sentences onto their representations in the putative internal code.

I mention this point because 'translation theories' of meaning have recently become the object of considerable philosophical disapprobation, much of it, I think, quite undeserved. Consider, for example, the following remarks of Professor David Lewis.

---

[15] One of the advantages of looking at things this way is that it makes clear why there *must* be linguistic universals. To learn a natural language, one must learn the correspondence between its sentences and their internal representations. But it is immediately obvious that there could be no general solution to the problem of devising a device which can learn just *any* arbitrary relation between the members of two infinite sets. The possibility of constructing a language learner depends on there being a priori constraints on the kinds of correspondences that it will be required to learn.

My proposals regarding the nature of meanings will not conform to the expectations of those linguists who conceive of semantic inter- pretation as the assignment to sentences and their constituents or com- ponents of 'semantic markers' or the like. (Katz and Postal (1964) for instance.) Semantic markers are *symbols*: items in the vocabulary of an artificial language we may call *Semantic Markerese*. Semantic interpre- tation by means of them amounts merely to a translation algorithm from the object language to the auxiliary language Markerese. But we can know the Markerese translation of an English sentence without know- ing the first thing about the meaning of the English sentence: namely, the conditions under which it would be true. Semantics with no treat- ment of truth conditions is not semantics. Translation into Markerese is at best a substitute for real semantics, relying either on our tacit com- petence (at some future date) as speakers of Markerese or on our ability to do real semantics at least for the one language Markerese. Translations into Latin might serve as well, except insofar as the de- signers of Markerese may choose to build into it useful features—free- dom from ambiguity, grammar based on symbolic logic—that might make it easier to do real semantics for Markerese than for Latin. . . . Markerese semantics [failed to deal with] the relations between symbols and the world of non-symbols—that is, with genuinely semantic rela- tions. (1972, pp. 169–170)

For the moment, I want to preserve an appearance of strict impartiality about the details of the semantic theory proposed in works such as Katz and Postal (1964). We shall return to such questions presently and at length. It seems pertinent, however, to comment on a certain unfairness that attaches to Lewis' remarks if they are taken as a general criticism of translational ap- proaches to semantics.

To begin with what is right about what Lewis says, it is true that the mere translation of the formulae of L into those of a canonical language does not provide an account of the way the formulae of L relate to the world. I am going to cede Lewis 'real' since he seems to want it very much. It follows that translational semantics, unlike real semantics, does not say how symbols relate to whatever it is they symbolize.

It is also true that "we can know the Markerese translation of an En- glish sentence without knowing the first thing about the meaning of the En- glish sentence." It's true, but it's a little beside the point. Since the canonical representation of S is itself a formula in some language, one can know what the canonical representation of S *is* without knowing what S *means*: e.g., if one doesn't understand the language in which the canonical representation is couched. But, of course, this will hold for absolutely any semantic theory whatever so long as it is formulated in a symbolic system; and, of course, there is no alternative to so formulating one's theories. We're *all* in Sweeney's boat; we've all gotta use words when we talk. Since words are not, as it were, self-illuminating like globes on a Christmas tree, there is no way in which a semantic theory can guarantee that a given individual will find its formulae intelligible.

So, the sense in which we can "know the Markerese translation of an English sentence without knowing . . . the conditions under which it would be true" is pretty uninteresting. And what is simply false is that we can *give* the Markerese translation of an English sentence without *representing* the conditions under which it is true. We have a guarantee that this is false built into the definition of 'Markerese translation of *S*' since no formula satisfies that definition unless it is true when, and only when, *S* is.[16]

Finally, how good is the criticism that goes 'Translating English into a canonical language is no better than translating English into Latin, except for whatever conveniences the theorist may have built into the former that God left out when he designed the latter'? Well, as Lewis admits, the conveniences may, for all practical purposes, be essential even for doing 'real' semantics. It might quite possibly turn out, for example, that one cannot characterize validity for arguments in English except as one first translates them into their canonical counterparts. Indeed, it seems quite certain that it *will* turn out that way since, on any account that I have heard of, an ambiguity-free notation is the least that such a characterization would require and, notoriously, 'surface' English provides no such notation.

But, second, the remark that *T* is a 'mere' translation scheme from

---

16 The real difference between real semantics and mere translation semantics is not that only the former provides a representation of the truth conditions of sentences in the object language; if *M* is the Markerese translation of *S*, then '*S* is true iff *M* is true' will be a logical consequence of the semantic theory. The difference lies, rather, in the way in which the two kinds of theory characterize the semantic properties of object language expressions. Roughly, translation theories characterize such properties by reference to metalinguistic expressions which share them; 'real' semantic theories do not.

Consider, e.g., reference itself. Translation theories typically specify, for each referring expression of the object language, some coreferring expression of the metalanguage. The reference of object language expressions is, therefore, determined, but only relative to a determination of the reference of the corresponding metalanguage expressions. 'Real' semantics, on the other hand, actually *says* what the object language expressions refer to; i.e., it names their referents. In effect, then, 'real' semantics defines a relation of reference, whereas 'mere' semantics defines only a relation of coreference.

What is certainly true is that a theory of a language must say, in some way or other, what the terms in the language refer to. For this reason, a 'real' semantic theory would have to be part of a theory of the internal code. This consideration does not, of course, make the specification of a translation procedure from formulae of the natural language to formulae of the internal language a dispensable part of the theory of the former.

English to Latin is unlikely to impress a Latin speaker who wants to know what some or other English sentence means. A mere translation scheme is just what his case requires. Now, we have been supposing that the nervous system 'speaks' an internal language which is neither English, nor Latin, nor any other human tongue. The formulae in this code represent the information that natural language sentences convey, so a theory which assigns the formulae to the sentences ipso facto represents the meanings of the latter. And, though such a theory doesn't in Lewis's sense, accomplish real semantics, it must nevertheless be internalized by any organism which can use a natural language as a vehicle of communication. For it is only by exploiting the correspondences that such a theory specifies that organisms can get the information which verbalizations convey into a form in which the nervous system can use it. All in all, a pretty healthy sort of unreality.[17]

The first half of this chapter was concerned with laying out a general account of the relation between linguistic and cognitive theories; to say the same thing in the material mode, with constructing a model of how linguistic and cognitive processes interrelate. The point of the exercise was to rationalize the use of facts about language to constrain theories about the structure of the representational system which mediates cognition. We can summarize the results as follows.

1. Specifications of messages represent the information that utterances of sentences communicate. To put this a different way, they represent the description under which the speaker primarily intends his verbalizations to be understood. To put it a third way, they represent the communicative intentions of the speaker insofar as his communicative intentions can be construed (just) from the form of words he utters.

2. Characterizing the correspondence between messages and the linguistic forms that express them is the proprietary business of linguistic theories.

3. The fact that speaker/hearers can effect such correspondences is to be explained by the assumption that they have internalized computational procedures which associate token messages with token sentences and vice versa. Characterizing the information flow through such procedures is the proprietary business of psycholinguistic theories.

4. Messages must thus be so represented as to provide appropriate domains for the computations involved in encoding and decoding speech. The theory of messages is therefore constrained by theory construction in psycholinguistics.

---

[17] Moreover, if a 'real' semantic theory is one which says how formulae in the *internal* code relate to the world, then speaker/hearers do *not* have to learn any such a theory; presumably the internal code is not learned but innately given. (See the discussion in Chapter 2.)

5. But messages must also be so represented as to provide appropriate domains for such *non*linguistic computational processes as verbally carried information enters into if, as item 1 asserts, messages are what verbalizations convey. The theory of messages is therefore constrained by cognitive psychology at large.

Philosophers sometimes say that ascriptions of intentions to people—especially ascriptions of communicative intentions to people—are so vastly underdetermined by the behavioral data that it is really misleading to describe them as in any important sense *empirical*. There is something to this, but not much. What is probably true is that what any organism *does* is compatible with a vast variety of hypotheses about what it intends and, a fortiori, with indefinitely many hypotheses about how its intentions should be represented. Our point has been, however, that the main constraint upon representations of communicative intentions is not compatibility with *behavior* but compatibility with reasonable, and independently motivated, models of the psychological processes of the speaker/hearer. There is, of course, a kind of diehard reductionist who supposes that all constraints of the latter kind must, in the long run, prove really to be constraints of the former kind. What is lacking is any plausible reason for thinking that what diehard reductionists suppose is true.

We thus arrive at a turning point in our investigation. For it is not enough to argue that the notion of an internal language is conceptually coherent, that it is demanded by such cognitive models as sensible people now endorse, and that, in principle, claims about the structure of that language connect with empirical issues in psychology and linguistics. What now needs to be shown is that some progress can in fact be made in the assessment of such claims. That is what the rest of this book will be about. I shall be reviewing some kinds of arguments that are quite familiar in linguistics (this chapter) and psychology (Chapter 4), but I shall interpret these arguments somewhat eccentrically: viz., as bearing on questions about the character of the internal code.

One kind of question it is often sensible to ask about a representational system is: What are the items in its vocabulary? There is, of course, no *guarantee* that this sort of question will prove to be sensible since some representational systems don't have vocabularies (assuming that to have a vocabulary is to have a finite inventory of discrete, meaningful elementary items); cf. 'analog' representational systems like pictures and the bee languages. It is, however, prima facie reasonable to suppose that a system rich enough to express the messages that natural language sentences can convey will have one. We shall, at any event, make that assumption for heuristic purposes and consider some of the linguistic evidence that bears on what the vocabulary of the language of thought is like.

THE STRUCTURE OF THE INTERNAL CODE:
SOME LINGUISTIC EVIDENCE

THE VOCABULARY OF
INTERNAL REPRESENTATIONS

It is a traditional observation that the sentences of natural languages could communicate what they do communicate even if their vocabularies were smaller than they are. The point is that some natural language vocabulary items can be 'eliminated' by defining them in terms of others, preserving at least the set of inferences that can validly be drawn from sentences of the language. Suppose, for example, that 'bachelor' means the same as 'unmarried man'. Then, roughly, whatever can be said in a language which contains both can be said in a language which contains only one or the other. Moreover, if one is to be dispensed with, it is clear which it will have to be: 'Unmarried' and 'man' occur in phrases other than 'unmarried man', and there is not much point in eliminating the phrase if we can't eliminate its constituents. If, in short, we eliminate 'unmarried man' in favor of 'bachelor', we have not reduced the number of items in the vocabulary of the language, though we have reduced the number of phrases it contains. But if we go the other way around, taking 'bachelor' as the defined expression, the language can make do with only two primitives where previously there were three. Applying this sort of argument wherever it will apply, we arrive at the notion of the *primitive basis* of the vocabulary of a language: viz., the smallest set of vocabulary items in terms of which the entire vocabulary can be defined.[18]

The interest of the notion of a primitive basis, for our purposes, is this: We have seen that the system of internal representations for the sentences of a natural language must at least capture the expressive power of those sentences. It now appears that the primitive basis of a language determines its expressive power insofar as the latter is a function of vocabulary. It is thus an open possibility that the vocabulary of the system used to represent the messages conveyed by the sentences of a natural language corresponds precisely to the primitive basis of that language. If this were the case, it would follow, for example, that 'He is a bachelor' and 'He is an unmarried man' receive identical representations at the message level assuming that 'bachelor' and 'unmarried man' are synonyms.

Of course, from the fact that the primitive vocabulary of the internal representational system *could be* smaller than the 'surface' vocabulary of a natural language, it does not follow that the primitive vocabulary of that system *is* smaller than the surface vocabulary of a natural language. It is possible, after all, that the vocabulary of the inner language is richer than it needs to be: i.e., richer than is necessary for purposes of expressing the content of natural language sentences. That, I take it, is a *strictly* empirical

[18] I assume, for the sake of simplicity, that there is exactly one such set. There is certainly going to be no more than one set of *psychologically* primitive vocabulary items, or psycholinguistics won't be worth doing.

issue, and it is the issue with which the following discussion is primarily concerned.

There seems to be considerable consensus in the recent linguistic literature that there is a 'semantic' level of grammatical representation—a level at which the meaning of sentences is formally specified—and that, whatever other properties this level may have, it is at least clear that it affords identical representations for synonymous sentences. Since psychological reality is usually—if wistfully—claimed for the structures that grammars enumerate, and since it is messages that semantic representations represent, this amounts, in our terms, to the claim that messages *are* couched in a vocabulary less rich than the surface vocabulary of natural languages. It is, then, common ground among many linguists that a process analogous to the replacement of *definiendum* by *definiens* occurs in the course of grammatical derivations, and that there are a variety of semantic and/or syntactic facts about natural languages that the occurrence of this process explains. I am, myself, pretty sure that this consensus is unwarranted, a point to which I shall presently return. First, I want to explore at some length the kinds of mechanisms that linguists have proposed for achieving the effect of eliminative definition, and the evidence for and against the postulation of these mechanisms.

Perhaps the earliest discussion of this complex of issues in the context of generative grammar is to be found in Katz and Fodor (1963). The basic proposal there has gone pretty much unchallenged by those generative grammarians who accept an 'interpretive' view of semantics: viz., that one of the computational devices that mediate the relation between semantic representations and surface sentences is a *dictionary* and that one of the things that the dictionary says about English is that 'bachelor' corresponds to the metalinguistic formula *unmarried man*.[19] This is, of course, to take the notion of eliminative *definition* very literally. The semantic level provides the same representation for the surface sentences 'He is a bachelor' and 'He is an unmarried man'. Moreover, it takes the second sentence as the more explicit of the two since the representation it provides for both will be some composite out of the representations it provides for 'He is unmarried' and 'He is a man'. In effect, the semantic level ignores the difference between 'bachelor' and 'unmarried man' but is sensitive to the fact that the latter has 'man' and 'unmarried' as its constituents. If, therefore, a speaker wants to get 'bachelor' into a surface sentence, or if a hearer wants to get it out, they must do so via their knowledge of the dictionary. For, on this account, there

---

[19] Wherever the distinction is important, I shall use single quotation marks for natural language expressions and italics for expressions in the vocabulary of semantic representations. Strictly speaking, then, the claim at issue is not that 'bachelor' is defined in terms of 'unmarried man', but that 'bachelor' and 'unmarried man' are both defined in terms of *unmarried man*.

is no item in the vocabulary of semantic representation that corresponds to 'bachelor' except for such items as directly correspond to 'unmarried man'.

Whatever disadvantages this sort of theory may have, it does at least accommodate the following sorts of facts:

1. 'He is a bachelor' and 'He is an unmarried man' are synonymous; i.e., they are alternative expressions of the same message.
2. 'Bachelor' should be defined in terms of 'unmarried man' and not vice versa.
3. Whatever follows from 'He is a bachelor' follows from 'He is an unmarried man' and vice versa. (This will be assured by the assumption that inferential operations are sensitive only to the *message* representation of a sentence; i.e., the domains in which inference rules apply are semantic representations rather than surface forms. Since 'He is a bachelor' and 'He is an unmarried man' have, by assumption, the *same* semantic representation, it follows that an inference will be represented as valid for the one iff it is represented as valid for the other.)

The most serious objection to this sort of theory to be found in the linguistic literature is, I think, just that it is too liberal. To say that the grammar contains a dictionary is, after all, only to say that it contains a finite set of pairs each consisting of a defined term from the natural language together with its defining formula in the representational system. The difficulty is that, unless we have some antecedent information about what formulae are well formed in the representational system, the interpretivist proposal will allow just *anything* to count as a possible definition, and this cannot be right. There must *be* some constraints on what can be a defining expression since there must be some constraints on what a word can mean. For example, *of and but* is not a possible definition (is not the meaning of a possible word) because, to put it crudely, *of and but* does not itself mean anything. But what about the semantic theory thus far described rules out *of and but* as a *definiens*? In effect, the suggestion that semantic interpretation involves the application of a dictionary is very nearly vacuous unless something can be said which constrains what may appear *in* the dictionary; i.e., something that specifies the form and content of possible definitions. (For a systematic attempt to formulate such constraints within the assumptions of "interpretive" semantics, see Katz, 1972, especially Chapter 3.)

Where we have gotten to so far is this: We could estimate a lower bound on the size of the vocabulary of the message level if we knew what natural language expressions are replaced by definitions in the course of computing representations at that level. We could say something about what expressions get replaced by definitions if we knew what definitions are and, in particular, what the constraints upon defining expressions are. Now, we do know this much: whatever formulae in the message language express definitions must at least be well-formed in that language. The recommended research strategy is thus to use what one can find out about conditions on well-formedness in the message language to constrain the class of possible definitions and to use what one can find out about the constraints on possible definitions to illuminate the conditions on well-formedness in the message language. This is what has been going on (more or less explicitly) in linguistic semantics for the last several years. (For an extensive review of this literature, see Janet Dean Fodor, to be published.)

The first point to notice is that the most obvious suggestions don't work. Consider, for example, the possibility that well-formedness in the message language satisfies the conditions upon surface well-formedness in whatever natural language is used to express the messages. This would mean, in particular, that definitions for the words in L have the syntax of well-formed formulae of L, so that, at least so far as syntactic constraints are concerned, every word in L that can be defined at all can be defined by some expression of L.

There is, of course, no a priori reason why conditions upon well-formedness of formulae in the internal language should mirror conditions upon well-formedness of surface sentences. On the contrary, if, as we have supposed, the language of thought is a system distinct from natural languages, then correspondences between their structure should be thought of as *surprising* facts, facts to be explained. In particular, there is no a priori reason why the definitions of terms in L should be expressible in L. I stress this because it is arguable that some sorts of garden-variety definitions *can* be so expressed. If, e.g., it is true that 'dog' means *domestic canine,* then that truth can be expressed by a grammatical formula of English (viz., ' "dog" means "domestic canine" '). 'Domestic canine' is a well-formed English noun, so surface English can serve as its own metalanguage for purposes of expressing this much of English semantics.

In fact, this point can be generalized. The definitions of lexical nouns (if, indeed, they have definitions) can usually be expressed by well-formed phrases of the structure (adjective + noun). Extrapolating from this, one might thus be inclined to say: Definitions of terms in L must be capable of being formulated as surface constituents of L. That, however, would probably be a mistake.

The serious problems arise in the case of what we can loosely call 'relational' expressions. Consider, e.g., 'or'. If one wants to say that 'or' standing alone is definable at all, the defining formula would presumably have to be something like 'not both ((not . . .) and (not . . .))'; and, whatever that formula is, it isn't a well-formed sequence in surface English. Similar difficulties arise for relational verbs like 'kill', which is supposed by some to mean *cause to die.* Notice that 'cause to die' cannot occur as a constituent in an English sentence: 'John caused to die Bill' is ill-formed.[20]

---

[20] 'Cause to die' is immediately recognizable as dictionaryese, which is to say that dictionaries do not, in general, honor the condition that definitions must be couched in the syntax of surface English. Of course, many entries that appear in dictionaries

THE STRUCTURE OF THE INTERNAL CODE:
SOME LINGUISTIC EVIDENCE

Philosophers interested in eliminative definition (but not, by and large, in psychological reality or linguistic plausibility) have, at least since Russell (1905), generally handled these sorts of cases by appeal to 'definitions in use'. On this treatment, one does not, in fact, define 'or' or 'kill'. Rather, one introduces rules for eliminating 'P or Q' in favor of 'not both ((not P) and (not Q))' and 'x killed y' in favor of 'x caused y to die'. Thus, where conventional definitions hold between defined *words* and defining *phrases*, definition in use relate *phrases* to phrases. Since the phrases so defined are allowed to contain variables which can be, as it were, carried over into the defining expressions, it is quite likely that a systematic employment of definitions in use will permit one to meet the condition that all definitions must be well-formed surface constituents. Certainly it will allow one to get a great deal closer to meeting that condition than the use of conventional definitions will.

For the purposes which philosophers have chiefly had in mind—viz., simplifying the primitive basis of a language—this does very nicely, so long as it is possible finitely to exhaust the syntactic contexts in which the eliminandum ('or', 'kill', or whatever) occurs. Taken as a bit of psychology, or of descriptive linguistics, however, it seems pretty unpersuasive. In effect, definitions in use are able to *tighten* the constraints on *defining* expressions (to insist that they must be constituents) precisely because they *loosen* the constraints on *defined* expressions (they allow that defined expressions may be phrases rather than words). To put it slightly differently, appeals to definitions in use affront the very strong intuition that, barring idioms, the definable expressions of a language are all drawn from the same linguistic level (say, words or morphemes). Indeed, the problem with definition in use is that it would treat 'P or Q' in something like the way it treats 'kick the bucket'; viz., as a string exhibiting internal syntactic structure but no decomposition into semantic elements with independently specifiable meanings. Until recently, philosophers have tended to be pretty cavalier about missing linguistically significant structure so long as doing so was consistent with finiteness of the semantic theories they purveyed. But linguists and psycholinguists can't be so tolerant; they are concerned not just with formality but also with empirical truth, and the empirical truth would seem to be that 'P or Q' isn't any kind of idiom.

Among the most interesting of the recent contributions to this tangle of problems about definitions and constraints on definitions is a group of pro-

---

are not definitions at all, assuming that definitions are phrases synonymous with the terms that they define. Funk and Wagnalls (1966) handles 'or' by listing its uses, not by saying what it means: "1. Introducing an alternative: stop *or* go. . . . 2. Offering a choice of a series: Will you take milk *or* coffee *or* chocolate? . . ." It will, in fact, be one of the morals of this chapter that the importance of the definition relation has been vastly overestimated in the literature on linguistic semantics.

posals associated with the epithet 'generative semantics'. The basic idea is that one might treat definitions as species of *syntactic* relations; specifically, that defined terms might be derived from their defining expressions by rules formally indistinguishable from syntactic transformations.[21] If this is true, it should be possible after all to use the syntax of the object language to constrain the possible defintions of its terms. For even though it isn't plausible that every definition must be a well-formed surface constituent of the object language, it *would* be required that every definition should be the output of a syntactic process of the object language. In particular, it would be required that every definition should be a well-formed formula at *some* point in a syntactic derivation. To put it more generally, if this proposal can be made to work, then some of the constraints on definitions would be 'inherited' from the constraints on syntactic transformations.

For example, it is pretty widely accepted as a constraint on transformations that they are allowed to move, delete, or substitute only for constituents; i.e., the objects which a transformation applies to must be constituents at the point in a derivation where the transformation applies to them. This requirement (hereafter the 'single node constraint' or SNC)[22] is deeply entrenched in generative theory, since a standard way of showing that something *is* a constituent at a certain point in a derivation is to show that some transformation moves, deletes, or substitutes for it at that point. Consider, for example, the pair of sentences (1) and (2).

(1)   Bill climbed over the fence.

(2)   Bill phoned up the man.

It is generally accepted that the first must be bracketed (Bill) (climbed) (over the fence), while the second is bracketed (Bill) (phoned up) (the man). That is, 'phone up' is a constituent of (2), but 'climb over' is *not* a constituent of (1). The argument which shows this appeals directly to SNC; viz., that there is a sentence (3) corresponding to (1), but there is no sentence (4) corresponding to (2). Since there is a transformation which

(3)   Over the fence climbed Bill.

(4)   *Up the man phoned Bill.

21 Strictly speaking, the suggestion is not that terms derive from their (object language) definition, but that both derive from a common (metalanguage) source; i.e., 'kill' and 'cause to die' both derive from *cause to die*. (See footnote 19 above.)

22 Strictly speaking, the principle at issue is that elementary transformations can apply only to subtrees of a constituent structure tree. A collection of nodes constitutes a subtree iff there is a node of the supertree which dominates them and them only.

applies to 'over the fence', SNC requires that that sequence be marked as a constituent.

So far, the discussion has gone like this: If defined terms are syntactically derivable from their defining expressions (*pace* footnote 19), then definitions will have to meet whatever constraints apply to objects that fall in the domain of transformations. In particular, they will have to meet SNC. But SNC requires that the objects that transformations apply to must be constituents at the point where the transformations apply. Hence, if the generative semantics account is true, we know at least the following about the constraints on definitions: Defining expressions must be well-formed constituents at some point or other in the course of object language syntactic derivations. This constraint is, of course, weaker than the requirement that definitions must be well-formed *surface* constituents of the object language; but it is, nevertheless, more than strong enough to be interesting.

Consider, then, how the present proposal might work for such definitional relations as the one between 'kill' and 'cause to die'.[23] One would start by assuming that (5) is among the well-formed syntactic deep structures of English. (Structure (5), is the one which in the obvious sense, directly underlies such sentences as 'John caused Mary to die', 'John caused Mary's death', etc.) We shall also have to assume two transformations. *Predicate raising* applies to the verb in the embedded sentence, with the effect of

(5)

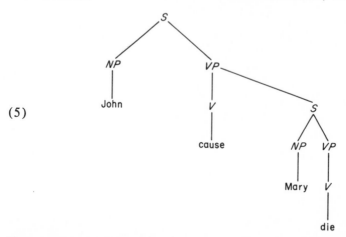

[23] What follows is a very much simplified version of the treatment of causatives proposed by Lakoff (1970a) and McCawley (1971) among others. For a detailed development of some difficulties with this treatment, see Fodor (1970), but it is worth emphasizing from the start that the proposed definition is surely defective since 'x caused y to die' doesn't entail 'x killed y'. Consider the case where x causes y to die by getting *someone else* to kill him.

It is usual to reply to this sort of objection by invoking a special relation of 'immediate causation' such that, by fiat, 'x immediately caused y to die' *does* entail 'x killed y'. It is this relation of immediate causation that is said to figure in the definition of verbs like 'kill'. It is a mystery (apparently one which is to remain permanently unexplained) what, precisely, this relation is. (In the most obvious

attaching it to the verb node in the embedding sentence. The application of *predicate raising* to (5) thus yields some such derived structure as (6).

(6)

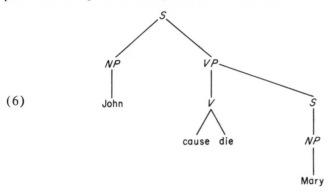

It should be noticed that, in (6) 'cause die' is analyzed as a compound verb; hence in particular, 'cause die' satisfies SNC and is, to that extent, a possible domain for further transformations. And, in fact, a further transformation will now apply. *Lexicalization* is a substitution transformation which converts structures like (6) into structures like (7); i.e., into surface trees which contain defined terms.

(7)

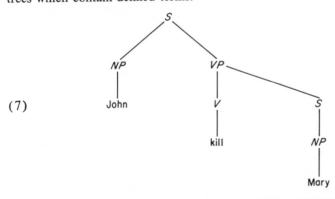

---

sense of 'immediately cause' what immediately causes one's death isn't, usually, what kills one. If it were, we should all die of heart failure.) But whatever the notion of immediate causation is supposed to come to, the reply misses the point. What counts is that, of all the species of x causing y to die, there is one and only one which is necessary and sufficient for making 'x killed y' true: viz., x's causing y to die by killing y. Similarly, of all the species of x causing the glass to break, there is one and only one which is necessary and sufficient for making 'x broke the glass' true: viz., x's causing the glass to break by breaking the glass. And so on, *mutatis mutandis,* for the rest of the causative verbs. I take it that this strongly suggests that *both* 'kill' and 'cause to die' (both 'break$_{transitive}$' and 'cause to break$_{intransitive}$') must be vocabulary items in a metalanguage rich enough to represent the truth conditions on English sentences. More specifically, it strongly suggests that NP_1 must be represented as the agent of $V_{causative}$ (and not as the agent of $cause_V$) in the semantic analysis of sentences of the surface form NP_1 $V_{causative}$ NP_2.

The important point to notice about *lexicalization* is that its function here is in some sense analogous to a definition of 'kill' and not to a definition in use of '*x* kill *y*'. What gets 'kill' into the right relation to its subject and object in surface sentences like 'John killed Mary' is not that it is defined in the context of variables (as it would be in definition in use); rather, the derivation is so arranged that, after *lexicalization,* the deep subject of 'cause' has become the derived subject of 'kill', and the deep subject of 'die' has become the derived object of 'kill'.

There are, in general, three kinds of questions that one wants to raise about this sort of proposal: Is it desirable, is it technically feasible, and is there any evidence for it? I think that there can be no doubt but that the answer to the first quesion must be yes. What we have been wanting all along is a way of constraining possible definitions in order to be able to estimate how rich the primitive basis of the system of semantic representations must be. If the present proposal is correct, it does supply such a source of constraints: We know at least as much about conditions on definitions as we know about conditions on transformations. Moreover, if there are analogies between constraints on well-formedness in the representational system and constraints on well-formedness in the object language, the present account explains them: The rules that relate words to their definitions are a special case of the rules that relate surface structures to deep structures.

I shall presently have something to say about the question of technical feasibility. It seems to me to be false that good candidates for definitions invariably satisfy such constraints on transformations as SNC, just as it seems to be false that good candidates for definitions invariably constitute well-formed surface phrases. For the moment, however, I want to look at the third question. It has been one of the central claims of generative semanticists that assuming that there are syntactic relations between *definiendum* and *definiens* permits us to account for a wide range of grammatical facts which cannot otherwise be explained. If this is true, it is obviously important since it provides empirical support for a syntactic treatment of definitions. It would thus be a prime example of the use of distributional linguistic data to choose between theories about internal representations, and it is the burden of this chapter that linguistic data *can* choose between such theories. Indeed, viewed from this prospect, the generative semantics proposal is important even if it *isn't* true, so long as there are data which show that it isn't. Our main point is that theories about internal representations are legitimate empirical theories. One way to show that they are is to find data which confirm them. But it would do equally well to show that there are data with which they are incompatible.

It is beyond the scope of this book to attempt a detailed survey of the evidence pro and con a syntactic treatment of definitions. What I shall do instead is work through an example. In particular, I want to show how some facts about English sentences might be resolved by any of three different assumptions about the character and content of the primitive vocabulary of the system of underlying representations. My conclusion will be that, for these data at least, the best solution assumes not only that there is no *syntactic* process of definition, but that there is no process for definition *at all*; i.e., that both the defined expression and its definition appear as items in the primitive vocabulary of the representational system.

It goes without saying that this sort of argument cannot refute the generative semantics case. If the present example does not support the existence of a transformational process of *lexicalization,* perhaps some other example will. My aim, however, is not to prove or disprove any given treatment of definition, but just to provide some examples of the kinds of considerations that are relevant. On the one hand, we shall see that the syntactic account of definitions apparently doesn't work in at least one case where, prima facie, it might have been expected to; and, on the other, we shall turn up some facts which look like being informative about the. character of semantic representations whatever view of definition one eventually accepts. Toward the very end, 1 shall review some considerations which do, I think, support a general moral. I shall argue that there probably is no semantic level in at least one traditional sense of that notion: i.e., that there is no psychologically real level of representation at which definable terms are replaced by their definitions. If this is right, then a fortiori both generative and interpretive views of semantics are wrong; the primitive vocabulary of the internal representational system is comparable in richness to the surface vocabulary of a natural language.

It is widely accepted that English contains a transformation *equi-NP deletion* (= *equi*) which deletes the subject of a subordinated sentence under conditions of identity with an *NP* in the immediately subordinating sentence. The existence of pairs like (8) strongly suggest such a rule, and the sug-

(8)   John$_1$ objects to his$_1$ being bitten.
       John objects to being bitten.

gestion is strengthened by the observation that 'John objects to being bitten' is understood to have 'John' as the logical subject of *both* verbs (i.e., it is *John's* being bitten that the sentence says that John objects to).

So far so good. The present point, however, is that *equi* runs into prima facie difficulties when in operates in the scope of such quantifiers as 'only'. Consider (9).

(9)   Only Churchill remembers giving the speech about blood, sweat, toil and tears.[24]

[24] Hereafter abbreviated to 'Only Churchill remembers giving the speech . . . ' . The example emerged in conversation with Professor Judith Jarvis Thomson, to whom thanks are due.

I assume that (9) is true if (a) only Churchill did give the speech and (b) Churchill remembers doing so. If (9) is true under these conditions, then so, too, must be the sentence from which (9) is derived by *equi*.[25] But what could that sentence be? Prima facie, there are three possibilities: (10–12).

(10)   Only Churchill remembers himself giving the speech. . . .

(11)   Only Churchill remembers his giving the speech. . . .

(12)   Only Churchill remembers Churchill('s) giving the speech. . . .

But, prima facie, none of these possibilities will do. Sentence (10) is out because, though it is equivalent to (9), it is itself presumably transformationally derived and the only available sources are (11) and (12); hence, to assume that (9) comes from (10) is simply to replace the question 'Where does (9) come from?' with the question 'Where does (10) come from?' But it is immediately evident that (11) and (12) must be out, too, since neither is equivalent to (9). It does not, for example, follow from the fact that only Churchill gave the speech and that Churchill remembers doing so that only Churchill remembers his giving the speech. What shows this is that *I* remember his giving the speech, and so, doubtless, do many others. Similarily, it does not follow from those premises that only Churchill remembers Churchill('s) giving the speech, since, once again, *I* remember Churchill's giving the speech; the same argument that precludes deriving (9) from (11) also precludes deriving it from (12). One might put it (for fun) that remembering giving the speech exhibits a curious kind of epistemic privacy: It is something that only whoever gave the speech can do. But remembering *his* giving the speech (or Churchill('s) doing so) is something that anyone who heard the speech is entitled to. It looks as though (9) can't derive from any of (10–12).

A solution of these data would require (a) saving *equi* (i.e., showing that (9) isn't a counterexample to it); (b) providing a source for (9) which isn't a possible source for (11) and (12); (c) explaining the relation between (9) and (10) (i.e., explaining why they are equivalent). I want now to consider three different solutions. What makes them different is primarily the assumptions they make (or, anyhow, tolerate) about the character of the vocabulary of the deepest representations to which transformations apply. All three solutions are compatible with the data proposed thus far, but we shall see that there are nevertheless plausible grounds for choosing among them.

---

[25] I am assuming that transformations are 'meaning preserving', whatever, precisely, *that* means.

Solution 1: 'Only' Decomposed

We commence with a line of analysis which suggests that the surface quantifier 'only' does not occur in the vocabulary of the deeper levels of linguistic representation. In particular, according to this analysis, (a) 'only' does not occur at the deepest level of representation for which transformations are defined; (b) 'only' is introduced into surface structures by a lexicalization transformation; (c) lexicalization has the effect of deriving surface sequences of the form 'only a is F' from underlying sequences of approximately the form 'a is F and no other x is F'. This is, in fact, a typical generative semantical analysis, though, so far as I know—and for reasons that will presently become clear—no generative semanticist has endorsed it.

We will assume, then, two base structures: Sentence (13) is to be the underlying representation for (9) and (10); and (14) is to be the underlying representation for (11) and (12).

(13) Churchill₁ remembers he₁ give the speech and (no other$_x$) (x remembers (x give the speech)

(14) Churchill₁ remembers he₁ give the speech and (no other$_x$) (x remembers $\begin{Bmatrix} he_1 \\ Churchill_1 \end{Bmatrix}$ give the speech)

The important point to notice is that both *equi* and *reflexivization* require identity between the *NP*s on which they operate, and while this condition is satisfied by the italicized items in (13) (viz. the variables), it is *not* satisfied by the italicized items in (14).

Given these structures, the derivations are routine. Either *equi* or *reflexive* can apply to (13), yielding, respectively, (15) and (16).[26]

(15) Churchill₁ remembers he₁ give the speech and (no other x) (x remembers (give the speech))

(16) Churchill₁ remembers he₁ give the speech and (no other x) (x remembers (himself give the speech))

As just remarked, however, neither of these transformations applies to (14), so the subordinate *NP* must remain as either a pronoun or a name.

What does now apply, both to (14) and to (15) and (16) is *conjunction reduction,* a transformation which optionally deletes the first of a pair

---

[26] I am not bothering, here or elsewhere, with the morphological adjustments required for tense, agreement, etc.

of identical *VP*s in conjoined sentences. The application of *conjunction reduction* to (15) and (16) yields, respectively, (17) and (18).[27]

> (17) Churchill and no other x (x remembers giving the speech)

> (18) Churchill and no other x (x remembers himself giving the speech)

The application of *conjunction reduction* to (14) yields (19). Notice that neither *equi* nor *reflexive* can apply to '$\begin{Bmatrix} he_1 \\ Churchill_1 \end{Bmatrix}$' in (19) because the subordinating (derived) *NP* is not 'Churchill' but 'Churchill and no other x'; i.e., the identity conditions on *equi* and *reflexive* are not satisfied in (19) any more than they are in (14).

> (19) Churchill$_1$ and no other x (x remembers $\begin{Bmatrix} he_1 \\ Churchill_1 \end{Bmatrix}$ give the speech)

Lexicalization now applies to introduce 'only' in all three structures. Sentence (17) becomes (9), (18) becomes (10)—thus deriving (9) and (10) from the same ultimate source, viz., (13)—and the two versions of (19) become (11) and (12), respectively.[28]

Could this story be right? I want, for the moment, to leave open the question whether 'only' is reduced to primitives at some level of linguistic representation *more* abstract than syntactic deep structure. For what does seem clear, in any event, is that *if* it is, it can't be put back together by any *transformational* operation. In particular, 'only *a* is *F*' cannot be a lexicalized form of '*a* and no other x is F' if lexicalization is a syntactic process. The point is that to accept that treatment would probably require abandoning widely acknowledged constraints on transformations, and that no one is prepared to do.

---

[27] The attentive reader may have noticed that, strictly speaking, we don't *have* identity between the *VP*s on which *conjunction reduction* is to operate in (15) and (16): In the former case it deletes 'remembers he$_1$ give the speech' in the presence of 'remembers give the speech', and, in the latter case, it deletes 'remembers he$_1$ give the speech' in the presence of 'remembers himself give the speech'. What has to happen, in fact, is that *equi* (in the one case) and *reflexive* (in the other) must operate on *NP*s in the left conjunct, yielding, respectively, 'Churchill remembers giving . . .' and 'Churchill remembers himself giving . . .'. *Conjunction reduction* can now operate under strict identity of the derived *VP*s to yield (17) and (18).

[28] If *lexicalization* has the effect of rewriting 'Churchill and no other x' as 'only Churchill', it will have the side effect of leaving an unbound variable in the residual structure. Sentence (17), e.g., would come out 'Only Churchill (x remembers giving the speech)'. There are fancy ways of avoiding this, but I shan't pursue them since, as we are about to see, the whole analysis lacks credibility.

SNC, for example, says that transformations (hence *lexicalization* in particular) must operate upon constituents. The trouble is that the transformation we need in the present case is one which rewrites 'and no other x' as 'only' inside the phrase 'Churchill and no other x'. But it is surely plausible the bracketing of that phrase is (20) and not (21).

(20) ((Churchill) (and) (no other x))

(21)* ((Churchill) (and no other x))

If this is right, then a transformation that works the way *lexicalization* would need to would ipso facto apply to a nonconstituent. The conclusion would have to be that there is no such transformation.

I have taken it for granted that (21) is the wrong analysis of 'Churchill and no other x', but it may be that there are some who would accept (21) rather than abandoning the syntactic decomposition of 'only'. Ross (1967) has, in fact, endorsed that bracketing on independent grounds. It may therefore be worth remarking that the possible violation of SNC isn't all that's wrong with the proposed analysis. For example, 'only' is a determiner in 'only Churchill', and whatever 'and no other x' is, it isn't that. So the kind of lexicalization involved will have to (a) substitute 'only' for what is, prima facie, a nonconstituent and then (b) change the labeling of this prima facie nonconstituent in a completely arbitrary way. All this looks as though the processes that would be required in order to substitute 'only' for its presumptive phrasal source would grossly violate standard conditions on transformations. Clearly, we should avoid acknowledging such processes if there is any way to do so.

Two further points before we turn to a consideration of some alternative solutions for the data proposed by (9–12). First, we could save *lexicalization and* SNC if, instead of deriving 'only' from 'and no other x' we derived 'only Churchill' from 'Churchill and no other x'. For, 'Churchill and no other x' is a constituent in (17–19), so an operation that substitutes for it satisfies SNC. This is, however, no comfort. The difficulties with this proposal are precisely the ones we mentioned above in connection with definitions in use.

It was supposed to be an advantage of the syntactic account of definitions that it allowed us to have independent introduction rules for what are, intuitively, distinct semantic items (thus, *lexicalization* was to introduce 'kill' into surface structures and not, e.g., 'x kill y'). But now, to make *lexicalization* conform to SNC we shall have to have a transformation which introduces (not 'only' but) 'only a' into structures of the form 'only a is F'. We thus violate the strong intuition that phrases like 'only Churchill' aren't idioms; i.e., that their meanings are constructs out of the meanings of their component terms. I should think that there would be general agreement among linguists that that would be too high a price to pay for lexicalization, just as it is generally agreed to be too much to pay for definition in use.

The final point is that 'only' isn't the only quantifier that makes trouble for lexicalization. There seems to be considerable philosophical agreement that 'the' can be defined in terms of 'a' at least in such constructions as '(the *x* such that *x* is *F*) is *G*'. Roughly, the definition is supposed to be the one in (22).

> (22) *There is an* x such that (x is F) & (x is G) & (y) (y *is F* ≡ (y = x)).

There is, as everyone knows, a variety of alternative notations for expressing this definition, and there is considerable disagreement about which, if any, of its clauses are presupposed when the *x* such that *x* is *F* is referred to. It seems clear, nevertheless, that any attempt to get 'the' into surface structures by a process of lexicalization would have, somehow or other, to substitute for (and *just* for) the italicized items in (22). I think it's safe to assume that any rule which brought this off would ipso facto not be a transformation.

Solution 2: Names as Quantifiers

It looks as though we would do well to search for a treatment of (9–12) that does not assume that 'only' is syntactically decomposed. In fact, such a treatment is already available in the literature.

McCawley (1970) has noticed that pairs like (23) and (24) are apparent exceptions to the reflexive transformation.

> (23) Only Lyndon pities Lyndon.

> (24) Only Lyndon pities himself.

For, on the one hand, (23) ought to fall in the domain of *reflexive* and, on the other, (23) and (24) are not equivalent: In our terms, (24) is not one of the surface forms which expresses the message expressed by (23). It turns out, in fact, that the failure of *reflexive* to apply in (23) is really the same phenomenon as the failure of *equi* to apply in (11) and (12); the Churchill phenomenon and the Lyndon phenomenon are basically identical, and a solution that works for one will resolve the other.

Consider, in particular, a solution somewhat like the one that Mc-Cawley proposed for (23) and (24).[29] Suppose we assume the availability, at some level of representation that is accessible to transformations, of the

---

[29] I want to emphasize that the proposal I'm about to sketch is *not* the one that McCawley endorses. The details of the present treatment are, in fact, dictated largely by expository convenience. The only part I care about, and the part that *is* borrowed from McCawley, is the suggestion that what blocks *reflexive* in (23) and (24) (and

usual cross-referencing mechanisms of first-order logic. In particular, we assume the distinction between free and bound variables on the one hand and constants on the other. We assume, moreover, that the vocabulary of the level acknowledges not only the standard variable binders *some* and *all,* but also a (presumably productive) class of 'restricted' quantifiers, which can be generated in a uniform way from proper names. Suppose, in particular, that 'a' names the individual a. Then the corresponding quantifier '(a_x)' is the formula such that '$(a_x) [F_x]$' is true iff all the members of the class whose single member is a are F. Correspondingly, we can define a complex quantifier '(only (a_x))', such that, if 'a' names a, then '(only $(a_x)) [F_x]$' is true iff all the members of the class whose single member is a are F, and nothing else is F. Thus, e.g., if 'John' names John, then '(John$_x$) $[F_x]$' is true iff John is F, and '(only (John$_x$)) $[F_x]$' is true iff John is F, and nothing else is F.

Given these conventions, it is possible to develop a reasonable treatment of the behavior of reflexive vis-à-vis pairs like (23) and (24). In particular, the deep representation of (23) is something like (25).

(25)   (only (Lyndon$_x$)) (x pities Lyndon)

Reflexive does not apply because the two arguments of 'pities' (viz., a bound variable and a constant) are not identical. There is, of course, a source for (24); viz., (26).

(26)   (only (Lyndon$_x$)) (x pities x)

In (26) the identity conditions on the arguments of 'pities' *are* satisfied (both arguments are variables and both are bound by the same quantifier), so reflexivization goes through.

It might be thought possible to embarrass this analysis by pointing out that (27), like (23), cannot be a source of surface reflexives.

(27)   Only Lyndon pities only Lyndon.

For, it might be supposed, (27) *does* satisfy the identity conditions on *reflexive* and so ought, on the present analysis, to yield (24) as a possible transform. That *would* be an embarrassment since (27) is no more equivalent to (24) than (25) is. In fact, however, the analysis can cope with (27) as McCawley has pointed out; (27) is treated as a case of multiple quantification, analogous to, say, (28).

---

would *mutatis mutandis,* block *equi* in (11) and (12)) is that the identity conditions on these transformations are not satisfied by pairs consisting of a constant and a bound variable.

(28)   Everyone hates everyone.

Notice that (28) cannot be the source of the surface reflexive (29), and that one way out would be to distinguish between the two quantifiers in deep syntax just as one would if one were 'formalizing' (28) in first-order logic.

(29)   Everyone hates himself.

In particular, (28) would have the deep analysis (30) with, as usual, *reflexive* not applying because of nonidentity of the arguments of the verb.

(30) (x) (y) $(x$ hates $y)$

Sentence (29), on the other hand, comes from (31), just as (24) comes from (26).

(31) (x) $(x$ hates $x)$

The symmetry seems striking and argues, prima facie, for the proposed assimilation of names to quantifiers.

The present point is that (27) can be handled as fundamentally analogous to (28). In particular, (27) doesn't reflexivize if we regard it as containing two *different* quantifiers, and the present proposal permits us to do that by deriving it from some such source as (32).

(32)   (only (Lyndon_x)) (only (Lyndon_y)) $(x$ pities $y)$

Notice that the truth conditions work out right. If (27) comes from (32), then it will be true iff all the members of the set whose only member is Lyndon pity all the members of the set whose only member is Lyndon.

The bearing of all this on our original problem—what to do about (9–12)?—can now be stated rather quickly. The fundamental point is that precisely the same mechanisms that were just used to prevent *reflexive* from applying to (23) can also be used to prevent *equi* from applying to (11) or (12). Thus, (11) and (12) could both be derived from something like (33), while both (9) and (10) are derived from something like (34), via *reflexive* and *equi*.

(33)   (only (Churchill_x)) $(x$ remembers Churchill give the speech)

(34)   (only (Churchill_x)) $(x$ remembers x give the speech)

The usual considerations about identity remain in force: i.e., neither *equi* nor *reflexive* apply to pairs consisting of a bound variable and a constant, but either can apply to pairs consisting of two variables bound by the same quantifier.

We have thus got a candidate solution for (9–12) which not only accounts for the data but also explains a number of other, apparently related, syntactic phenomena. What we pay for this treatment is the postulation of the mechanisms of variable binding at some level of *syntactic* analysis (i.e., at some level for which transformations are defined). But the analysis is arguably cheap at the price since, presumably, we will have to have these mechanisms *somewhere* in the theory (e.g., at the level where the ambiguity of strings like 'Everybody loves somebody' is displayed). We might thus tentatively conclude that we have learned quite a lot about the vocabulary of the internal representations of sentences from the discussion thus far: that 'only' is available at least as far 'up' in derivations as syntactic deep structure and that the mechanisms of quantification are available at least as far 'down' in derivations as syntactic deep structure. I think, however, that conclusions based on the present analysis are premature, since I think that there are strong reasons for doubting that this analysis is right. Let's have one last fling at (9–12).

Solution 3: *Self* in Deep Structure

We began the discussion of the Churchill cases by rejecting the proposal that the transformational source of (9) is (10). For though these sentences are presumably equivalent, reflexives are themselves traditionally treated as derived forms.[30] If the traditional treatment is right, and if (9) is the result of applying *equi* to (10), what is the transformational source of (10)?

But this argument is only as good as the assumption that there is no reflexive element is syntactic deep structure. Suppose, for the moment, that that assumption is false. In particular, suppose that *self* is an item in the base vocabulary, and that *equi* applies *only* to it (i.e., no NP other than *self* can be deleted by *equi*). So far as I can see, these assumptions resolve all the data we have examined so far: Sentences (9) and (10) are synonymous, with the latter derived from the former by the application of *equi*; neither (11) nor (12) can provide a source for (9) because *equi* applies only to *self*; neither (11) nor (12) can provide a source for (10) because there is no *reflexive* transformation. The Lyndon cases follow suit. In particular, if *reflexive* is a base form, there is no problem about blocking the derivation of (24) from (23). In fact, so far as I know, if this proposal is correct, there is no direct evidence at all for the existence of quantificational mechanisms at any specifically *syntactic* level of linguistic representation. For the

---

30 But not any more. The general account of the relation between *reflexive* and *equi* that I am about to propose has been independently suggested by several linguists, though their reasons for endorsing it aren't the ones that I shall give (cf. Helke, 1971.)

alleged evidence would appear to be exhausted by the nonequivalence of pairs like (28) and (29) and the ambiguity of sentences like 'Everyone loves someone.' On the present view, however, (28) and (29) are both base forms, and it is left open whether ambiguities of mixed quantification are syntactically resolved.

How plausible, then, is the claim that *self* is a deep structure element? What I shall argue is pretty clear is that *self* is an element at whatever level of representation inferential relations are defined for. For a generative semanticist that ought to settle the question since, by definition, a generative semanticist identifies that level with the deepest one at which transformations apply. If one prefers one's semantics interpretive, however, the situation is a little more complicated. It is conceptually possible that *self* should appear at the semantic level, disappear at the deep syntactic level, and then turn up again, transformationally introduced, in surface sentences. But though this position is, in principle, open, I shouldn't have thought that anyone would want to hold it.

So, I now want to argue that *self* is an element at that level of representation to which rules of inference apply. To begin with, consider argument (35). I take it that this argument is (roughly) valid, and that it is (roughly) of the form (36).

(35)   a. John believes that Bill is a pothead.

       b. Mary believes what John believes.
       _____

       c. Mary believes that Bill is a pothead.

(36)   a. John believes S_i
       b. $(\exists S_x)\,((\text{Mary believes } S_x \,\&\, (S_x = S_i))$
       _____

       c. Mary believes S_i

That is, argument (35) turns on substituting the syntactic object of 'believes' in premise (35a) for the syntactic object of 'believes' in premise (35b), and the substitution is licensed by the identity of what Mary believes with what John believes. For present purposes, I don't much care about the further details.

Now consider argument (37).

(37)   a. The cat wanted to eat the cheese.
       b. The mouse got what the cat wanted.
       _____

       c. The mouse got to eat the cheese.

I assume that this argument, too, is roughly valid and that it is of essentially the same form as (35). In particular, I assume that, in both (35) and (37), the relevant rule of inference applies to move the syntactic object of the main verb of the first premise.

Now, in the case of (35) these assumptions are reasonably unproblematic. In (37), however, there *are* problems. In particular, one wants an answer to the question: What *is* the syntactic object of 'want' in (37a) at the point where the inference rule that licenses (37) applies?

To begin with, there are two arguments that suggest that the object of 'want' must be a *sentence* at that level. The first is that, if it isn't a sentence, we lose the identity of logical form between (35) and (37) and that would be both uneconomical and counterintuitive. We would like to fix things up so that (35) and (37) fall under the same rule of inference, and, patently, the rule that governs (35) applies to formulae with sentential objects.[31] Second, there seems to be wide agreement that inferential operations are defined for objects *at least* as abstract as 'standard' (i.e., *circa* Chomsky, 1965), deep structures. But it is pretty clear that (37a) has a sentential object at the level of standard deep structure. What shows this is that sentences like (37a) have counterparts which contain passivized complements; cf. (38). Since *passive* applies to structures of the form $(NP_1 \text{ V } NP_2)s$, we will have

(38)   The cat wanted the cheese to be eaten.

to assume that 'eat' has a subject *NP* in the syntactic source of (38) and parity of analysis will require a sentential complement in the syntactic source of (37a). It presumably follows that both sentences have sentential complements at levels of representation still more abstract than standard deep structure (e.g., at the semantic level) if, indeed, there *are* levels of representation more abstract than standard deep structure.

But now, what could the embedded subject *NP* be in the underlying representation of (37a)? So far as I know, the available notational options, including those provided by the standard formalizations of quantificational logic, amount to (39a–c).

(39)   a. the cat_1 wanted (the cat_1 eat the cheese)
        b. the cat_1 wanted (he_1 eat the cheese)
        c. (the cat_x) (x wanted (x eat the cheese))

(39a) corresponds to the assumption that *equi* applies to lexical *NP*s; (39b) corresponds to the assumption that *equi* applies to deep pronouns; (39c)

---

[31] Strictly speaking, the object of 'believe' in (35) is presumably a sentential *NP*: i.e., (believe (that $(S))_{NP}$); parity of analysis suggests (want (that $(S))_{NP}$) for (37). It doesn't, however, affect the present argument one way or another.

corresponds to the assumption that *equi* applies to deep variables. I don't care, for present purposes, which, if any, of these proposals ought to be taken seriously. The present point is that none of them provides an appropriate domain for the inferential operations that license (37). To put it the other way round, the available mechanisms for representing binding and cross-referencing will not permit an adequate treatment of the validity of (37).

Suppose that (37a) is represented by (39a) at the level where inference rules apply. Then the substitution of the syntactic object of 'want' in the underlying representation of (37a) for '(what the cat wanted)' in the underlying representation of (37b) will yield as conclusion 'the mouse got (the cat eat the cheese)'. But clearly, this isn't what the conclusion of (37) says; what the mouse got was (the *mouse* eat the cheese).

(39b) and (39c) fare no better. If the conclusion of (37) is the mouse got (he_1 eat the cheese), then either (39b) suffers from the same defects as (39a) (assuming that 'he_1' cross-references to 'the cat') or 'he_1' is functioning as an unbound variable, and (37c) is represented as an open sentence, which, of course, it isn't. Finally, since subscripting of pronouns and conventional binding of variables are, for these purposes, essentially the same mechanism, the considerations that rule out (39b) apply, *mutatis mutandis,* to rule out (39c) as well.

That problem is that, if the rule that makes (37) valid is to apply by 'moving' the complement of the underlying representation of (37a), then what we need as subject of that complement is, in effect, not a variable but a variable variable. That is, we need a variable which cross-references to 'the cat' in (37a) and to 'the mouse' in (37c). The assumption that *self* is an element in the vocabulary of the representations that the rule applies to, and that it is interpreted as cross-referencing to the *NP* which syntactically commands it, provides precisely the resources we require.[32] Thus, the underlying representation of (37a) is 'the cat wanted (self eat the cheese)' at the level where inferential operations are defined. The rule involved moves the subordinated sentence into the direct object position in (37b) yielding, as conclusion, 'the mouse got (self eat the cheese)'. The binding conventions for *self* assure that it cross-references to 'the cat' in the former sentence and to 'the mouse' in the latter, yielding just the representation of the argument that we wanted.

I take it that these considerations suggest very strongly that *self* is an unanalyzed element at the level of semantic representation; hence that it either is, or very probably is, an unanalyzed element at the deepest level of syntactic representation (depending on whether or not one assumes that

---

[32] That is, the conditions which are thought of as sufficient for NP_1 reflexivizing NP_2 on transformational treatments of 'self' will now be thought of as sufficient for NP_2 (= *self*) cross-referencing to NP_1; on this treatment, the structural analysis of the putative reflexive transformation is thought of as specifying structural conditions on the binding of *self*.

these levels are identical). I take it, too, that it follows that the mechanisms that a semantic theory of English uses for the representation of cross-referencing of *NPs* are *richer* than the mechanisms that standard formulations of quantificational logic use to represent the cross-referencing of variables.

We can now summarize the main discussion. We have seen that a syntactic decomposition of 'only' is not demanded by the evidence under review and is probably ruled out on grounds of conflict with SNC and other constraints on transformations. We have also seen that a nonsyntactic treatment (one which assumes that 'only' is primitive at the level to which transformations apply) will account for the kinds of data we have surveyed, so long as the standard mechanisms of variable binding are assumed to be available at that level. However, the main arguments for the existence of such mechanisms in deep structure depend on their interaction with the alleged reflexive transformation, and the evidence of (37) makes it plausible that the reflexive morpheme is not, after all, tranformationally introduced. Taking these considerations together, the indicated conclusions seem to be these:

a. *Self* is a deep structure element; there is no reflexive transformation.
b. The syntactic source of (9) and (10) is 'only Churchill remembers (self give the speech)'; (9) and (10) differ only in that *equi* has applied in the derivation of the former.
c. *Equi* can apply only to *self;* in particular, *equi* cannot apply to derive (9) from (11) or (12).
d. Pairs like (23) and (24) (or (24) and (29)) offer no particular evidence for the existence of quantifiers and variables at the level of deep syntactic structure. Perhaps there is no such evidence.

I want presently to draw some morals. Before doing so, however, it is worth noticing a certain spiritual affinity between the semantic phenomenon illustrated by cases like (37) and the (putative) syntactic phenomenon known as 'sloppy identity'.

Looked at from the point of view of standard quantificational notation, in which one has variables but no variable variables, what seems to be happening in (37) is that the inference rules are, as one might say, 'blind' to the shape of the variables in the subjects of the embedded sentences. That is, one is allowed to infer '(mouse_x) (x gets (x eat the cheese))' from a premise of the form '(cat_y) (y wants (y eat the cheese))' despite the non-identity of x and y. Now it has often been suggested (see Ross, 1967) that a similar blindness to the requirement of strict identity is exhibited by certain syntactic transformations. For example, there is a rule of *do so* transformation which, in the untendentious cases, derives sentences like (40) from sentences like (41) under the condition that the *VPs* of the source sentence are identical.

> (40) John ate Cracker Jacks and so did Mary.
> (41) John ate Cracker Jacks and Mary ate Cracker Jacks.

The present point is that it looks as though this condition of strict identity is violated in the derivation of sentences like (42) since, taking the meaning into account, it appears that (42) will have to come from (43) and, the *VP*s in (43), are not identical.

> (42) John broke his arm and so did Mary.
> (43) John broke his arm and Mary broke her arm.

Such cases suggest that *do so* is blind to the shape of variables too.

Now, it seems clear that (37) does not itself turn upon sloppy identity since its premises are not so much as syntactically related. So, either there are parallel, distinct phenomena which explain (37), on the one hand, and (42), on the other, or the treatment of (42) will have to be reduced to the treatment of (37). The latter course seems to me preferable though not, so far as I know, mandatory. That is, assume that (42) comes not from (43) but from (44), with *do so* applying under strict identity but with the two *selfs* interpreted by the sort of cross-referencing principles suggested above.

> (44) John broke self's arm and Mary broke self's arm.

This requires assuming that *self* + *possessive* + *gender* has the surface realization 'his/her', but that assumption is independently plausible: There is no surface form '$\left\{ \begin{array}{c} \text{his} \\ \text{her} \end{array} \right\}$ self's'.

We commenced this discussion by assuming—along with most of current linguistics, generativist and interpretivist—that there is a level of representation at which words are replaced by their defining phrases. Our intention was to consider several of the possible procedures for effecting this replacement using 'only' as a test case. From this point of view, the results of the investigation are a little unsettling. For we not only found no clearly acceptable procedure for eliminating 'only', but we ended by advocating a solution which recognizes 'only' at the deepest level to which transformations apply, and which acknowledges a richer system of cross-referencing than standard quantificational logic employs at the level for which inference is defined.

Of course, the example was chosen with malice aforethought, and of course it is silly to generalize from a single case. But one can at least say this: There is nothing in the data we have considered so far which suggests that the primitive vocabulary of the higher levels of linguistic representation is importantly less rich than the surface vocabulary of English. In particular, none of these data suggest that the replacement of *definiendum* by *definiens* is a significant process in the decoding of wave forms into messages. I think there are, in fact, several serious grounds for being skeptical of the existence of such a process, quite independent of the inferences one might feel inclined to draw from the 'only' case. I now want to say something brief about them.

The first point is that any theory which holds that understanding a sentence involves replacing its defined terms by their defining expressions appears to require that the definitional complexity of the vocabulary of a sentence should predict the relative difficulty of understanding the sentence. For, on any such account, the canonical representation of a sentence containing W must be more elaborate than the canonical representation of a corresponding sentence containing W' given that W' is a primitive in terms of which W is defined and given that everything else is held constant. (Thus, for example, 'John is unmarried' ought to be a simpler sentence that 'John is a bachelor' on the assumption that 'bachelor' is defined as 'unmarried man'. For the semantic representation of 'John is unmarried' is *John is unmarried*; but the semantic representation of 'John is a bachelor' is *John is unmarried and John is a man*.) Presumably, this sort of asymmetry ought to show itself in measurable psychological effects, since, on the stated assumptions, the semantic representation of the W-sentence may plausibly take more steps to compute and will certainly take more memory space to display than will the semantic representation of the W' sentence.

But, in fact, the predicted correspondence between definitional and perceptual complexity doesn't seem to hold.[33] Indeed, as Dr. Michael Treisman

---

[33] The only cases I know about where evidence for such a correspondence has been alleged involve very special phenomena like linguistic markedness. Thus, Clark and Chase (1972) have shown that sentences containing the marked member of a pair of words tend to be harder to cope with than the corresponding sentences which contain the unmarked member of the pair (e.g., a sentence containing $\left\{ \begin{array}{l} \text{far} \\ \text{tall} \\ \text{high} \end{array} \right\}$ is easier, *ceteris paribus,* than its control sentence which contains $\left\{ \begin{array}{l} \text{near} \\ \text{short} \\ \text{low} \end{array} \right\}$. Clark and Chase want to explain this asymmetry by arguing that the marked form is semantically analyzed as (negative + unmarked form); e.g., 'near' = 'not + far$_{\text{unmarked}}$'. On this analysis, the observed difference in ease of processing could be a special case of the putative general correspondence between psychological complexity and definitional complexity.

Even if Clark and Chase are right in this, it is dubious how much can be inferred from a phenomenon as parochial as markedness. But, in fact, it seems unlikely that Clark and Chase *are* right, since it seems unlikely that their analysis of markedness can be sustained. The issues are very complicated, and I shan't go through them here. But, roughly, if 'short' = 'negative + tall$_{\text{unmarked}}$', where 'tall$_{\text{unmarked}}$' is the name of the height dimension, then 'John is short' is analyzed as meaning 'it's false that John has a height' which, of course, it doesn't. This suggests that we need to acknowledge has pointed out (in conversation), if there *were* such a correspondence it is hard to see how explicit abbreviatory definition could have the heuristic value it does have in facilitating reasoning. Abbreviations (and, for that matter, recoding schemes in general; see Miller, Galanter, and Pribram, 1960; Norman, 1969; Paivio, 1971) wouldn't be of much use if understanding a formula required replacing its defined terms by the complex expressions that define them. On the contrary, if abbreviation facilities comprehension, that would seem to be precisely because we are able to understand sentences that contain the abbreviations *without* performing such replacements.

It should be emphasized, in light of all this, that the objection under discussion holds equally against generative and interpretive accounts of semantic representations. For the issue between these schools concerns (primarily) the mechanisms whereby definitions replace definables at the semantic level; on the generative (but not the interpretive) account, these mechanisms are held to be special cases of syntactic transformations. The present point, however, is that there is no clear reason to credit the psychological reality of any level of representation on which definable expressions have been defined away. We shall return presently to the question of how one might construct a semantic theory which does not take definition to be a fundamental semantic relation; hence, a theory which postulates internal representations whose vocabulary is comparable in richness to that of the surface sentences of a natural language.

The next point, too, is intended to hold against both generative and interpretive accounts of semantics. It is this: Both kinds of theory posit an unwarranted distinction in kind between formulae true by virtue of definitions and certain other kinds of 'analyticity.'

Definitional truths are, by their nature, symmetrical. If 'bachelor' means 'unmarried man', then 'unmarried man' means 'bachelor', and it follows that 'x is an unmarried man' entails 'x is a bachelor' iff 'x is a bachelor' entails 'x is an unmarried man'. But now, to put it roughly, there would seem to be some semantic relations that are just like the one that holds between 'bachelor' and 'unmarried man' except that they are *not* symmetrical, and the definitional theory of analyticity simply has no resources for representing this fact. The classic case is the relation between, say, 'red' and 'colored'. If it is a linguistic truth that bachelors are unmarried, then it would seem to be equally a candidate for analyticity that red is a color. But the two cases differ in the following way. It is plausible to say that 'bachelor' entails 'unmarried' because 'bachelor' means 'unmarried man' and 'unmarried man' entails 'unmarried'. But there is no predicate P such that it is plausible to

---

three terms to each markedness relation: e.g., 'short$_{marked}$' as in 'John is short', 'tall$_{unmarked}$' as in 'How tall is John?', and 'tall$_{marked}$' as in 'John is tall'. On this account, 'John is tall' and 'John is short' should be *equivalent* in definitional complexity. Hence, such computational asymmetries as they exhibit can't be explained by appeal to definitional complexity.

say that 'red' entails 'colored' because 'red' means 'a color and P'. I mean not only that there *isn't* such a predicate in English, but that there *couldn't be* such a predicate in any language; there would be no coherent meaning for such a predicate to have. Notice, for example, that it makes perfect sense to speak of *x*s which are just like bachelors except for not necessarily being unmarried. This would just be a circumlocutory way of referring to men. But it makes no sense that I can grasp to talk of *x*s which are just like red except for not necessarily being colors. What would such things *be*?

The notion that linguistic truths derive from definitions requires that wherever Fx analytically entails Gx and not vice versa, there will always be some H or other such that G and H are logically independent and such that Gx *and* Hx entails Fx. But this doesn't seem to be true. The result is that definitional theories of analyticity either ignore the contrary cases (as they have generally been ignored by generative semanticists) or treat them by essentially ad hoc means (as in Katz, 1972).[34] A way of putting this is that a semantic theory should represent the relation between 'bachelor' and 'unmarried man' as the bidirectional counterpart of the unidirectional relation between 'red' and 'colored'. But neither generative nor interpretive accounts of semantics have the resources to do so. In fact, neither theory provides principled grounds for claiming that the two relations have anything in common at all.

If entailments that derive from terms in the 'nonlogical' vocabulary of a natural language do not depend on a process of definition, how *are* they determined? A standard proposal (since Carnap, 1956) is that if we want F to entail G (where one or both are morphologically simple expressions of the object language) we should simply *say* that F entails G; i.e., we should add $\ulcorner F \rightarrow G \urcorner$ to the inference rules. Such nonstandard rules of inference have come to be called 'meaning postulates', so the present proposal is that it is meaning postulates that do the work that definitions have usually been supposed to do.[35]

---

[34] I suspect that this class of cases extends well beyond sensation terms. (In fact, what I *suspect* is that it includes pretty much the entire nonlogical, nonsyntactic vocabulary.) It is, in general, considerably easier to state logically necessary conditions on natural language expressions than to define them. We remarked above that 'kill' doesn't, of course, *mean* cause to die, though, very likely, it is analytically impossible to kill someone without causing his death. I think one ought to take such facts seriously: The best examples of linguistic truths tend to be *a*symmetric, which is just what the definitional account of analyticity doesn't predict. (For further discussion, see J. D. Fodor, to be published.)

[35] From a formal point of view, meaning postulates might well look precisely like definitions in use: i.e., they might apply to expressions under syntactic analysis and in the context of variables. Since meaning postulates don't purport to *define* the expressions they apply to, allowing a complex expression to fall in the domain of a meaning postulate is *not* tantamount to claiming that that expression has no internal semantic structure. Meaning postulates thus permit us to use the formal mechanisms of definition in use without inviting the sorts of objections discussed above.

I don't want to discuss this proposal at length: There is getting to be a considerable literature on the possible role of meaning postulates in the semantic analysis of natural languages, and the reader is hereby referred to it. (See, in particular, Fillmore, 1971; Lakoff, 1970b; Fodor, Fodor, and Garrett, to be published.) Suffice it to mention here three of the more striking advantages.

1. The meaning postulate treatment does not require the theory to posit a sharp distinction between the logical and the nonlogical vocabulary of the object language; the logical behavior of 'bachelor' is not, on this view, treated fundamentally differently from the logical behavior of 'and'. Both occur in the vocabulary of the metalanguage, and the entailments they engender are determined by the inference rules under which they fall.

2. Unlike definition-based theories, the meaning postulate approach does *not* predict a correspondence between the complexity of a sentence and the complexity of the definitions of the words that it contains. 'John is a bachelor' and 'John is unmarried' can be allowed to exhibit any complexity relations they choose to, since 'bachelor' and 'unmarried' *both* occur in the vocabulary of the level of representation at which messages are specified. True, the rules of inference which govern the relation between formulae at that level determine that the first sentence entails the second; but *applying* those rules is not part of *understanding* the sentence (as, according to both generative and interpretive semantics, recovering the semantic representation of the sentence is supposed to be).

It should be borne in mind that understanding a sentence involves computing a representation of the sentence that *determines* its entailments; it doesn't involve computing the entailments. (It couldn't; there are too many of them.) But the representation of 'John is a bachelor' *does* determine the entailment 'John is unmarried' if (a) the representation of 'John is a bachelor' is *John is a bachelor* and (b) the inference rules which apply to that representation include *bachelor → unmarried*.

We are supposing, in effect, that the surface vocabulary of a natural language is identical to, or at any event not much larger than, the vocabulary in which messages are couched. Since it is messages which must be displayed if sentences are to be understood, it is hardly surprising if there is no co-variation between the computational demands that understanding a sentence imposes and the complexity of the definitions of the words that the sentence contains. Learning a definition principally involves learning a meaning postulate. It thus adds to the constraints (not on computing memory but) on long-term memory; it adds a rule of inference to the list that is stored there. That is why, according to the present view, abbreviatory definition and other recoding schemes make formulae easier to understand: Computing memory is expensive, but long-term memory is cheap.

I think this point is sufficiently important to bear some elaboration. A theory of the hearer can reasonably be expected to contain two distinguishable components. The first of these is concerned with explaining sentence comprehension proper; i.e., with characterizing the computations which effect the correspondence between wave forms and messages; i.e., with specifying those mental operations which eventuate in a display of the information that utterances of sentences convey; i.e., with showing how hearers reconstruct the communicative intentions of speakers. Call this component a 'sentence understander'. The second component is concerned with representing the data processes (including the drawing of inferences) which are *defined over* the information that utterances of sentences convey; i.e., those data processes which mediate the hearer's use of the information he gleans from the utterances he hears. Call this component a *logic*. Then, roughly (abstracting from feedback and the like) the output of the sentence understander is the input to the logic. Equivalently, the (or a) function of the sentence understander is to represent utterances in the normal form for which operations in the logic are defined.[36]

Now, given the usual idealizations, the operations of the sentence understander are on-line operations. We understand an utterance when we hear it. But the operations of the logic may take any amount of time at all. It may take minutes, or days, or weeks to notice some of the implications of what we have heard. And since there are typically an infinity of such implications, we are guaranteed that there are some implications that we will never notice.

The point is that somebody has to carry the baby. Suppose we allow the relation between wave forms and messages to be very abstract. Suppose, in particular, that we assume that the substitution of *definiens* for *definiendum* occurs *in the process of assigning a message to a wave form*. What this assumption buys us is the corresponding simplification of the logic; the logic need now contain no rules that specify the behavior of the *definiendum* since, by hypothesis, the *definiendum* has been defined away before we get to a representation that the logic applies to. But we buy this at a price: the simpler the logic is, the more complicated the processes which assign messages to wave forms will have to be.

In short, we have two broad theoretical options: We can acknowledge definitions instead of meaning postulates and thereby simplify the logic at the cost of complicating the sentence understander, or we can acknowledge meaning postulates instead of definitions and thus simplify the sentence understander at the cost of complicating the logic. The present point is that, *ceteris paribus,* we would be well advised to go the second route. For the important thing about sentence understanding is that it is *fast*; too fast, in

---

[36] It seems to me, by the way, to be a conclusive objection to 'network' models of the hearer that they neither make nor admit of this distinction between understanding a sentence token and recognizing what it implies. See, e.g., Collins and Quillian (1969) and their spiritual heirs.

fact, for any psycholinguistic theory that is currently available to explain.[37] We make this mystery worse in proportion as we make the relation between wave forms and messages abstract, since it is this relation that the sentence understander is required to compute. Conversely, we mitigate the mystery insofar as we assume a 'shallow' theory of messages, since the more structural similarity there is between what gets uttered and its internal representation, the less computing the sentence understander will have to do. The interest of meaning postulates is that they provide a general procedure for complicating the logic in ways that reduce the strain on sentence comprehension. That is, they let us do what psychological theories need to do: simplify the representation of computations that must be carried out on-line.

3. There is no reason why, on the present account, analyticity must rest upon symmetrical relations. Some rules of inference go one way, other rules of inference go both ways. There is nothing special about the latter.

I want to close this section by ironing out some apparent incompatibilities between what I've said here and some of the things I said at the end of Chapter 2.

I argued in Chapter 2 that the internal language must be able to express the extension of any predicate that can be learned: i.e., that for any such predicate, there must be a coextensive predicate of the internal language. But I did *not* want to argue that children are born with concepts like 'airplane' ready formed. Rather, I suggested, what they must have innately are the elements into which such concepts decompose, together with the appropriate combinatorial operations defined over the elements. In effect, one can reduce the nativistic commitments of the internal language story if one assumes that definition is among the processes that go on in concept learning. OK so far. But I have wanted to claim in the present discussion that, probably, natural language predicates aren't internally represented by their definitions after all: The message representation of 'bachelor' is *bachelor* and not *unmarried man*. How are these claims to be squared?

I think the following is a serious possibility: *bachelor* gets into the internal language *as an abbreviation for a complex expression of the internal language*: viz., as an abbreviation for *unmarried man*. The abbreviatory convention is stored as a principle of the logic (i.e., as *bachelor* $\rightleftarrows$ *unmarried man*). Since, in the course of learning English, 'bachelor' gets hooked onto *bachelor* and 'unmarried man' gets hooked onto *unmarried man, bachelor* $\rightleftarrows$ *unmarried man* can be used to mediate such inferential relations as the one between '*x* is a bachelor' and '*x* is an unmarried man'.

I want to emphasize that, though this may be wrong, it isn't a fudge.

---

[37] For an estimate of how fast it is, see the work on semantic influences on shadowing by Marslin-Wilson (1973). These studies suggest that at least *some* information about the content of linguistic material is available within a quarter of a second of its reception.

On the contrary, it licenses a number of straightforward empirical predictions. On the present model, we would expect (a) that there *won't* be a correlation between the definitional complexity of a term and the difficulty of understanding a sentence which contains the term (see above); but (b), in certain cases there *will* be a correspondence between the relative definitional complexity of a pair of terms and the order in which they are learned. Since we are now supposing that the process of definition is, as it were, ontogenetically real, we would expect that the child should master terms corresponding to the *definiens* before he masters terms corresponding to the *definiendum*. If, e.g., *only* is defined in terms of *all,* we would expect 'all' to be learned before 'only'. Which, in fact, it is.

It might be argued that it can be shown on empirical grounds that this prediction is false in the general case, Thus, Brown (1970) has remarked that the kind of nouns the child uses first tend to be of middle-class abstractness; 'dog', for example, enters the vocabulary before 'animal' or 'poodle' do. And since 'dog' is presumably defined in terms of 'animal', the ontogenetic pattern Brown observed would appear incompatible with the theory I have just espoused.

There are, however, several problems with this line of argument. First, though children use 'dog' before they use 'animal', it's not out of the question that what they *mean* when they say 'dog' is approximately what *we* mean when we say 'animal', hence that the present observations don't show that the meaning of 'dog' is available before the meaning of 'animal' is. Certainly children's early use of kind terms appears wildly overgeneralized from the adult's point of view. Vygotsky's remark that *extensional* consensus mediates communication between children and adults would seem to be precisely what is not the case.

Second, the whole discussion has proceeded on the assumption that what one learns when one learns a term like 'dog' (or 'airplane', or other such kind terms) is appropriately represented as a set of logically necessary and sufficient conditions. But that, as we remarked in Chapter 2, would seem to be extremely dubious. It seems sufficiently plausible that much conceptual knowledge is organized around stereotypes, exemplars, images, or what have you, and not, at least in the first instance, around definitions.[38] (The issues here are terribly difficult: How, for example, does one *access* an exemplar? If your concept of a dog is, in large part, a representation of a stereotypic dog, how do you go about determining what *falls under* the concept?) Still, the general point would seem to be well taken. What mediates the child's first use of 'airplane' is, surely, not the knowledge that airplanes are flying machines. Rather, things are airplanes insofar as they are like other

---

[38] For discussion, see Heider (1971), Putnam (to be published), and Paivio (1971). What all these otherwise quite different theorists agree upon is the inadequacy of definitions to express what we know about kinds.

things that the child has seen go buzz across the sky. The definitional theory of concepts clearly takes too little account of the role of ostension in fixing what one knows.

It may, in short, be true as I've suggested that, *insofar as a concept is internally represented as a definition,* the order of the acquisition of terms parallels the order of definitional complexity of the concepts that the terms express. But we won't be able to test that claim until we know which (if any) concepts are internally represented as definitions, and such information as is currently available suggests that many of them are not.

Here's a summary of where we've gotten to:

1. The linguistic evidence we have looked at is compatible with the view that the vocabulary of messages (and, a fortiori, the vocabulary of internal representations at large) is very rich.
2. If this is true, then the data processes which operate on messages (viz., the logic) must be correspondingly elaborate. For there must be something which determines the conceptual relations between 'nonlogical' terms in the natural language vocabulary, and if the sentence understander doesn't do it, the logic will have to.
3. Meaning postulates are plausible candidates for enriching the logic.
4. Tentatively, then, the relation between natural language *definiendum* and natural language *definiens* is expressed by meaning postulates defined for their respective innerlanguage translations.
5. In particular, the replacement of definables by their definitions is *not* one of the processes that mediates understanding a sentence; *definiens* and *definiendum* typically have distinct message-level representations.
6. The dispute between generative and interpretive semantics, insofar as it is a dispute over the syntactic treatment of definitions, is a tempest in a teapot. In the sense of 'definition' at issue, definition is not a central notion in semantic theory.
7. In particular, there is no level of representation (including the semantic level) at which 'kill' and 'cause to die', 'only' and 'none but', etc., receive identical representations.
8. These views are generally compatible with considerations concerning the speed of sentence comprehension. Since sentence processing is very fast we should prefer theories which hold that the representation of a sentence that must be recovered in understanding it is relatively *un*abstractly related to the surface form of the sentence. Such theories place the computational load where it is most easily accommodated: on *off*-line processes.

The point of this chapter was primarily to illustrate some kinds of arguments which bring facts about natural languages to bear upon hypotheses about internal representations. The general approach was to assume that some internal representations represent sentences, so if we know how sentences are represented we know what some internal representations are like.

Our conclusion is that, very likely, much of the lexical elaboration of surface sentences may also be available at the level of representation where messages are made explicit. This may seem a surprisingly late-Wittgensteinian view for any discussion which accepts the methodology of generative grammar to endorse, so a methodological remark is in order before we conclude.

Theorists—both philosophers and linguists—who have taken seriously the possibility of formalizing natural languages have tended to make two assumptions about the system of representations they were trying to construct. As compared to natural languages, the representational system is supposed to be both explicit and simple.

I suppose that the requirement of explicitness just *is* the requirement of formality. The semantic properties of object language sentences are to be literally definable over their translations in the representational system. Rules for manipulating the information conveyed by sentences are to apply mechanically to the semantic representations that sentences receive. Simplicity, on the other hand, constrains the *basis* of the representational system rather than the relations between its formulae and the rules that they fall under. A simple system (in at least one important sense of that notion) is one with a relatively small primitive vocabulary and a relatively uncomplicated syntax.

The present point is that strictly speaking, the satisfaction of the goal of explicitness is not conceptually connected to the satisfaction of the goal of simplicity. For the latter implies what the former does not: that the communicative resources of a natural language could, in principle, be captured by a system which is structurally less elaborate than natural languages are. The assumption that English can be formalized in some representational system or other does not, in short, require that it can be formalized in a system whose syntax and vocabulary are interestingly different from the surface syntax and vocabulary *of English*.

This sort of consideration must, of course, be taken quite seriously by anyone who wants to discover semantic representations that are psychologically real. There are, after all, constraints on internal representations other than maximizing the simplicity of basis of the formalism in which they are couched; the most important is maximizing the computational efficiency of the data processes defined over them. Philosophers have tended to hold not only that the sentences of a natural language have a determinate logical form, but also that their logical form can be expressed in a system rather like first-order quantificational logic. Linguists have tended to hold not only that semantic rules can be defined over base structures, but also that the vocabulary and syntax of base structures is fundamentally simpler than the vocabulary and syntax of surface strings. The present point is that the formalist and the reductionist assumptions could, at least in principle, come unstuck. If the kinds of arguments we have been surveying are right, unsticking them would seem to be the thing to do.

There may, then, really be some point to the late Wittgensteinian insistence upon the surface richness of natural languages; one has, at any event, no right simply to take it for granted that their complexity is *merely* superficial in the sense that we could communicate as well—or better—with formally simpler systems. Of course, this works both ways. If one cannot assume that an appropriate language for semantic representations must be less complex than natural languages, one also cannot argue against the possibility of formalizing natural languages on the ground that they are very complicated. If sentences are complex objects, this may show only that we need a correspondingly complicated metalanguage to represent their logical form. If, in short, the independence of reduction and formalization has not always been clear to the formalists, it has not always been clear to their critics either.

The upshot of these remarks is a suggestion that I regard as entirely speculative but very interesting to speculate about: viz., that the language of thought may be very like a natural language. It may be that the resources of the inner code are rather directly represented in the resources of the codes we use for communication. The least that can be said in favor of this hypothesis is that, if it is true, it goes some way toward explaining why natural languages are so easy to learn and why sentences are so easy to understand: The languages we are able to learn are not so very different from the language we innately know, and the sentences we are able to understand are not so very different from the formulae which internally represent them.

It is pertinent to finish by emphasizing that these views may very well all be wrong: even, that is, if the general animus of this chapter can be sustained. The thesis I care most about is that claims (or, anyhow, some claims) about the character of internal representations are empirical in the sense that empirical data would tend toward their confirmation or disconfirmation. I have tried to show this by arguing that data about natural languages bear directly upon, and tend to choose between, competitive hypotheses about the vocabulary of the internal representations that the speaker/hearer assigns to utterances of sentences. The present point is that it is not necessary that these arguments should be decisive in order that the demonstration should succeed. All that is necessary is that they should be arguments. It is entirely in the cards that the solutions I have proposed for the examples under review may prove to be inadequate. But, if they do, the proof will have to advert to further examples or better solutions. In either case, it will assume that theories about the form and content of internal representations must compete in respect of methodological adequacy and adequacy to the facts, just as other kinds of scientific theories do. That, in a nutshell, is what this chapter was about.

4
THE STRUCTURE OF THE INTERNAL CODE: SOME PSYCHOLOGICAL EVIDENCE

E pluribus unum.

If much of what I have been saying in previous chapters is true, then the causal relation between stimulus and response is *typically* mediated by the organisms's internal representation of each. And if *that* is true, then almost every result in psychology—from psychophysics to psychometrics—can probably be made to bear, in one way or another, upon hypotheses about what the system of internal representations is like. The epistemic situation is thus normal for a live science: In principle, the data underdetermine the theories; in fact, we have more data than we know what to do with—far more than our theories are able to handle.

I do not, of course, propose to review the whole of psychology in aid of demonstrating this point. What I shall do instead is concentrate upon just one of the morals that seem to emerge from the experimental literature. Moreover, I shall stick largely to my last. Many of the results to be discussed come from the investigation of psycholinguistic processes. I think it is quite likely that these findings can be generalized to other areas of psychology, but I regard that as an open empirical question. It will do, for the purposes of this book, if I can show that there are at least some kinds of psychological findings which constrain the theory of the internal representations that mediate at least some mental processes.

The claim I want to argue for is this: It is probably a mistake to talk of *the* system of internal representations that the organism has available for the analysis of environmental events or behavioral options. Rather, in the general case, organisms have access to a variety of types and levels of representation, and which one—or ones—they assign in the course of a given computation is determined by a variety of variables, including factors of motivation and attention and the general character of the organism's appreciation of the demand characteristics of its task. If the moral of Chapter 2 was the richness of the representational system which must underlie perception and the integration of behavior, the moral of this chapter will be the flexibility of that system and the rationality of the mechanisms by which it is exploited.

Let us begin by reviewing some points about sentences and sentence recognition that were mentioned in Chapter 2. We remarked there that it is a main tenet of modern linguistics that every sentence in a natural language has an analysis at each of a fixed number of descriptive levels. Each such level has itself got the properties of a formal language: It has its proprietary vocabulary and syntax, and there exists a proprietary class of abstract entities which are the designata of its terms under their intended interpretations.

If the structural description that a given grammar assigns to a given sentence is correct, then the properties it marks should be precisely those by virtue of which utterances of the sentence conform to the conventions of the language that the grammar describes. In particular, what utterances of the sentence standardly communicate is determined by (a) what the conventions of the language are and (b) what the structural description of the sentence is. It is thus reasonable to assume a priori that understanding token sentences probably involves assigning token structural descriptions to them. And, as we also remarked in Chapter 2, there is now quite a lot of a posteriori evidence which suggests that this assumption is true. Since the same points also hold, *mutatis mutandis,* for the *production* of sentences, we are in a position to propose a first approximation to a theory of psycholinguistic processes: The perceptual recognition of an utterance involves assigning it a series of increasingly 'abstract' representations (one for each level of linguistic description acknowledged by the grammar of the language), and the production of an utterance involves representing the intended behavior as satisfying the corresponding series of *de*creasingly abstract representations, the last member of which can be read directly as a phonetic matrix.[1]

---

[1] I am assuming that the parameters of a phonetic matrix determine the set of *inputs* to the vocal apparatus insofar as the *output* of the vocal apparatus is interpretable as speech (i.e., insofar as it is phonetically interpretable). Similarily, a given set of simultaneous values of such parameters (as specified by the distinctive feature representation of a speech sound) corresponds to a given state of excitation of the articulators (though the current evidence is that it does so only very indirectly—via a series of subphonetic transformations of values of the matrix; for details, see Liberman, Cooper, Shankweiler, and Studdert-Kennedy, 1967). The effect of such assumptions is to provide the general outlines of an answer to the question: 'How do *behavioral intentions* get translated into *behavior* in the course of speech production; in particular, how does the speaker manage to produce utterances that *do* satisfy the phonetic descriptions that he *intends* them to satisfy?'

The suggested answer is that when behavioral intentions are behaviorally efficacious it is because (a) one of the descriptions under which the behavior is intended is interpretable as a set of instructions to the relevant effector organs, and (b) the physiological organization of the system is such that, all other things being equal, the neurological event which encodes the instructions causally excites the

Even at this early point in the discussion we can see that 'the' representation that gets assigned to an utterance in a speech exchange must be a very heterogeneous sort of an object. It is, in effect, the logical sum of representations drawn from a number of different sublanguages of the internal language. It is an empirical question what, if anything, these sublanguages have in common, and some of the most important results in modern linguistics have been contributions to answering that question (e.g., the discovery that the morphophonological and phonetic levels make do with the same set of distinctive features).

But, in fact, this account is far too simple, and the ways in which it departs from the facts are edifying. To begin with a fairly trivial point, the present model acknowledges only two relations between a perceiver and a sentence token: Either he understands the token (in which case he assigns it a full structural description) or he does not understand it (in which case he assigns it no representation at all). But, clearly, this is very crude. Understanding is a graded notion and it is possible to recover more or less of what a given utterance was intended to convey.[2] There are a number of ways in which one could imagine liberalizing the model to accommodate this fact. One of the most appealing derives from suggestions made by Broadbent (1958).

Suppose that we assume that the various linguistically relevant representations of an utterance token are literally computed in series in ascending order of abstractness. Assume, too, that once that ith-level representation of the input has been computed (for any $i > 1$), the hearer must choose either

---

effector organs to perform in a fashion compatible with the instructions (i.e., normally, to obey them). Thus, in the present case, one of the descriptions which verbal behavior is normally intended to satisfy is given by a phonetic matrix. But (a') a phonetic matrix is interpretable as a set of instructions to the vocal apparatus, and (b'), all other things being equal, being in the state of intending one's utterance to satisfy phonetic description D is causally sufficient to excite the vocal apparatus to produce an utterance which *does* satisfy phonetic description D. (All other things being equal requires, e.g., that there are no contrary and overriding intentions, that the vocal apparatus is in working order, and so on.) As we have previously remarked, the bedrock upon which the possibility of computational explanations of behavior is founded is the (presumed) fact that the *causal* relations among the physiological states of the organism respect the *semantic* relations among formulae in the internal code.

[2] It is useful (and probably true) to assume that one of the things that an utterance is normally intended to communicate is its own structural description. (This is, of course, a stronger assumption than that an utterance is normally intended to *satisfy* its structural description.) We intend, when we speak, that our utterance should be construed as an utterance of one or another form of words, i.e., as a token of one or another linguistic type. If the general drift of contemporary linguistic theory is true, this intention can be identified with the intention that the hearer should assign to the utterance whatever structural description individuates the type in question. The present point is that such intentions may, in a given case, be satisfied entirely, or to some extent, or not at all.

to discontinue the computation or to go on and compute the representation of the stimulus at level $i + 1$. Each level of representation is thus associated with a decision point at which the hearer has the option of not bothering to compute further. Moreover, at any given level (a) the decision whether to go on with the analysis has to be made in light of such information about the stimulus as is available at that level, and (b) the decision has to be made in real time—presumably within the time available for the display of representations of the stimulus in short-term memory.

This sort of model seems intuitively plausible, it comports with the fact that there are levels of understanding an utterance, and there even exists some experimental and anecdotal evidence for the view of sentence processing that it commends. The model suggests three main predictions. First, if there really are 'gates' between adjacent levels of analysis such that input receives a full structural description only if it gets through all the gates, one would expect that different stimuli would have different probabilities of getting recognized and that the probability for any given stimulus is somehow a function of its overall interestingness. Second, if representations of inputs are computed in increasing order of abstractness, one would expect that only relatively concrete information would be reportable in the case of stimuli which *don't* get a full analysis (e.g., stimuli that are only partially attended). Finally, as I suggested above, if the decision whether to continue the analysis is made in real time, one would assume that the amount of ith-level representation that could be relevant to determining whether to go on to the $i + 1$th level would be comparable to the amount of ith-level representation that can be simultaneously displayed in short-term memory.

There is reason to believe that each of these predictions is true. The evidence for the first is largely anecdotal: It seems to be everyone's experience that there is a differential sensitivity to utterances containing one's own name, or to utterances in a familiar voice, or to utterances containing 'key' words like 'analytic' or 'tenure'. Such utterances seem to emerge from their background in noisy situations. The present view is that that is because there is literally a bias for their recognition and for the full analysis of utterances that contain them. The cocktail party seems to be a sort of natural experiment in support of this claim.

In the case of the second two predictions, we can appeal to well-known experimental results. Anne Treisman (1964) did a number of studies of sentence perception in which she employed what is now known as a 'shadowing' paradigm. The subject in this sort of study listens to tape-recorded signals presented dichotically through headphones, with a different signal in each phone. S is instructed to attend to one channel only. At the end of the presentation, however, S is questioned about the material in the *un*attended channel. The usual finding is just what the preceding predicts: S can report only such features of the unattended input as are relatively directly determined by its gross acoustic properties: e.g., that the signal was speech and what the sex of the speaker was, but *not* the content of what was said. This finding is, of course, quite compatible with a 'bottom-to-top' view of speech perception, such that representations of the signal are computed in increasing order of abstractness starting with the recovery of its acoustic/phonetic properties. Apparently attentional mechanisms interact with utilities to determine how complete an analysis a given signal gets. (In the situation Treisman investigated, the utilities of the subject are presumably determined primarily by his intention to comply with the experimental instructions to attend to one channel only.)

One of the permutations of Treisman's paradigm has special relevance to the third of the predictions enumerated above. In this design, the material in the unattended channel is the *same* as the material in the channel to which *S* is instructed to attend. However, the latter signal lags behind the former by an interval that the experimenter can vary. It turns out that *S*'s recognition that the two channels carry the same signal is critically dependent upon the size of this interval. *S*s rarely notice the identity of the signals when the interval is more than about 2 seconds and rarely fail to notice it when the interval is less.

It seems reasonable to assume these 2 seconds represent the period during which the unattended signal is available in short-term memory. This interpretation fits nicely with the Broadbent model, which requires some mechanism that holds (relatively) uninterpreted information for long enough to permit decisions about the desirability of further processing. To extend the previous metaphor, if attention is a gate through which input information must pass in order to be recognized, then Treisman's results suggest that, in the case of linguistic material, the gate opens about 2 seconds wide. It is of some interest that this estimate of about 2 seconds as the critical interval is at least broadly compatible with assessments of the span of short-term memory for linguistic materials made with independent experimental paradigms. See, e.g., Jarvella (1970), which suggests that on-line storage of syntactically structured material will hold units of up to about one clause in length, and Crowder and Morton (1969), which estimates a span of about 2 seconds for the 'echoic' storage of linguistic stimuli.

We started out with the fact that not everything one hears is fully understood. The Broadbent-Treisman model accounts for this fact by assuming that, though some inputs receive representations at every level of description, many do not. The model thus stresses the *incompleteness* of the analysis that some utterances receive. We also remarked, however, that there are alternative approaches to the facts, and at least one of them should be mentioned here.

For Broadbent and Treisman, there is a gate between adjacent levels of description and only fully attended inputs get through all the gates. Recent work by Lackner and Garrett (1973) suggests, on the contrary, that even unattended inputs get descriptions at the highest levels, but that representations are *accessible* (e.g., available for the subject to report) only in the case of signals that are objects of attention.

Like Treisman's subjects, Lackner and Garrett's heard linguistic materials on both channels of stereo headphones. And, again as in the shadowing paradigm, S's attention was directed to one of the two channels. Moreover, Lackner and Garrett sought to ensure the relative unavailability of the unattended material by substantially lowering its volume as compared to that of the attended channel. In fact, the volume of the two channels was sufficiently mismatched that, in the posttest interviews, many of the subjects could not even report that the unattended channel contained speech.

The stimulus materials in the two channels that Lackner and Garrett presented to their subjects differed not only in volume but also in content. In particular, in the critical cases, the attended channel contained an *ambiguous sentence*, while the unattended channel contained a *disambiguating context*. For example, for a given subject on a given trial, the attended channel might contain a sentence like (1) while the unattended channel contained (2). Such a subject's performance would be compared with that of subjects who had the same sentence in the attended channel but for whom the unattended channel contained (3) (i.e., a context which favors the alternative disambiguation of (1)). All Ss were required to paraphrase the attended sentence at the end of each trial so that the experimenters could determine which interpretation they had imposed upon it.

(1)   The spy put out the torch as our signal to attack.
(2)   The spy extinguished the torch in the window.
(3)   The spy showed the torch from the window.

Garrett and Lackner reasoned as follows: If no information from the unattended channel was getting analyzed, or if only relatively low-level information was, then the content of the unattended channel could have no effect on the character of the paraphrase S gave for the attended sentence; of the two possible readings, the paraphrases Ss give should reflect one or the other interpretation in about the same proportion as do those of control subjects for whom the content of the unattended material is neutral to the interpretation of the attended sentence. If, on the other hand, high-level representations are being computed for the unattended material, then some of that information might 'get through' to bias Ss' paraphrase of the attended sentence, which would thus be skewed in the direction of the disambiguating signal. Rather surprisingly, it is the latter prediction that the data support. Even subjects who are quite unable to *report* the content of the unattended channel show an influence of its content on their choice of a paraphrase for the attended sentence. Apparently, some information about the semantic content of the unattended sentence is computed even though little or none is consciously available to the subject.

These results suggest a quite different picture of the relation between perception and attention than the one that Broadbent and Treisman proposed. If Garrett and Lackner are right, attention functions not to determine how full a representation the input gets, but rather how much of the representation can be reported. There is still a 'gate', but, on the Garrett and Lackner view, it is between the temporary memory (in which the structural analysis of the input is computed) and a relatively permanent memory in which the results of the computations are available for conscious access. Only attended material gets through from temporary to permanent storage, and only what is in permanent storage can be reported.

It is, as things stand, quite unclear which—if either—of these accounts is right. For present purposes, however, it doesn't matter, since what the data uncontrovertibly show is that the all-or-none model (either a full representation of the input is available or nothing is) won't do. If Broadbent and Treisman are right, we do not always compute the full analysis of what we hear. If Garrett and Lackner are right, then much of what we do compute does not get stored for long enough to be reported. In either case, the hearer apparently has a good deal of freedom in deciding how the internal representation of an impinging stimulus is to be handled. Remember that, in both the Treisman and the Garrett and Lackner studies, the difference between what happens to the competing stimuli is a function of *instructional* variables; i.e., the processing differences are determined, at least in part, by S's decision to attend to the material in one channel and to ignore the material in the other.

It has been a main argument of this book that if you want to know what response a given stimulus is going to elicit, you must find out what internal representation the organism assigns to the stimulus. Patently, the character of such assignments must in turn depend upon what kind of representational system is available for mediating the cognitive processes of the organism. The present point, however, is that that's not all that it depends on. On the Broadbent-Treisman model, it is attentional mechanisms which determine how the available representational capacities are exploited. On the Garrett-Lackner model, it is whatever mechanisms affect the transfer of information from computing memory to long-term memory. On either model, the psychological states of the organism are implicated in determining which of the potentially available representations of the stimulus is the one that in fact mediates the production of behavior. To put the point more generally, the organism's exploitation of its representational capacities is, in some systematic way, responsive to its utilities. Part of what a theory of the representational system must do is help in explicating this interaction.

Consider another line of evidence for these remarks. One of the earliest experiments on the psychological reality of generative grammars was performed by Mehler (1963). A detailed discussion can be found in Fodor, Bever, and Garrett (1974). Suffice it to say here that Mehler used a paradigm in which subjects were required to memorize lists of sentences of a variety of different syntactic types (e.g., simple active declaratives, passives, negatives, questions) and that the results strongly suggested that syntactic type is a determinant of level of recall. Roughly speaking, the probability that a sentence would be remembered correctly was inversely related to the complexity of its syntactic structural description and the probability that a pair of sentences would be conflated was proportional to their syntactic similarity. (For a similar study with comparable results, see Clifton and Odom, 1966.) So Mehler concluded that the syntactic structural description of a sentence is—or is, anyhow, part of—the representation of the sentence that gets stored in long-term memory.

On the other hand, Jacqueline Sachs (1967) presented subjects with running text, testing recall for selected sentences at the end of each presentation. The stimulus sentences she used varied along the same sorts of syntactic dimensions as Mehler's, yet the results of her experiment were sharply different. Sachs found practically no effect of the syntactic variables; the only thing that counted was content. That is, synonymous sentences tended to be conflated regardless of their syntactic form, and syntactically similar sentences were distinguished so long as they differed in meaning.

What is one to make of this sort of anomaly? In particular, if Mehler's work argues *for* a specific engagement of syntactic structure with permanent memory, do Sachs's results argue against it? The answer seems to be: The salience of structural variables depends on the nature of the experimental task. Specifically, it depends on what the subject takes the point of performing the task to be. Wanner (1968) showed that one can switch the Mehler effect on and off *holding the stimulus materials constant* depending on how the subject is instructed. Ss who are told that they are participating in a memory experiment show the effect of syntactic detail; Ss who are told to read the text for content don't. (Similar findings are reported in Johnson-Laird and Stevenson, 1970). This is, after all, not very surprising. One knows from one's own experience that one treats a text differently when one is trying to memorize it than when one is just reading it. Given instructions to recall one tries to remember all of what one reads; given instructions to read for content one discards everything except the gist. One has a shrewd suspicion that the difference in treatment works; that the two kinds of attitudes to the material do typically yield different stored representations of the stimulus. In effect, Wanner's study confirms this suspicion.

It seems to me that all these considerations point towards a fundamental and pervasive feature of higher cognitive processes: *the intelligent management of internal representations.* Serious psychology begins with the recognition that it matters how the organism specifies impinging stimuli and response options. It thus presupposes an internal language rich enough to represent whatever inputs can affect behavior and whatever outputs the organism can deploy. But it now appears that there is a range within which the organism can choose how its representational resources are to be exploited; the reiterated moral of the findings just reviewed was that the subject can control what representations get assigned to sentence tokens and/or which of the assigned representations get stored. By exerting such control, the subject affects a rational correspondence between his performance and (what he takes to be) the demand characteristics of the experimental task.

But now we are back in a well-worn groove. If the subject is to choose between ways of representing the stimulus and the response, he will have to have ways of representing his options; i.e., he will have to have ways of representing his ways of representing the stimulus and the response. But to have ways of representing ways of representing inputs and outputs is to have a *layered* representational system. Some expressions in the internal language refer to (potential or actual) inputs and outputs. Some expressions in the internal language refer to expressions *in the internal language*. Computations whose consequences determine how the subject's representational resources are to be deployed presumably make essential use of expressions of the latter kind.

The general view of (some) higher mental processes implicit in these remarks is sufficiently familiar from the work of cognitive psychologists whose speculations have been influenced by the organization of computers (cf. Miller, Galanter, and Pribram, 1960; Newell and Simon, 1972). One imagines a hierarchy of 'executive' programs which function to analyze macrotasks into microtasks. Such programs may 'call' both one another and lower-level problem-solving routines, though the extent of such cross-referencing is limited by the ingenuity of the program and, of course, the overall computational capacity of the machine. When things go well the results of lower-level processes can be integrated to yield a solution of whatever macroproblem the system was originally posed. Whether, in a given case, things *do* go well is partly determined by whether the executive programs manage to select the right subroutines and to apply them in the right order.

Our present concern is not, however, to endorse the generality of this sort of model or even to examine its details. It is rather to emphasize what such theories imply about the character and recruitment of the representational system over whose formulae the postulated computations would have to be defined. The relevant implications would appear to be twofold. In the first place, as we have seen, there must be resources for representing representations. If one of the executive functions is to decide what lower-level descriptions get computed, then the language that the executive talks (i.e., the language over which executive computations are defined) must have ways of referring to such descriptions as lower-level routines are able to assign. Second, it is implicit in the model that the character of the representations deployed at any given level will often depend, in part, on the outcome of *higher*-level computations. In the technical jargon, the flow of information in such systems exhibits feed-*back* from high-level decisions as well as feed-*forward* from low-level decisions.

It is worth pausing to reflect on these two points. On the one hand, internal representations are labile and the effectiveness with which they are deployed may, in given cases, significantly determine the efficiency of mental processing. On the other hand, we know of no general constraints on how information flows in the course of the computations which determine such deployments: To say that we are dealing with a feedback system is simply to admit that factors other than the properties of the input may affect the representation that the input receives. In particular, what internal representations get assigned is sensitive to the cognitive state—for all we know, to the *whole* cognitive state—of the stimulated organism. Perhaps there are bounds to the options that organisms enjoy in this respect, but if there are no one now knows where to set them. Psychology is very hard.

Consider just one more kind of example which illustrates the flexibility with which the resources of the system of internal representation are exploited. We have seen that the analysis of macrotasks into microtasks is often employed as a primary strategy in standard models of problem-solving. The result of such a decomposition of the task is typically to establish a hierarchy of long and short term computational goals, and the flow of information within the hierarchy will normally require the solutions of lower-level problems as inputs to higher-level processes. (See, e.g., the concept of nested TOTE-units developed in Miller, Galanter, and Pribram, 1960; and Miller and Johnson-Laird, to be published.) Where such requirements are strictly observed, every ith-level computation must be run before any $i + n$th-level computation can be initiated. In fact, however, one can often get away with less than strict compliance with such requirements so long as one is willing to tolerate occasional mistakes. Suppose, for example, that the results of some of the ith-level computations are partially redundant with the results of some of the others. We can then *predict* the results of the latter computations on the basis of having actually *performed* only the former ones. Since the probability that the prediction is true varies directly with the magnitude of the redundancy, we will have reason for accepting the prediction whenever we have reason to suppose that the redundancy is high. Clearly, there could be cases in which accepting the prediction would be the rational thing to do, since one thereby reduces the number of computations that need to be performed overall.

In short, the computational load associated with the solution of a class of problems can sometimes be reduced by opting for problem-solving procedures that work only *most* of the time. Reliability is wagered for efficiency in such cases, but there are usually ways of hedging the bet. Typically, heuristic procedures are tried first; relatively slower, but relatively algorithmic, procedures are 'called' when the heuristics fail. This way of marshaling the available computational resources can often provide the optimal trade-off between the speed of computation and the probability of getting the right results.

These are, of course, just the familiar considerations which underlie the notion of heuristic programing. Our present point is that they have considerable significance for theories of internal representation. Since heuristic routines typically beg off computations that algorithms are required to perform, they also often yield relatively impoverished analyses of their inputs. A fail-proof procedure must represent every property of its input that *could be* task relevant. A heuristic procedure can make do with representing just those properties of its input which *probably are* task relevant. But what this means, from the point of view of our concerns, is that whether a given input gets a given description on a given occasion depends, *inter alia,* on how the utilities of the organism are arranged: on the relative weights assigned to reliability and efficiency in coping with the task at hand. I want to work briefly through a case which illustrates these principles.

We have seen that a model of sentence comprehension is, in effect, a device which associates token wave forms with messages. Very little is known about how such a device might operate, though I would guess that, if we started now and worked very hard, we might be able to build one in five hundred years or so. In any event, one or two things do seem clear; among them that any fail-proof recognition procedure would have to infer the message that a token of a sentence encodes from a specification of the grammatical relations that obtain among its constituents. That is, if such a device is to work for *every* sentence in the language, then whatever subroutine actually outputs a representation of a message must have, among its inputs, a representation of the grammatical relations exhibited by the sentence to which the message is assigned. On the convenient (though probably false) assumption that a sentence recognizer is an entirely serial device, this can be translated into a claim about the order of operations in real time: A representation of grammatical relations must be assigned to a token *before* a representation of a message is assigned.

It is, I suppose, some sort of conceptual truth that, given the appropriate idealizations, a fluent speaker of L is a fail-proof device for recognizing the sentences of L. If, for example, there are sentences of English that no English speakers can understand, that must be because of limitations on their time, memory, or attention and not, surely, because of limitations on their grasp *of English.* To a first approximation: To be a sentence of English *is* to be something that English speakers *qua* English speakers can understand. So, if it is true that fail-proof sentence recognizers *must* infer messages from representations of grammatical relations, it seems to follow that English speakers *can* infer messages from representations of grammatical relations.

But though they presumably can, they demonstrably often don't. What apparently happens is that grammatical relations are computed only when all else fails. There exist heuristic procedures for sentence recognition which, in effect, ignore grammatical relations and infer messages directly from lexical content, accepting, thereby, the penalties of fallibility.

So-called self-embedded sentences provide a clear case though, as we shall see, there are other cases that are more interesting.

To begin with, it *is* possible to work out the meaning of a sentence like 'The boy the girl the man knew wanted to marry left in a huff'. All that's needed is time, patience, and the insight that that sentence is structurally analogous to, e.g., 'The girl my friend married makes pots'. That what one is doing in working out such sentences is, in fact, a computation of the grammatical relations among their phrases is witnessed by the kinds of mistakes one is likely to make en route. Thus, if you got hung up on 'The boy the girl the man knew wanted to marry left in a huff', the odds are that (a) you tried to read 'the boy the girl the man' as a compound noun phrase (see Blumenthal, 1966), and/or (b) you tried to read 'wanted to marry' as the object complement of 'know' (see Fodor, Garrett, and Bever, 1968). Advanced students may now work on hearing *'Bulldogs bulldogs bulldogs fight fight fight'* as a sentence rather than, say, a Yale football cheer. (Hint: Take the first two verbs as transitive.)

The present point is that there is a shorter way with some self-embeddings. Consider the relative transparency of 'The boat the sailor the dog bit built sank'. What seems to be going on here is this: The sentence is taken as an anagram, and the message intended is inferred from such considerations as the following. Boats (but not dogs or sailors) often sink; sailors (but not dogs) often build boats; dogs (but not sailors) often bite, and when they do it's more likely to be a sailor than a boat that gets bitten. And so on. It seems plausible that no syntactic structural description ever does get assigned in recognizing a sentence like this one. Or if it does, the intended structural description is probably inferred from the analysis of the message rather than the other way around. (For relevant experiments, see Schlesinger, 1968.) We are back where we started: If one wants to know what representation a given input gets assigned, one needs to know something about the kinds of computational procedures (including heuristic short cuts) the subject has available for assigning representations to inputs. And one needs to know something about which of these procedures have actually been activated.

Self-embeddings are psycholinguistic curiosities, so it is worth remarking that the same moral can be drawn from other kinds of examples. Consider passives. It is a standard (if not unchallenged) finding that passive sentences tend to be measurably harder to understand than their active counterparts. The usual explanation of this fact assumes (a) that the assignment of grammatical relations to passives precedes the assignment of messages and (b) that the assignment of grammatical relations to passives is complicated by properties of their surface form. In particular, the surface *subject* of a passive is in fact its grammatical *object,* while the true grammatical subject appears as the surface object of a preposition. All this has to be untangled in the course of assigning grammatical relations, and grammatical relations have to be assigned in order to assign messages. So passives *ought* to be harder to understand than actives.

Interestingly, however, there is some evidence that this computational asymmetry between actives and passives is found only in special cases. For details, see Slobin (1966) and the experimentation by Wall presented in Walker, Gough, and Wall (1968). But the gist can be grasped as follows. Suppose that we distinguish between 'reversible' and 'irreversible' sentences on the following principle: A sentence is reversible iff (or, rather, to the extent that) its plausibility is not reduced by switching its grammatical subject with its grammatical object; irreversible sentences are the ones that aren't reversible. (That isn't howlingly precise, but it will do for the purposes at hand.) So, 'Mary was bitten by John' is a reversible passive, and 'John bit Mary' is a reversible active (*vide* 'John was bitten by Mary' and 'Mary bit John', both of which are OK). But 'The ice cream was eaten by the child' and 'The dog bit Mary' are, relatively, irreversible (because of *?the child was eaten by the ice cream* and *?Mary bit the dog*).[3]

The available data suggest[4] that one finds a computational asymmetry between active and passive only when one compares *reversible* passives with *reversible* actives. Presumably this can be explained along the lines we explored in the discussion of self-embedded sentences. If one can infer the intended message directly from the vocabulary of the input sentence one does so, thereby saving the need for computing grammatical relations. This is possible in the case of irreversibles, so asymmetries of computation load produced by syntactic factors tend to wash out for such sentences. With reversibles, however, there is no way of recovering the intended message except the long way; one must compute the syntactic analysis that the utterance was intended to satisfy. So syntactic features predict computational load when sentences are reversible.

We have been reviewing some psychological evidence for the proposition that higher cognitive processes characteristically exhibit the organism's intelligent management of its representational resources. Within limits (and by means) that are currently unknown, the organism is able to shape its assignment of representations in ways that reflect its estimates of what will contribute to its goals. I conclude this survey by remarking that this capacity for managing the representational resources apparently has an interesting ontogenetic career.

---

[3] It should be clear that reversibility is not a *syntactic* phenomenon; i.e., whether a string is reversible is *not* determined by its formal properties. Reversibility has to do with speakers' expectations about what is *likely to be true,* and so belongs to 'pragmatics' if anything does.

[4] Or, at least, most of them do. For evidence to the contrary, see Forster and Olbrei (1973).

Consider, again, the asymmetry between reversible and irreversible sentences. We suggested above, in effect, that the hearer can by-pass the computation of syntactic relations in cases where the speaker's intended message can plausibly be inferred from (a) the lexical content of his utterance and (b) background information about what messages speakers are *likely* to intend to convey. Obviously, reliance upon such inferences will occasionally lead one astray. But, by definition, the more irreversible a sentence is, the more unlikely to fail the heuristics are so long as speakers generally intend to say what it is plausible to say. In any event, the employment of this sort of short cut clearly presupposes a degree of sophistication not only about the contents of the lexicon but also about the probable intentions of partners to a speech exchange. The data suggest that it takes time to acquire such sophistication and that children make characteristic kinds of mistakes along the way.

Bever (1970) presents the results of a number of studies of the development of heuristic sentence-processing procedures by young children. Consider, e.g., the data summarized in Figure 4–1. The two top curves represent, respectively, the performance of children on fully reversible actives (e.g., 'the cow kisses the horse'); and on plausible *ir*reversible actives (e.g.,

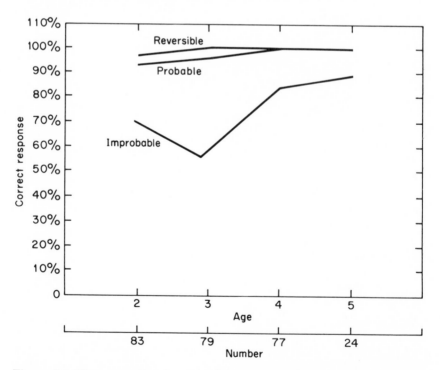

Figure 4-1 The proportion by age of correct responses to reversible active sentences, probable active sentences, and improbable active sentences. From Bever 1970, p. 304.

The mother pats the dog). The lowest curve represents performance on, as it were, reversed irreversible actives (i.e., irreversible actives with an *implausible* reading such as *'The dog pats the mother'*). The gross configuration of the results is not surprising. Subjects' performance is near perfect on plausible irreversibles, as one might expect on the assumption that the basic procedures for analyzing simple NP V NP sentences are available to children by age 2. It is, similarly, not surprising that performance on reversed irreversibles is relatively poor at the outset and tends to improve with age; these are precisely the sentences where heuristics based upon assumptions about the speaker's probable intentions will lead the child *wrong*. The relatively poor performance on the implausible sentences thus probably represents the child's overreliance upon such heuristics, and the tendency of his performance to improve with age probably represents his developing knowledge of how to hedge his heuristic bets. What is of special interest, however, is the dip in performance on the implausible irreversibles at age 3. Three-year-olds apparently do *worse* on such sentences than their 2-year-old controls. Bever thinks that a specially heavy reliance upon heuristic strategies for perceptual analysis is a typical feature of 3-year-old mentation; in effect, that it determines a developmental 'stage' which shows up across a wide variety of experimental tasks. If this account is right, then the anomalous disadvantage that 3-year-olds display stems from their having abandoned relatively algorithmic sentence-processing routines in favor of chancier (but quicker) heuristic procedures. Somewhere between ages 3 and 4 they begin to learn to control their exploitation of these procedures; to strike a more realistic balance between efficiency and reliability.

If anything like this is true, then Bever's data show a rather detailed modulation of the child's performance as a result of his developing skill in managing his representational resources. On any account, the child's linguistic apprenticeship must eventuate in a grasp of the kinds of structural descriptions that the sentences of his language satisfy; for as we have seen, it is only *because* they satisfy such descriptions that utterances of sentences can serve as conventional vehicles for the expression of communicative intentions. But, apparently, the child learns more than this. He also learns that, when the circumstances are right, communicative intentions can be estimated from a very gross analysis of the linguistic character of the utterance. And he also learns, within the limits of human fallibility, how to tell when the circumstances are right.[5]

Some consolidation is now in order. My primary purpose in this book

---

[5] The preceding remarks connect, in fairly obvious ways, with a long tradition of psychological work on stereotyping, prejudice, and 'perceptual bias'. What all this work reveals is the tendency of the subject to 'fill in' such features of the percept as can be plausibly inferred from (what the subject takes to be) background knowledge. The general moral is S's willingness to purchase computational efficiency at the cost of occasional inaccuracy and misrepresentation. For some studies, see Bartlett (1961), Bruner (1957), and Heider (1971).

has been to argue for the existence of an internal language in which the computations that underlie cognitive processes are carried out. In this chapter, however, the emphasis has shifted from the existence of this system to its deployment. The main conclusions, thus far, are these: First, there would seem to be a variety of representations that a given input may receive, and which representation it *does* receive depends, *inter alia*, on the demands of the subject's task. Second, the subject's achievement in matching the exploitation of his representational capacities to the exigencies of the experimental situation is itself a form of intelligent behavior. I don't mean to suggest that such performances are conscious; I suppose, on the contrary, that they usually are not.[6] Rather, the point is that, when things go right, what the subject effects by the management of internal representations is a rational correspondence between his performance and his goals. Looked at the other way round, the point is that the internal representation of a stimulus depends not only on the character of the stimulus and the character of the representational system, but also on the utilities of the subject.

If the main line of this book is right, then the language of thought provides the medium for internally representing the psychologically salient aspects of the organism's environment; to the extent that it is specifiable in this language—and only to that extent—does such information fall under the computational routines that constitute the organisms cognitive repertoire. These routines are, as it were, defined only for formulae in the internal language. But now I want to add that some organisms, at least, appear to have considerable freedom in determining how this representational system shall be employed and that that freedom is typically rationally exploited. For adult human beings, at least, the deployment of representational resources appears often to be a calculated strategy for the achievement of behavioral goals. As we remarked above, however, the existence of such strategies has important implications for the character of the code in which they are carried out. If subjects really do *calculate* how internal representations are to be deployed, then these calculations, too, must be defined over representations; i.e., over representations of representations. Some properties of the language of thought must, in short, be represented in the language of thought since the ability to represent representations is, presumably, a precondition of the ability to manipulate representations rationally.

These reflections raise a series of questions which one might hope that

---

[6] There are, of course, plenty of cases of the conscious, voluntary, and, indeed, studied manipulation of internal representations in the service of some or other gain of computational efficiency. Of particular interest is the use of mnemonic systems to facilitate the recall of otherwise disorderly stimulus materials; many such systems rely precisely on a disciplined manipulation of the internal representations assigned to the stimuli. See, e.g., rhyming mnemonics of the 'one is a bun, two is a shoe' variety. (For discussion, cf. Miller, Galanter, and Pribram, 1960; Paivio, 1971; Norman, 1969. For exotica, see Luria, 1968.)

a developed cognitive psychology will some day answer: How rich is the capacity of the internal code for self-representation? To what extent is this capacity actually exploited in the integration of one or another kind of behavior? To what extent do individuals differ in this respect? To what extent do species?

But however such questions may ultimately be answered, we have come far enough to see how profoundly a reasonable theory of cognition must differ from even the most sophisticated treatments available within the confines of associationism. That is a good note on which to end this section.

It might be thought that talk of internal representations comes, in the long run, to not much more than the addition of a link or two to stimulus/response chains. Something of the sort has been a traditional view in 'mediational' psychology, which thought to interpose *representations* of the stimulus and the response between the Ss and the Rs that strictly behavioristic theories acknowledge. (See, e.g., Hull, 1943; Osgood, 1957; Berlyne, 1965.) But mediational associationists *are* associationists for all that. Like unblushing behaviorists, they postulate mechanical (or probabilistic) linkages between psychological states and assume that the links are forged by whatever laws determine the strength of habits. Internal representations, in particular, are supposed to be associated to Ss and Rs in just the way that Ss and Rs are (supposed to be) associated to one another.

Our present point is that this view is wrong in every way it can be. Internal representations are typically paired with what they represent by computational (rather than associative) processes. That is, representations are not *elicited* but, as it were, assigned; and *which* representation is assigned is determined by calculations which rationally subserve the utilities of the organism. There may be—perhaps there must be—some end to this hierarchy of rational decisions. But the end is not in sight. For all we now know, cognition is saturated with rationality through and through.

Thus, far the discussion in this chapter has concerned itself with aspects of what is sometimes called the theory of 'performance'. That is, we have assumed that a very powerful, but conceivably monolithic, representational system is available as the medium of cognitive processes, and we have remarked upon some of the options that are apparently exploited in determining how this representational system is employed. Theories in linguistics, and some theories in psychology, tend to abstract from the existence of such options precisely because the goal is to characterize the *full* representational capacities of the organism. Thus, linguists study full structural descriptions even though they may cheerfully acknowledge that the computation of full structural descriptions is perhaps a strategy of last resort in understanding sentences. Psycholinguists typically do experiments in which only last-resort strategies will work; perhaps because they assume that such strategies are what members of a speech community must share, whereas heuristic procedures may vary extensively from subject to subject. In any event, though we have argued for considerable flexibility in the ways in which the language of thought is *used*, everything we have said so far is compatible with the view that it is *a* language; that the modes of internal representation constitute, in some reasonable sense, a uniform and systematic whole.

There is, however, reason to doubt that this is true. It is a traditional claim that, alongside whatever discursive representational mechanisms may be available to organisms, there exists also a capacity for imagistic representation and that the exploitation of this capacity is central to a variety of cognitive functions. I think that the best current evidence is that some such claim is very likely to be true. So something needs to be said about imagery in even the most cursory discussion of the ways that empirical findings in psychology can constrain theories of internal representations.

Among those psychologists who take it seriously that thought implies a representational system, the question that has been most discussed is the relation between items in that system and the things that the items stand for; roughly, the question of how thoughts refer to the objects of thought. The ur-doctrine in this field is inherited from the British empiricist tradition in philosophy: Thoughts are mental images and they refer to their objects just insofar as (and just by virtue of the fact that) they resemble them.

This is, of course, a very strong doctrine—much stronger than the claim that there are mental images and that they play an occasional, or even an essential, role in some cognitive processes. I stress the distinction because there are pretty decisive arguments against the former view. If an image resembles what it refers to, then thinking cannot be just a matter of entertaining images. But it adds to the confusion (which is, anyhow, epidemic in this area) to suppose that because thinking can't be having images, it somehow follows that there aren't any images or that, even if there are, they can't play an essential role in thinking. What I want to do first in this discussion is review briefly the kinds of considerations which show that thinking and imaging can't be the same thing. Then I want to look at the status of the weaker hypothesis, that imaging plays some interesting role in thought. I'll end with some speculations on what that role might be.

There probably aren't now any cognitive psychologists who think that *all* thoughts are images. It is more usual these days to postulate a dimension of 'abstractness' along which thoughts can vary, with images occurring mainly at the 'concrete' end.[7] Some concrete thoughts are images (so the story goes), but the vehicle of abstract thinking is discursive.

---

[7] It may be that there are images that are conjured up by abstract terms. But, even if there are, they cannot resemble what those terms denote (e.g., in the way that an image of John conjured up by utterances of 'John' might resemble John). Nothing could look like, say, virtue since virtue doesn't itself look like anything. I take it that the arguments against the identification of abstract ideas with images are sufficiently

THE STRUCTURE OF THE INTERNAL CODE:
SOME PSYCHOLOGICAL EVIDENCE

If one wants to find the image theory full-blown, one has to look in the developmental literature. Bruner, Werner, and Piaget (in certain of his works) have all proposed variants of the view that the child's cognitive development is conditioned by a shift from imagistic to discursive modes of internal representation. Very roughly, in the early child the vehicle of thought bears some nonsymbolic relation to its objects; early thoughts *resemble* the things that they are thoughts about. But the course of development is toward increasing abstractness in the relation of thoughts to things. Fully adult thoughts are (or, anyhow, can be) fully symbolic; i.e., there may be arbitrarily little resemblance between the vehicle of thought and its object; i.e., adult thoughts may be arbitrarily unlike images.

In Bruner's work, e.g., we are invited to view the child as proceeding through three more or less distinct developmental stages, each characterized by its typical mode of internal representation.[8] In the earliest stage, the vehicle of thought is an internalized motor-schema. (In this Bruner is explicitly endorsing Piaget's notion of 'sensori-motor' intelligence.) At the second stage, thoughts are images (described by Bruner as displays organized in space rather than time and which preserve perceptual features of their objects). Finally, in mature thought, the medium of representation is symbolic in the sense that words are: There need be no resemblance between the vehicle of representation and the thing it represents. As Bruner sometimes says, at this highest level of representation "one cannot tell what a symbol stands for by sensing it" (1966, p. 31).[9] Clearly, the major break in ontogeny is between stages two and three. For at both of the earliest stages, it is the putative similarity between thoughts and their objects which, to put it crudely, glues the one onto the other. But it is precisely the *lack* of such similarity which is the distinguishing property of stage three representations.[10]

---

familiar from Berkeley, though a tendency to get confused on these points is still occasionally evident in the literature. Paivio (1971) offers edifying examples.

[8] This does less than justice to the subtlety of Bruner's views since he holds both that there may be overlap in the representational capacities that are available at a given point in a child's ontogenetic career, and that translation relations may obtain between the different forms of representation. However, my concerns, here and elsewhere in the text, are not to review the literature but just to examine some of the theoretical options.

[9] Since images—iconic or motoric—are ideally unsuited to be the vehicles of abstract thought (see footnote 7), the child's progress through the stages is also progress in the direction of increasingly abstract representational capacities 'Abstract' and 'symbolic' tend to get used interchangeably in Bruner's theorizing.

[10] Bruner, like most other writers who have concerned themselves with the nature of symbolism, assumes that there is a principled distinction between 'iconic' symbols (viz., images) and 'discursive' symbols (viz., words or descriptions). I'm inclined to consider that reasonable though, notoriously, it is extremely difficult to say what the principled distinction consists in (see Goodman, 1968, and Bruner's own discussion in *Studies in Cognitive Growth*). I shan't, in any event, raise these issues here. For

It is notable, to begin with, that this rather elaborate theoretical apparatus is supported primarily by observations that are fragmentary and impressionistic by anybody's standards. The tenuous connection between the data and the theory is best illustrated by direct quotation. In *Studies in Cognitive Growth,* Bruner cites such observations as the fellow from Piaget (1954).

> At 0:6 Lucienne . . . grasps the material covering the sides [of her bassinet]. She pulls the folds toward herself but lets them go at each attempt. She then brings before her eyes her hand which is tightly closed, and opens it cautiously. She looks attentively at her fingers and recommences. This goes on more than ten times.
>
> It is therefore sufficient for her to have touched an object, believing she grasps it, for her to conceive of it as being in her hand although she no longer feels it. Such a behavior pattern . . . shows the degree of tactile permanence the child attributes to objects he has grasped. (p. 22)

Not, one might have thought, the sort of data which will bear a lot of theoretical weight. Here, however, is what Bruner makes of them:

> For the infant, then, the actions evoked by stimulus events may serve in major part to 'define' them. At this age he is unable to differentiate clearly between percept and response. Lucienne expects to see the fold of cloth in her hand, having clenched her hand 'as if' the cloth were still in it. In later childhood this first technique of representation does not fully disappear, and it is very likely the origin of confusion between thinking something and doing it. (1966, p. 12)

One might reasonably wonder what kind of argument could get conclusions like that from premises like those. Doubtless, many of Piaget's observations do suggest that there is a period during which the child is specially concerned with objects viewed as manipulanda; i.e., that very young children characteristically attend to those properties of objects that determine what can be done with them. And there are rather firmer data which suggest that, later on, children are specially concerned with properties of objects that can be imaged—with visual properties of objects, whatever precisely that may mean. For example, children often categorize things by form, color, and

---

it will presently be clear that even if we take the notion of resemblance for granted, the sense in which thoughts *could* refer to their objects by resembling them will have to be pretty attenuated. That is, even if the difference between iconic and discursive symbols is principled, the distinction between the ways in which iconic and discursive symbols *refer* is not. Roughly, as we shall see, you can *never* tell what a symbol refers to (just) by sensing it, and that is true whether or not the symbol is iconic.

mere propinquity, even when that way of sorting seems unnatural to adults (see Vygotsky, 1965); the vocabulary of young children typically exhibits a preponderance of words for concrete objects over words for abstractions and relations (Brown, 1970), etc. Such considerations may argue for a special salience of perceptibles in the child's psychological economy. If so, they tell us something interesting about what children think *about*. But it doesn't follow that they also tell us something about what children think *with*. On the basis of the sorts of facts that I've just mentioned, Bruner concludes: ". . . we have seen that representation can be effected *in the media* of symbols, images and actions and that each *form of representation* can be specialized to aid symbolic manipulation, image organization, or the execution of motor acts" (1966, p. 11; emphasis mine). The inference is, I think, quite unwarranted. One cannot, in general, infer from *what* is represented to the nature of the *vehicle* of representation. Information about enactive or perceptual properties of the environment *could,* after all, be stored as descriptions (i.e., 'symbolically' in Bruner's sense of the term). For this reason, to demonstrate an ontogenetic shift in the features of the environment that the child attends to is not more than the first step in demonstrating the very radical thesis that the medium of internal representation changes with development. Yet, so far as I can tell, no other sort of argument has been given.[11]

If I have been unsympathetic about the empirical basis for the existence of stagelike changes in modes of internal representation, it is because I think it would be appalling if the data really did somehow require us to endorse that sort of view. I am, in fact, strongly inclined to doubt the very *intelligibility* of the suggestion that there is a stage at which cognitive processes are carried out in a medium which is fundamentally nondiscursive. I am not, of course, denying the empirical possibility that children may use images more than adults do, or that their concepts may be, in some interesting sense, more concrete than adult concepts. What I do deny, however, is that the difference could be qualitative in the kind of way that Bruner seems to require. That is, I don't think that there could be a stage at which images are the vehicle of thought in the strong sense that thinking is *identifiable* with imaging at that stage; not, at least, if images are representations that refer by resembling. All this needs considerable sorting out.

Imagine, *per impossible*, that adults think in English; i.e., that English sentences provide the medium in which adult cognitive processes are car-

---

[11] We shall see, as we go along, that there *are* fairly persuasive ways of using data to implicate imagery in cognitive processes. The present point is just that the ones Bruner appeals to aren't among them.

It may be that Bruner thinks that children use images because he takes it to be obvious that there are no means of discursive representation available to them; after all, very young children can't talk. If that is the argument Bruner has in mind, however, it's a bad one. One might as well claim that very young children don't have *images* on the grounds that they can't *draw*.

ried out. How, on this assumption, would children have to differ from adults if Bruner's ontogenetic doctrines are to hold? That is, if we take thinking in English as a clear case of thinking in symbols, what is to count as the corresponding clear case of thinking in icons? Well, one possibility is that the children use a representational system just like the one that the adults use except that the children have *pictures* where the adults have *words*. This suggestion surely *is* coherent; one can, for example, imagine devising a hiero- glyphic orthography for English. English sentences would thus be sequences of pictures (rather than sequences of phones) but everything else stays the same. So we have assigned *a* sense to the proposal that children's thought is iconic and adults' thought is symbolic.

But, of course, it isn't the sense that Bruner has in mind. For icons, in Bruner's sense, aren't just *pictures*; they are pictures that resemble what they stand for. That is, it's not just that symbols *look* different from icons; it's also that they are differently related to what they symbolize. The reference of icons is mediated by resemblance. The reference of symbols is mediated by conventions. Or something.[12]

So English in hieroglyphs won't quite do. But we can fix things up. We can imagine a language just like English except that (a) words are replaced by pictures and (b) the only pictures allowed are such as resemble what the corresponding words refer to. Of course, the representational capacity of such a language would be very limited since we can only use it to refer to what we can picture. Still, it is a coherent suggestion that there could be such a language, and it is a coherent hypothesis that that is the language that children think in. The point of the exercise is that one way of understanding the idea that children think in icons is this: Children think in a language in which *pictures* (not just hieroglyphs) take the role that words play in natural languages.

I am pretty sure that this is not, however, the sort of account of chil- dren's mental processes that Bruner wants to commend either. For one thing, if the difference between children and us were just that we think in some- thing like standard English while they think in (call it) Iconic English, then the difference between us and children might not come to much. For though Iconic English can refer to fewer things than standard English can, they can both express some of the same semantic relations among the things they do refer to. After all, some such relations are carried by grammatical fea-

---

[12] Bruner stresses the *conventionality* of noniconic representational systems (like English), but, surely, it isn't their conventionality which makes them noniconic; En- glish would be a discursive (i.e., a symbolic; i.e., a noniconic) representational system even if it were innate (i.e., nonconventional). It is, in fact, a major problem in the philosophy of language to give a plausible account of the relation between symbols and what they symbolize. What Bruner's theory comes to is that icons refer by resem- bling and symbols refer in some other—as yet unspecified—way. The latter claim is certainly true.

tures of standard English, and standard English and Iconic English have the same grammar. Since agency, predication, possession, and the rest are presumably expressible in Iconic English, it looks as though much of the cognitive incapacity that would be involved in using it would be a relative paucity of *vocabulary*. Bruner makes it pretty clear, however (1966, Chap. 2), that he takes the availability of grammatical structure in representations to be a proprietary feature of symbolic (i.e., noniconic) representational systems.

The preceding remarks are intended as something more than a commendation of syntax. The point is that we can make sense of Iconic English as a representational system precisely *because* the switch to Iconic English leaves the grammar of standard English unaltered. One way to put the point is this: In Iconic English, *words* resemble what they refer to, *but sentences don't resemble what makes them true*. Thus, suppose that, in Iconic English, the word 'John' is replaced by a picture of John and the word 'green' is replaced by a green patch. Then the sentence 'John is green' comes out as (say) a picture of John followed by a green picture. But *that* doesn't look like being green; it doesn't look much like anything. Iconic English provides a construal of the notion of a representational system in which (what corresponds to) *words* are icons, but it provides no construal of the notion of a representational system in which (what corresponds to) *sentences* are. Nor do I think that this can usefully be patched up; the notion that sentences could be icons *has* no construal. But if sentences couldn't be icons, thoughts couldn't be either.

The structure of the argument is this: If the role that images play in a representational system is analogous to the role that words play in a natural language, then having a thought *cannot* be simply a matter of entertaining an image, and this is true whether the image is motoric or iconic and quite independent of any particular empirical hypothesis about the nature of cognitive development. For thoughts are the kinds of things that can be true or false. They are thus the kinds of things that are expressed by *sentences,* not words. And, while (barring considerations to be reviewed below) it makes a sort of sense to imagine a representational system in which the counterparts of words resemble what they refer to, it makes no sense at all to imagine a representational system in which the counterparts of sentences do.

We have hypothesized a representational system—Iconic English— which differs from standard English in that all the words are pictures but where everything else stays the same. We have remarked that in *that* representational system there is a *non*iconic relation between sentences and what makes them true. Can we do better? What *would* it be like to have a representational system in which sentences are icons of their truth conditions?

For example, what would it be like to have a representational system in which the sentence 'John is fat' is replaced by a picture? Suppose that the picture that corresponds to 'John is fat' is a picture of John with a bulging tummy. But then, what picture are we going to assign to 'John is tall'? The same picture? If so, the representational system does not distinguish the thought that John is tall from the thought that John is fat. A different picture? But John will have to have some shape or other in whatever picture we choose, so what is to tell us that having the picture is having a thought about John's height rather than a thought about his shape? Similarly, a picture of John is a picture of John sitting or standing, or lying down, or it is indeterminate among the three. But then, what is to tell us whether having the picture is having the thought that John is tall, or having the thought that John is sitting, or having the thought that he is standing, or having the thought that he is lying down, or having the thought that one doesn't know whether John is sitting, standing, or lying down?[13]

There are lots of ways of making this sort of point. Suppose that John *is* fat and suppose that John's name is a picture of John. So thinking of John is having a picture which, presumably, shows John fat. And thinking that John is fat is *also* having a picture that shows John fat. But then: What, on this account, is the difference between (just) thinking of John, on the one hand, and thinking that John is fat, on the other?[14]

Let's see where we have gotten to. The notion that thoughts are images —or that they were images when we were very young—is really viciously ambiguous. On the one hand, the proposal might be that we should identify having an image with thinking *of* something, and, on the other, it might be that we should identify having an image with thinking *that* something. These two proposals don't, by any means, come to the same thing. The former amounts to the suggestion that images might be the vehicle of *reference,* while the latter amounts to the suggestion that images might be the vehicle of *truth.*

So, e.g., if Iconic English were the language of thought, then *thinking* of John might consist of entertaining John's image; just as, in the standard use of ordinary English, *mentioning* John (referring to him) might consist just in uttering John's name. It is, in this sense, no more problematic that there should be a language in which reference is defined for images than that there should be a language in which reference is defined for words. I suppose it is just a matter of brute fact that all the natural languages that there are happen to be of the latter kind. But I see no way of construing the notion that there might be a language in which *truth* is defined for icons instead of symbols; in which, i.e., 'formulae' of the system are true of what they resemble. The trouble is *precisely* that icons are insufficiently abstract to be the vehicles of truth.

---

[13] This form of argument is owing to Wittgenstein (1953). It is, I think, entirely convincing.

[14] The obvious way out of this won't do. Suppose thinking of fat John *doesn't* involve having a picture that shows John fat. Still, the picture one has will have to show John *somehow;* i.e., as having some properties or other. And then what will be the difference between just thinking of John and thinking that John has those properties?

To a first approximation, the kind of thing that can get a truth value is an assignment of some property to some object. A representational system must therefore provide appropriate vehicles for expressing such assignments. Under what conditions, then, is a representation adequate to express the assignment of a property to an object? Well, one condition which surely must be satisfied is that the representation specify *which* property is being assigned and which object it is being assigned to. The trouble with trying to truth-value icons is that they provide no way of doing the former. Any picture of a thing will, of necessity, display that thing as having indefinitely many properties; hence pictures correspond (or fail to correspond) in indefinitely many ways to the things that they resemble. Which of these correspondences is the one which makes the picture true?

But if pictures correspond to the same world in too many different ways, they also correspond in the same way to too many different worlds. A picture of John with a bulging tummy corresponds to John's being fat. But it corresponds equally to John's being pregnant since, if that is the way that John *does* look when he is fat, it is also, I suppose, the way that he *would* look if he were pregnant. So, if the fact that John is fat is a reason to call a picture of John with a bulging tummy true, then the fact that John isn't pregnant is as good a reason to call a picture of John with a bulging tummy false. (A picture which corresponds to a man walking up a hill forward corresponds equally, and in the same way, to a man sliding down the hill backward; Wittgenstein, 1953, p. 139.) For every reason that we might have for calling a picture true, there will be a corresponding reason for calling it false. That is, there is no reason for calling it either. Pictures aren't the kind of things that can have truth-values.

Notice that symbols (as opposed to icons) are exempt from these worries; that's one of the respects in which symbols really *are* abstract. A picture of fat John is also a picture of tall John. But the sentence 'John is fat' abstracts from all of John's properties but one: It is true if he's fat and only if he is. Similarly, a picture of a fat man corresponds in the same way (i.e., by resemblance) to a world where men are fat and a world where men are pregnant. But 'John is fat' abstracts from the fact that fat men *do* look the way that pregnant men *would* look; it is true in a world where John is fat and false in any other world.

Taken together, these sorts of considerations strongly suggest that there isn't much sense to be made of the notion that there might be an internal representational system in which icons are the vehicles of truth; i.e., in which entertaining an image is identical to thinking *that* such and such is the case. But we've seen that a certain kind of sense *can* be made of the suggestion that there is an internal representational system in which icons are the vehicles of reference; i.e., in which thinking *of* such and such is identical with entertaining an image. It should now be remarked that even this concession needs to be hedged about.

In Iconic English, John's name is a picture of John. So if the language of thought were Iconic English, then thinking of John might consist of entertaining an image of John, in just the sense that, in real English, referring to John might be identical with uttering 'John'. But what sense is that?

Clearly not every utterance of 'John' *does* constitute a reference to John. For example, I just sat back from my typewriter and said 'John'. But I referred to no one; a fortiori, I did not refer to John. One might put it as follows: In the case of natural languages, utterances of (potentially) referring expressions succeed in making references only when they are produced with the right intentions. I cannot, as it were refer by mistake; no utterance of 'John' counts as a reference to John unless it was at least produced with the intention of *making* a reference.

In natural languages, to put it succinctly, the vehicles of reference are utterances that are taken under (i.e., intended to satisfy) descriptions. In paradigm cases of referring to John, I utter 'John' intending, thereby, to produce a form of words, and moreover to produce a form of words standardly used to refer to John, and morever to refer to John by producing a form of words standardly used to refer to John. But on other occasions when I make the sound 'John' none of these things are true, and in those cases (though not only in those cases) my utterances of 'John' don't count as references to John.

So sometimes uttering 'John' constitutes making a reference to John, but only when the speaker intends his behavior to satisfy certain descriptions; only when he intends his utterance in a certain way. I think the same kinds of remarks apply, *mutatis mutandis,* to the use of images as vehicles of reference in systems like Iconic English: If Iconic English were the language of thought, then there might be cases in which entertaining an image of a thing constituted thinking of it; but only when the image is taken to satisfy certain descriptions; only when it is entertained in the right way. Iconic English is, by hypothesis, a language where the referring expressions are images. But even in Iconic English resemblance wouldn't be a sufficient condition for reference since, even in Iconic English, what refers aren't images but images-under-descriptions. Iconic English doesn't succeed in being *very* nondiscursive after all.

Figure 4–2 is a picture of a pinwheel sort of thing. Close your eyes and form an image of it. If thinking is forming an image of a thing, and if images refer to whatever they resemble, then you must just have been thinking of a cube viewed from one of its corners. For the image you just entertained does, in fact, resemble a cube viewed from one of its corners, just as (and in just the same way that) Figure 4–3 resembles a cube viewed from one of its edges. But, surely, many readers will have formed the image and *not* have thought of the cube. Having the image will have constituted thinking of a cube only for those readers who both formed the image and took it in a

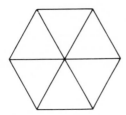

Figure 4-2 A pinwheel sort of thing. See text.

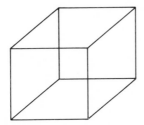

Figure 4-3 Schematic cube.

certain way: i.e., took the point in the center to be a corner of the cube, took the lines radiating from the point to be edges of the cube, etc.

The moral is: Yes, we can make a certain sort of sense of children having icons where we have symbols; viz., they have pictures where we have words (N.B.: words, not sentences).[15] But no, we cannot make much sense of the notion that the relation between thoughts and their objects is basically different for children and for us. To make sense of that, we would need to suppose that images refer by resembling while symbols refer by convention. (Or, as we remarked above, something.) And that they patently do not do. (Images usually don't *refer* at all. But when they do—as, e.g., in Iconic English—they do so in basically the same way that words and phrases do: viz., by satisfying, and by being taken to satisfy, certain descriptions.)

This is not, of course, to deny that pictures look like the things that they are pictures of. It is rather to deny that *looking like a thing* could be a sufficient condition for *referring* to that thing, even in a language like Iconic English, where pictures are the referring expressions. There is, in fact, a perfectly good way of using a picture to make a reference: viz., by embedding it in a description. So one might say 'I am looking for a man who looks like this . . .' and show a picture of a man. It's true that, in such a case,

---

[15] I want to emphasize that I am not *endorsing* the view that the thinking of children is iconic in *any* sense. I am simply trying to make clear what a coherent version of that view might come to. As will be apparent by now, I find that proposal a good deal less transparent than some of the psychologists who have sponsored it seem to do.

the form of words wouldn't usually succeed in communicating a reference unless the picture of the man looks like the man one is seeking. But, equally, the picture is no use without the description which tells you how it is intended to be taken. Compare the ways in which the picture would be used in 'I am looking for a man who $\begin{cases} \text{looks like} \\ \text{dresses like} \\ \text{is taller than} \end{cases}$ this . . . (picture of a short man wearing a toga)'. What carries the reference here is the picture *together with the 'symbols' that interpret it.*

I can, in short, see no way of construing the proposal that there might be a representational system in which resembling is a *sufficient* condition for referring; still less that there might be a representational system in which resembling and referring come to the same thing. To put it briefly, even if Bruner is right and the *vehicles* of reference are different for adults and children, the *mechanisms* of reference—whatever they are—must be pretty much the same for both.

I have been trying to undermine two notions about images that have played a long and dubious role in cognitive psychology: that thinking might *consist* of imaging, and that the means by which images refer to what they are images of might be fundamentally different from the means by which symbols refer to what they denote. But, of course, nothing I have said denies that images exist or that images may play an important role in many cognitive processes. Indeed, such empirical evidence as is available tends to support both claims. This is interesting from the point of view of the major preoccupations of this book. The fact that the data come out the way they do throws light on the nature of the representational resources that people have available. And the fact that the data come out *at all* supports the view that the nature of such resources is a bona fide empirical question.

The relevant studies have recently been extensively reviewed (see, in particular, Paivio, 1971; Richardson, 1969). Suffice it here to sketch one or two of the findings which seem to argue forcibly for the psychological reality of images.

1. If there are images, and if, as introspection suggests, imaging is very like visual perception, one might plausibly expect that experimental tasks which elicit images should produce mode-specific interference with other cognitive processes in which vision is implicated. Tasks which require visual imagery, e.g., should induce decrements in the performance of simultaneous tasks which require visually guided responses. An elegant series of experiments by Brooks (1968) suggests that they do so. In one condition, Ss are asked to form a memory image of a figure like Figure 4–4. They are then asked to trace around the memory image following the arrows and indicating, for each corner, whether it occurs on a top edge of the figure. (The appropriate responses for Figure 4–4 are thus: 'no, yes, no, no, no, yes, yes, no, no, no'.) Depending on the experimental group to which the subject is

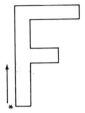

Figure 4-4 Stimulus diagram of the kind used by Brooks (1968)

assigned, responses are indicated either by pointing to written yeses and noes or by some form of nonvisually guided gesture (like tapping or saying 'yes' or 'no'). The relevant result is that performance is significantly better for subjects in the latter (nonvisually guided) groups. Visual images interfere with visually guided tasks.

Moreover, they interfere selectively. Brooks had another condition in which S's task was to produce sequences of yeses and noes depending on the form class of the words in a previously memorized sentence. A subject might be given a sentence like 'Now is the time for all good men to come to the aid of the party' and told to indicate 'yes' for each word that is a noun or verb and 'no' for each word that is neither. In this condition, the effect of response mode upon performance reversed the relation found in the visual image case: Performance was best for subjects who point or tap, worst for subjects who gave their responses verbally. Visually guided responses don't, apparently, much interfere with auditory images .

2. If there are images, and if, as introspection suggests, images are very much like pictures, then there ought to be demonstrable similarities between the processes of comparing an object with an image of that object and comparing two objects that look alike. There are, in fact, a number of experiments in the literature which suggest that this is so. (See, e.g., Cooper and Shephard, 1973.) The paradigmatic study is owing to Posner, Boies, Eichelman, and Taylor (1969).

To begin with, it is possible to show that there is a reliable difference in the speed with which subjects can make judgments of type identity in the case where the tokens are physically *similar,* on the one hand, and in the case where the tokens are physically *different,* on the other. Thus, e.g., Ss are presented with tachistascopic displays consisting of two letters and asked to respond 'yes' if the letters are the same and 'no' if they are different. In this situation, Ss are faster when the members of the positive pairs (i.e., the pairs for which the correct response is 'yes') are of the *same case* (like PP or pp) then when they are of *difference case* (like Pp or pP).

Now suppose the paradigm is changed. Instead of presenting S with two letters in the visual mode, we present him first with an auditory case-and-letter designation, then with a *single visual* letter to match to the auditory description. So the subject might hear 'capital P' and then see P (to which his response would be 'yes') or *p* or *Q* or *q* (to all of which the right response would be 'no'). It turns out that *S*s performance in this situation depends critically on the length of the interval between the auditory and the visual stimulus. Subjects for whom the visual stimulus comes on immediately after the auditory stimulus give response latencies comparable to those for visually presented letter pairs whose members *differ* in case. If, however, the interstimulus interval is increased to about 0.7 second, the response latencies *de*crease and approximate those for visually presented letter pairs whose members are *identical* in case. It is not mandatory, but it is extremely natural, to assume that what happens during the 0.7 second of interstimulus interval is that the subject constructs a letter image to fit the auditory description, and that it is that image which gets matched to the visual display. If this is true, and if, as we have supposed, matching images to things is fundamentally similar to matching things that look alike, we have some sort of explanation of the behavioral convergence between *S*s who judge the relation between pairs of letters both of which they *see,* and *S*s who judge the relation between pairs of letters one of which they only hear described.

The studies just reviewed are by no means the only possibilities for the empirical investigation of the psychological reality of mental images.[16] Consider just one further line of argument.

Discursive symbols, as Bruner remarked, are deployed in time. Or, rather, *some* discursive symbols are (viz., spoken sentences). Pictures (and written sentences), on the other hand, are deployed in space. There may be conventions for determining the order in which information is retrieved from a picture (as in certain kinds of didactic paintings which 'tell a story' and are meant to be scanned in a certain order) but, in general, there needn't be. In principle, all the information is available simultaneously and can be read off in whatever order the observer chooses.[17]

---

[16] The most impressive finding is perhaps that stereoptic depth perception can be produced by imposing an idetic memory image upon a visual stimulus. (See the very remarkable findings reported by Stromeyer and Psotka, 1970. For a general discussion of ideticism, see Haber, 1969.) It seems hard to deny that imaging is like perceiving when it is possible to produce typical perceptual illusions whose objects are images rather than percepts. It's worth remarking, in this respect, that it has been known for some time that there are circumstances in which subjects can be induced to confuse (*non*idetic) images with percepts (Perky, 1910; Segal and Gordon, 1968).

[17] This point is related to one that Kant makes in the *Critique of Pure Reason.* Kant distinguishes between 'subjective' and 'objective' temporal sequences, where the latter, but not the former, are independent of the scanning strategies of the perceiver. Thus, we may choose to examine the facade of a building from portal to pediment. But since all of the bits of the building are in fact contemporaneous, we could equally have chosen to go the other way around. Events which constitute an objective sequence, on the other hand, can be scanned in one order only. The same kind of point applies, *mutatis mutandis,* to the contrast between recovering information from pictures and from spoken sentences.

Suppose, then, that subjects *can* employ mental images to display the information pertinent to performing an experimental task, and suppose that mental images are relevantly similar to real pictures. One should then predict that *S*s who can use images ought to enjoy considerable freedom in the order in which they can report the information that their images present, while *S*s who use discursive forms of representation (e.g., sentences) ought to be relatively restricted in the order in which their information can be accessed. To take an extreme case, imagine an experiment in which the subject is shown a red triangle and then asked about what he has seen. *S*s who stored an *image* ought to be about equally quick in answering 'Was it red?' and 'Was it triangular?' *S*s who stored the sentence 'It was a red triangle' ought to be faster in answering the first question than in answering the second.[18]

As things stand this is, alas, largely a *gedanken* experiment; I mention it primarily as a further illustration of techniques that might be used to subject hypotheses about the nature of internal representations to experimental test. It is worth mentioning, however, that precisely this interpretation *has* been suggested by Paivio (1971) to account for differences in order-of-report effects exhibited by subjects in an experiment by Haber (1966). Paivio remarks that "while the implications of the present analysis have not been independently tested using the appropriate perceptual tasks, evidence from several sources is consistent with the hypothesis" (p. 130).

The preceding should suggest that the existence and functioning of mental images can be handled as an experimental issue and that techniques more subtle than brute appeals to introspection can be employed in the experiments. This may strike the philosophical reader as surprising, since it has recently been fashionable to treat the nonexistence of images as demonstrable a priori. Before we round off this discussion, it is worth digressing to see what can be said for so implausible a view.

Dennett (1969) has put succinctly what appears to be the paramount philosophical worry about images.

Consider the Tiger and his Stripes. I can dream, imagine or see a striped tiger, but must the tiger I experience have a particular number of stripes? If seeing or imaging is having a mental image, then the image of the tiger *must*—obeying the rules of images in general—reveal a definite number of stripes showing, and one should be able to pin this down with such questions as 'more than ten?', 'less than twenty?'. If,

---

[18] *S*s who stored, as it might be, the sentence 'It was a triangle and it was red' ought, of course, to show the reverse asymmetry. The point is that *some order of report effect or other* should be associated with any form of discursive representation, while imagists ought to be relatively free from such effects. If *S*s who claim that they are imaging turn out to be the ones who exhibit relatively weak order of report effects, that would be a reason for taking the hypothesis that they *are* using images seriously.

however, seeing or imagining has a descriptional character, the questions need have no definite answer. Unlike a snapshot of a tiger, a description of a tiger need not go into the number of stripes at all; 'numerous stripes' may be all the description says. Of course in the case of actually seeing a tiger, it will often be possible to corner the tiger and count his stripes, but then one is counting real tiger stripes, not stripes on a mental image. (pp. 136–137)

A number of philosophers appear to hold that this sort of argument provides something like a *demonstration* that there aren't mental images. If they are right it is an embarrassment since, as we have seen, there is some persuasive empirical evidence in the field, and it suggests that what goes on in imaging is very like picturing and very unlike describing. Moreover, the introspective plausibility of the image theory is enormous, so if the striped tigers do show what they are alleged to show we are without an explanation of either the introspections or the experimental data. Any theory is better than none; clearly, we should undermine the striped tiger argument if we can.

There are, I think, at least three ways that one might attempt to do so. I don't suppose that any of these counterarguments is conclusive, but I do think that, between them, they suggest that striped tigers don't clinch the case against images. Given the persuasiveness of the a posteriori arguments for imagery, that should be good enough.

To begin with, one might try simply denying what the striped tiger argument primarily assumes. That is, one might argue that there *is* some definite answer to 'How many stripes does the image-tiger have?' but that, because our images are labile, we usually can't hold on to them for long enough to count. It's to be said in favor of this view (a) that it seems introspectively plausible to many people who claim to have images (if you don't believe it, ask a few)[19]; (b) it makes everyday mental images qualitatively like idetic images, from which even Dennett admits "the subject *can* read off or count off the details" (p. 137); (c) this view is anyhow less hard to swallow than the alternative suggestion: that what goes on when I think that I am picturing a thing is that I am, in fact, describing it to myself.[20]

This is, I think, the kind of suggestion that sophisticated philosophers take to be naive; perhaps because they are impressed by the following sort

---

[19] I *will not* get involved in the question whether introspection is infallible; but it seems to be perverse to hold that the deliverances of introspection are eo ipso always wrong. The subject's views about what he's doing appear to have as good a right to be considered as yours or mine or the experimenter's.

[20] What's still harder to believe is that what goes on in typical cases of *perceiving* a thing is significantly like what goes on in typical cases of describing it. This is pertinent because the natural view of imaging is that to image a thing is to be in a psychological state qualitatively similar to the state that one would be in if one were perceiving the thing. If, therefore, imaging is like describing, perceiving must be too.

of argument. 'Having images is supposed to be part of the perceptual process. But now, if images themselves have to be perceived (scanned, etc.) to recover the information they contain, then surely we have taken the first step in a regress which will eventually require the postulation of images without number and endless perceivers to look at them'. This is, however, a bad argument. It assumes, quite without justification, that if recovering information from the external environment requires having an image, recovering information from an image must require having an image too. But why should we assume that? Moreover (and more to the present point), even if this were a *good* argument it would be no good here. For the most it could show is that images don't play a certain role in perception (i.e., that perceiving a thing couldn't always and everywhere require forming an image of that thing). It shows nothing about whether having and scanning an image might play a role in *other* mental processes (such as, e.g., comparing, remembering or imagining things).

The second point that one might want to make about striped tigers is this: It simply isn't true that a picture of a striped tiger must be determinate under such descriptions as 'has *n* stripes'.[21] Of course the *tiger* has to have precisely *n* stripes for some *n* or other (barring problems about the individuation of stripes), but there are all kinds of cases in which a picture of an *n*-striped tiger may not show any definite number of image stripes. Blurring is the main (but not the only) problem.[22]

What *is* true, what does follow from what Dennett calls "the rules of images in general" is that if what you've got is an image, then necessarily there will have to be *some* visual description under which it is determinate. For a picture in a newspaper, e.g., the pertinent description is one which specifies a 'gray-matrix'; an assignment of a value of black or white to each of the finitely many points that comprise the image. So far as I can see, this is the *only* kind of visual description under which newspaper pictures are *always* determinate. Whether a given such picture happens also to be determinate under some *other* visual description (as, e.g., has *n* stripes) will depend on such matters as what it's a picture of, the angle from which the picture was taken, how good the resolution is, etc.

If this is right, it means that the striped tiger argument is a good deal weaker than it started out to seem. What that argument shows *at most* is that there are *some* visual descriptions under which mental images *aren't* fully determinate. But what would need to be shown to prove that mental images fail to satisfy 'the rules of images in general', i.e., to prove that they aren't images, is that there are *no* visual descriptions under which they *are* fully

21 By stipulation, a picture is *determinate under a description* iff the statement that the picture satisfies the description has a determinate truth value.

22 Think of an out-of-focus photograph of a page of type. There is a definite answer to 'How many letters on the page?' Need there be a definite answer to 'How many image letters on the photograph?'

determinate. Surely nothing that strong follows from the sort of observations Dennett makes.[23]

The third point to make against the striped tiger is that it is more dogmatic about the distinction between images and descriptions than there is any need to be. A paradigmatic image (say a photograph) is *nondiscursive* (the information it conveys is displayed rather than described) and *pictorial* (it resembles its subject). The present point, however, is that there is an indefinite range of cases in between photographs and paragraphs. These intermediate cases are, in effect, images under descriptions; they convey *some* information discursively and *some* information pictorially, and they resemble their subjects only in respect of those properties that happen to be pictured. In particular, they are determinate under the same visual descriptions as their subjects only for such properties.[24]

An example may help to make this clear. Dennett says: "Consider the film version of *War and Peace* and Tolstoy's book; the film version goes into immense detail and in one way cannot possibly be *faithful* to Tolstoy's words since the 'picture painted' by Tolstoy does not go into the details the film cannot help but go into (such as the colors of the eyes of each filmed soldier" (1969, p. 136)). There are, however, other kinds of images than photographs. Consider, for example, *maps*. Maps are pictorial in respect of some of the information they convey; geographical relations are pictured when the map is oriented right. But they are, or may be, nonpictorial in respect of other information. Population densities or elevations above sea level may be given by coloring or shading, and then we need to use the legend to determine what the image means.

To put it briefly, since images under descriptions are images, they are typically pictorial vis-à-vis, some set of visual properties, and, of course, they will be determinate vis-à-vis any set of properties they picture. But since it is in part the description that determines what such an image is an image *of,* the properties for which the image has to be determinate can have arbitrarily little in common with the visual properties of whatever the image images. Images under descriptions share their nondiscursiveness with images

[23] My discussion begs the question of what is to count as a 'visual' description. However, the striped tiger argument does too since, presumably, it is only for visual descriptions that it follows from 'the rules of images in general' that images must be determinate.

[24] It isn't even the case that images under descriptions are necessarily pictorial in respect of all the information in respect of which they are nondiscursive. Taking 'nondiscursive' and 'pictorial' as coextensive is one of the root sources of confusion in thinking about images. Thus, the line on the globe that shows where the equator is presumably conveys information nondiscursively. But it doesn't look like the equator. Such cases suggest how rough-and-ready the unanalyzed contrast between images and descriptions really is. For present purposes, I am using the materials at hand, but serious work in this area would require sharpening (and perhaps ultimately abandoning) the framework of distinctions that I have been assuming.

tout court. What they share with descriptions is that they needn't look much like what they represent.

We can now say what all this has to do with the tiger's stripes. Suppose that what one visualizes in imaging a tiger might be anything from a full-scale tiger portrait (in the case of the ideticist) to a sort of transient stick figure (in the case of poor imagers like me). What makes my stick figure an image of a tiger is not that it looks much like one (my drawings of tigers don't look much like tigers either) but rather that it's *my* image, so I'm the one who gets to say what it's an image of. My images (and my drawings) connect with my intentions in a certain way; I *take* them as tiger-pictures for purposes of whatever task I happen to have in hand. Since my mental image *is* an image, there will be some visual descriptions under which it is determinate; hence there will be some questions whose answers I can 'read off' the display,[25] and the more pictorial the display is the more such questions there will be. But, in the case of any given image, there might be arbitrarily many visual properties which would not be pictured but, as it were, carried by the description under which the image is intended. The image will, ipso facto, not be determinate relative to these properties. We thus return, by a different route, to the conclusion mooted above: To show that mental images violate 'the rules of images in general', one would have to show not just that they are indeterminate under some visual description or other, but rather that they are determinate under no visual descriptions at all. There *may* be a way of showing this, but I doubt it and the striped tiger argument doesn't do it.

All this points toward some plausible speculations about how images may integrate with discursive modes of internal representation. If one recalls the Posner *et al.* experiment discussed above, one notices that there are two psychological processes postulated by the proposed explanation of the results. In the first phase, an image is constructed in accordance with a description. In the second phase, the image is matched against a stimulus for purposes of perceptual identification. The explanation thus implies (what common sense also suggests) that we have psychological faculties which can construct images which display the information that corresponding descriptions convey discursively; i.e., faculties which permit us to construct images *from* descriptions. The experiment demonstrates that having the information displayed *as* an image facilitates performance in certain kinds of tasks. (In effect, using the image rather than the description permits the subject to do the job of perceptual categorization in parallel rather than in series; he can check letter case and letter type *at the same time*.)

These remarks about the Posner experiment fit very well with the view

---

[25] It is, presumably, because images do allow some information to be 'read off' that people bother with constructing images in memory tasks. A standard psychological anecdote concerns the man who can't tell you how many windows his house has unless he constructs an image of the house and then counts.

that images under description are often the vehicles of internal representation. For insofar as mental images are constructed *from descriptions,* the descriptions can function to determine what the images are images of, and how their properties are to be interpreted. Here, then, is the general outline of the picture I have been trying to develop:

1. Some behaviors are facilitated when task-relevant information is non-discursively displayed (e.g., when it is displayed as an image).

2. One of our psychological faculties functions to construct images which accord with descriptions. That is, we have access to a computational system which takes a description as input and gives, as output, an image of something that satisfies the description. The exploitation of this system is presumably sensitive to our estimates of the demand characteristics of the task at hand.

3. The image that gets produced may be quite schematic since how the image is *taken*—what role it plays in cognitive processing—is determined not only by its figural properties but also by the character of the description it is paired with. We have seen that this point is important for evaluating the striped tiger argument. It may now be added that it goes some way toward meeting one of the empirical arguments that is frequently urged against taking mental images very seriously.

Psychologists who don't think that images could play any very important role in internal representation often insist upon the idiosyncratic character of the images that subjects report (see, e.g., Brown, 1958). Clearly the content of images does vary quite a lot from person to person, and it might well be that a given image can function to effect different representations in different computational tasks (what counts as the image of a duck for one purpose might count as the image of a rabbit for another). The present point is that if mental images are images under descriptions, then their idiosyncrasies might have very little effect on the role they play in cognitive processes. Suppose your image of a triangle is scaline and mine is isosceles. This needn't matter to how we use the images to reason about triangles so long as we agree on how the images are to be taken; e.g., so long as we agree that they are to represent *any* closed three-sided figure whose sides are straight lines.

This is, in fact, quite a traditional sort of point to make. The empiricists were on to it, though the significance of their views has frequently been overlooked. Thus, Hume acknowledged Berkeley's insight that images can't resemble the referents of abstract ideas, but held that there is a sense in which entertaining an abstract idea might be identical with having an image all the same. Hume says: "the image in the mind is only that of a particular object, tho' the application of it in our reasoning be the same as if it were universal" (1960 ed., p. 28). Viewed one way, this is tantamount to the abandonment of the image theory of thought, since the vehicles of internal representation are taken to be (not images *tout court* but) images under one or another interpretation; what we have been calling images under descriptions. What has been abandoned, in particular, is the doctrine that mental images refer to what they resemble and resemble what they refer to. But, viewed the other way, Hume's point is that the abandonment of the resemblance theory of reference is compatible with preserving the insight that (some) internal representations are, or may be, nondiscursive. The importance of distinguishing between these two claims—and the failure of lots of latter-day psychologists and philosophers to do so—has, of course, been one of the main themes of our discussion.

What we have so far is not more than a sketch of a theory: The questions it leaves open are more interesting than the ones that it proposes answers to. For example, granted that there is such a thing as mental imagery, is there any reason to suppose that it plays more than a marginal role in internal representation? What kinds of tasks are facilitated by the availability of nondiscursive displays? What is it about nondiscursive displays that makes them useful in such tasks? How much freedom do we have in opting for nondiscursive representation in given cases? What are the mechanisms by which images are constructed from descriptions?[26] Above all, it would be interesting to know whether *all* mental images are generated from descriptions, or whether some psychological processes are, as it were, nondiscursive from beginning to end.[27] If, for example, I use images to recall the look or smell of a thing, do I invariably recruit information which was discursively represented at some stage in its history? Was what Proust had stored a

[26] Some hints might be garnered from an examination of 'digital to analog' computer routines. It argues for the possibility of psychologically real devices which map descriptions onto images that machines can already be built to realize such functions. See Sutherland (1970).

[27] I assume, for the kinds of reasons just discussed, that insofar as internal representations are images, they must be images-under-descriptions. What I regard as an open empirical question is the mechanisms by which descriptions and images are related. One way to relate them—the one sketched above—would be to generate the images *from* the descriptions. The present question is whether there are other ways and, if so, what they are.

It may be worth remarking, by the way, that there are similarities between what I have been saying about how images might be deployed in recognition tasks and the so-called 'analysis by synthesis' theories of perceptual categorization. The point of such theories is precisely that representations—in effect, templates—are generated from descriptions and then matched to the input that needs to be categorized. The description from which the template is generated then provides the perceptual analysis of the input. It is an attractive feature of such models that they provide for an infinite stock of templates, so long as the formation rules for the descriptions are iterative. (For discussion, see Halle and Stevens, 1964; Neisser, 1967.) I very much doubt that analysis by synthesis could yield anything like a general theory of perception, but it is quite plausible that such mechanisms are involved in perception *inter alia*.

description of how madeleines taste soaked in tea? Or are there psychological mechanisms by which nondiscursive engrams are established and deployed? Certainly the enormous amounts of information which get handled in some tasks where images are implicated makes it implausible that the information displayed went through a stage of digital encoding. The discussion has, in any event, returned to an area of straightforwardly empirical psychological research, and I propose to leave it there. Interested readers are referred to Pribram (1971), and Penfield and Roberts (1959).

Many psychological processes are computational; they essentially involve the transformation of such information as the perceptual (or genetic) environment of the organism places at its disposal. But information must be represented somehow, and some forms of representation may be better than others; better adapted, i.e., to whatever task the organism is engaged in. The biological problem in designing the psychology of organisms is thus to assure, as much as may be, that modes of representation are optimally matched with kinds of tasks. People are one sort of solution to this problem, and so, I suppose, are any other organisms that have a mental life.

I have wanted, in this chapter, to say something about what kind of solution people are. The key appears to lie in flexibility. Human beings apparently have access to a variety of modes of representation, and can exert a rational control over the kinds of representations they employ. That is: How the available representational resources are exploited in any given case depends on what the agent takes the exigencies of the task in hand to be. The efficient deployment of computational capacities is itself a computational problem, and it is one which human beings are, apparently, pretty well equipped to solve.

This result may be discouraging for psychologists who are in a hurry. One seeks to run experiments which engage the brute, involuntary mechanisms of cognition; intellectual reflexes, as it were, with which the mind responds willy-nilly to the task. But what one often finds instead are merely the local, special-purpose strategies that subjects devise in order to comply efficiently with their instructions. What the experiment thus primarily reveals is the subject's capacity to figure out the experimenter's goals, and his willingness, by and large, to do the best he can about promoting them. (The recent literature on 'verbal conditioning' provides an edifying case in point. See Brewer, to be published; Dulaney, 1968.)

We are told that science seeks to explicate the uniformities that underlie the surface jumble of events. So it is depressing to dig below the complex and shifting cognitive resources that human subjects bring to problem-solving tasks, only to find, ever and again, further layers of shifting and complex resource. But *just* to be depressed would be to miss the point. It is, after all, not uninteresting that our cognitive capacities are layered in the way they are. On the contrary, it seems increasingly clear that a theory of the rational management of computational resources will be a significant part of any explanation of why we are so good at what we do. And if I am right in what this chapter says, the management of the means of representation is part of what such theories will have to be about.

In the long run—in the *very* long run—we shall want to get down to those brute reflexes of cognition. For in that long run, we want a theory, not just of one rational process or other, but of rationality per se. As Dennett has remarked, we won't have such a theory so long as our explanations still have " 'mentalistic' words like 'recognize' and 'figure out' and 'believe' in [them, since such explanations] presuppose the very set of capacities—whatever the capacities are that go to make up intelligence—[they] ought to be accounting for" (unpublished). I am, however, assuming that we all are middle-run psychologists and that our interim goals are rather less ambitious than the wholesale elimination of intentional predicates from psychological explanations. For our more modest purposes, the aim is not to explain rationality away, but simply to show how rationality is structured. It will thus do, for these purposes, if psychological theories exhibit the ways in which rational processes depend upon each other. If the mind is after all a mechanism, such theories won't have the last word in psychology. But saying the last word isn't the problem that currently confronts us. Our problem is to find something—almost anything—-that we can say that's *true*.

CONCLUSION:
SCOPE AND LIMITS

*I always think that when one feels
one's been carrying a theory too
far, then's the time to carry it a
little further.*
*A little? Good heavens man! Are
you growing old?*

MAX BEERBOHM

Like the rest of the sciences, psychology starts in the middle of things. This
is to say not just that psychologists inherit from the culture at large a legacy
of presystematic and only partially articulate beliefs, explanations, and
theories about the way the mind works, but also that the questions about
mentation which define their field are, in the first instance, simply those that
informal inquiry has raised but failed to answer: How do we learn? How
do we perceive? What is thinking? How are thoughts expressed in words? . . .

The various schools of psychology are distinguished, *inter alia,* by the
attitudes with which they view this legacy. Behaviorism, e.g., was explicit
in rejecting it. What made behaviorism seem so radical was the claim that the
traditional questions have no answers in the terms in which they are traditionally posed: that progress in psychology requires a full-scale overhauling
of the assumptions, the vocabulary, and most particularly the ontology of
commonsense accounts of mental processses.

Had the behaviorists been able to make this claim stick, they would
indeed have effected one of the major conceptual revolutions in the history
of science. That they didn't make it stick is not, perhaps surprising. What
they set out to do was to replace from whole cloth the intricate and elaborate
fabric of mental concepts that is the consequence of our literally millennia
of attempts to understand each other and ourselves. It's not, of course,
beyond dispute that the results of scientific inquiry *will* eventually show that
this tradition needs to be replaced. But one would expect the process to be

197

piecemeal—an operation from the inside out. It would really be extraordinary if we could make do, in accounting for behavior, with explanatory categories dreamed up *de novo* and, as John Austin says in a related context, of an afternoon.

Contemporary cognitive psychology is, by contrast, by and large conservative in its approach to the commonsense tradition. No doubt, the flora and fauna of psychology have proliferated vastly, and surprising mental processes are postulated right and left. Nevertheless, at the heart of the picture, the fundamental *explicandum,* is the organism and its propositional attitudes: what it believes, what it learns, what it wants and fears, what it perceives to be the case. Cognitive psychologists accept, that is, what the behaviorists were most determined to reject: the *facticity* of ascriptions of propositional attitudes to organisms and the consequent necessity of explaining how organisms come to have the attitudes to propositions that they do.

What is *un*traditional about the movement, if I have reconstructed it correctly, is the account of propositional attitudes that it proposes: To have a certain propositional attitude is to be in a certain relation to an internal representation. That is, for each of the (typically infinitely many) propositional attitudes that an organism can entertain, there exist an internal representation and a relation such that being in that relation to that representation is nomologically necessary and sufficient for (or nomologically identical to) having the propositional attitude. The least that an empirically adequate cognitive psychology is therefore required to do is to specify, for each propositional attitude, the internal representation and the relation which, in this sense, correspond to it. Attitudes to propositions are, to that extent, 'reduced' to attitudes to formulae, though the formulae are couched in a proprietary inner code.

So having a propositional attitude is being in some relation to an internal representation. In particular, having a propositional attitude is being in some *computational* relation to an internal representation. The intended claim is that the sequence of events that causally determines the mental state of an organism will be describable as a sequence of steps in a derivation if it is describable in the vocabulary of psychology at all. More exactly: Mental states are relations between organisms and internal representations, and causally interrelated mental states succeed one another according to computational principles which apply formally *to the representations.* This is the sense in which internal representations provide the domains for such data processes as inform the mental life. It is, in short, of the essence of cognitive theories that they seek to interpret physical (causal) transformations as transformations of information, with the effect of exhibiting the rationality of mental processes. In somewhat similar fashion, the coherence of a text emerges when a sequence of orthographic/geometric forms is interpreted as a sequence of sentences in a language. If, as Quine suggests, translation is that enterprise in which we do our best for the rationality of texts, cognitive psychology is the one in which we do our best for the rationality of mental processes at large.

This is, I take it, a framework for a science. As such, it makes demands upon the world. It won't be possible to construct a psychology of the kind that I have been envisioning unless organisms have pertinent descriptions as instantiations of some or other formal system. It's 'pertinent' that does the work, of course. What pertinency requires is (a) that there be some general and plausible procedure for assigning formulae of the system to states of the organism; (b) that causal sequences which determine propositional attitudes turn out to be derivations under the assignment; (c) that for each propositional attitude of the organism there is some causal state of the organism such that (c1) the state is interpretable as a relation to a formula of the formal system, and (c2) being in the state is nomologically necessary and sufficient for (or contingently identical to) having the propositional attitude.

It is, I assume, just obvious that points (a)–(c) constitute *substantive* constraints on psychological theories: Not every assignment of expressions in a formal system to causal states of an organism will succeed in displaying sequences of such states as derivations, and this remains true even if we don't fret much over what's to count as a formal system or what's to count as a derivation. We could imagine, e.g., an assignment of sentences of English to our own physiological states such that whichever such state is nomologically necessary and sufficient for believing that it will rain is paired with, say, the sentence 'there aren't any aardvarks any more'. In effect, according to this assignment, believing it will rain is being in a certain relation to the sentence about aardvarks. Patently, *this* assignment of formulae to causal states won't satisfy points (a)–(c) because, roughly, the *causal* consequences of believing that it will rain can't be paired in any coherent way with the *logical* consequences of 'There aren't any aardvarks any more'. The causal relations among states of the organism don't, in that sense, respect the semantic relations among sentences of English under the proposed assignment. What points (a)–(c) demand of psychological theories is, however, precisely that they should preserve this relation of respecting. So if we want to satisfy points (a)–(c), we had better at least ensure that being in the causal state that we pair with 'There aren't any aardvarks any more' is by and large nomologically sufficient for being in whatever state we pair with 'There aren't any aardvarks' since, by and large, people who believe what the first sentence expresses also believe what the second sentence does.

The real work starts here: What kind of formal system will be rich enough to provide the vehicle for internal representation? What kinds of operations upon the formulae of that system can count as computational operations? Which sequences of such formulae constitute 'derivations' in the sense required? What relations between organisms and formulae are such that being *in* those relations explicates entertaining propositional attitudes, and which propositional attitudes go with which of the relations? What principles assign formulae to causal states? Which causal states (and under what descriptions) are the ones to which the formulae get assigned? Very little is known about how to answer any of these questions, nor have I, in this book, shown how to answer them. My contentions have been modest: The program is far from fully clear, but there's no obvious reason to believe that it is fundamentally confused; the program engages issues that are abstract by anybody's standards, but there is no obvious reason to deny that it's a program of empirical research.

In fact, however, I think it's pretty clear that the program will not—can't—be carried out with the generality that points (a)–(c) envisage. There would seem to be some glaring facts about mentation which set a bound to our ambitions. I want to end by mentioning a few of these.

Mental states, insofar as psychology can account for them, must be the consequences of mental processes. Mental processes, according to the view that we've been entertaining, are processes in which internal representations are transformed. So, those mental states that psychology can account for are the ones that are the consequences of the transformation of internal representations. How many mental states is that? The main argument of this book has been that it comes to more than none of them. The present point, however, is that it also comes to less than all of them. If that is true, then points (a)–(c) cannot be satisfied with full generality because, in particular, (b) cannot.

It is, I think, the next thing to dead certain that some of the propositional attitudes we entertain aren't the results of computations. This isn't, of course, to say that they aren't caused; it's just to say that their causes aren't psychological: The events which fix such states have no interpretation under that assignment of formulae which works best overall to interpret the etiology of our mentation. An idea pops, suddenly, into one's head; or one finds oneself thinking, obsessively, of Monica Vitti; or one keeps wondering whether one locked the cellar door. Sometimes, no doubt, such states may be appropriately represented as the causal consequences of subterranean processes of inference. If the Freudians are right, that's true more often than the innocent suppose. But it surely isn't *always* true. Some mental states are, as it were, the consequence of brute incursions from the physiological level; if it *was* the oysters that one ate that were to blame, then there will be no *computational* interpretation of the causal chain that leads from them to one's present sense that things could, on the whole, be better.

The mental life is, as Davidson (1970) suggested, gappy.[1] Those of one's propositional attitudes that are fixed by computations form the subject matter for a science of the kind that we have been examining. But those that aren't don't, and that fact provides for the possibility of bona fide

[1] As is the domain of any other of the special sciences. If the world *is* a continuous causal sequence, it can be so represented only under physical description. (See the discussion in the Introduction.)

mental phenomena which a theory of cognition cannot, literally in principle, explain.

I want to emphasize this point because there is no reason to believe that the kinds of mental phenomena which are thus excluded from the domain of theories of information flow are restricted to occasional detritus of the mental life. On the contrary, some of the most systematic, and some of the most interesting, kinds of mental events may be among those about whose etiology cognitive psychologists can have nothing at all to say.

The most obvious case is the causal determination of sensation. Presumably the perceptual integration of sensory material is accomplished by computational processes of the general sort discussed in Chapter 1. But the etiology of sensory material must typically lie in causal interactions between the organism and sources of distal stimulation, and such interactions have, almost by definition, no representation in the psychological vocabulary. Cognitive psychology per se knows nothing about the stimulus except what is given in one or another of its *proximal* representations.

What *can* be psychologically interpreted is, then, certain of the *effects* of the causal interactions between the organism and its environment; viz., those effects that form the sensory basis of perception. The etiology of sensations must be handled by a different kind of science—one which predicts the sensory state of the organism from physical descriptions of impinging stimulations. That is, of course, what psychophysics has classically tried to do. Cognitive psychology starts, as it were, where psychophysics leaves off, but the methodologies of the disciplines differ radically. Psychophysical truths express the lawful contingency of events *under psychological description* upon events *under physical description*; whereas the truths of cognitive psychology express the computational contingencies among events which are homogeneously (psychologically) described. Cognitive psychology is concerned with the transformation of representations, psychophysics with the assignment of representations to physical displays.

The etiology of sensory material thus seems to be a clear case where the causal sequence which determines a mental state has no useful description as a rule governed sequence of transformations of representations. There are other cases which are more interesting even if less clear.

Thus, e.g., some of the most striking things that people do—'creative' things like writing poems, discovering laws, or, generically, having good ideas—don't *feel* like species of rule-governed processes. Perhaps, of course, they are; perhaps there are procedures for writing poems and psychology will become increasingly articulate about such procedures as time goes on. Or, perhaps more plausibly, there are computational procedures which govern the writing of poems under *some* description but not, as it were, under *that* one. That is, it may be that the processes we think of as creative don't form a natural kind for purposes of psychological explanation, but that, nevertheless, every *instance* of such a process is an instance of rule-guided, computational activity of one sort or another. People who prove theorems and people who cook soufflés are, I suppose, both involved in creative activities. It doesn't follow that what the cook is doing and what the mathematician is doing are similar under the descriptions that are relevant to their psychological explanations. The categories *creative/boring* may simply cross-classify the taxonomy that psychology employs.

My main point, however, is that the mere fact that creative mental processes are *mental* processes does not ensure that they have explanations in the language of psychology under *any* of their descriptions. It may be that good ideas (some, many, or all of them) are species of mental states which don't have mental causes. Since nothing at all is known about such matters, I see no reason to dismiss the intuitions creative people have about the ways in which they get themselves to act creatively. The anecdotes are, I think, remarkably consistent on this point. People with hard problems to solve often don't go about solving them by any systematic intellectual means (or, at least, if they do they often aren't conscious of the fact that they are doing it). Rather, they seek to manipulate the *causal* situation in hopes that the manipulated causes will lead to good effects.

The ways that people do this are notoriously idiosyncratic. Some go for walks. Some line up their pencils and start into the middle distance. Some go to bed. Coleridge and De Quincy smoked opium. Hardy went to cricket matches. Balzac put his nightgown on. Proust sat himself in a cork-lined room and contemplated antique hats. Heaven knows what De Sade did. It's possible, of course, that all such behaviors are merely superstitious. But it's surely equally possible that they are not. Nothing principled precludes the chance that highly valued mental states are sometimes the effects of (literally) nonrational causes. Cognitive psychology could have nothing to say about the etiology of such states since what it talks about is at most (see below) mental states that have mental causes. It may be that we are laboring in quite a small vineyard, for all that we can't now make out its borders.

So far I've been concerned with cases where mental states aren't (or, anyhow, may not be) contingent upon mental causes. The point has been that the etiology of such states falls, by definition, outside the domain of the explanatory mechanisms that cognitive psychologists employ; cognitive psychology is about how rationality is structured, viz., how mental states are contingent on each other.

But, in fact, the situation may be worse than this. Cognitive explanation requires not only causally interrelated mental states, but also mental states whose causal relations respect the semantic relations that hold between formulae in the internal representational system. The present point is that there may well be mental states whose etiology is precluded from cognitive explanation because they are related to their causes in ways that satisfy the first condition but do not satisfy the second.

There would seem, prima facie, to be a superfluity of such cases, though, of course, any claim one makes about the etiology of a mental state is at the mercy of what turns out to be empirically the fact; the best that one can do is offer plausible examples. Here's one: A man wishes to be reminded, sometime during the day, to send a message to a friend. He therefore puts his watch on upside down, knowing that he will glance at it eventually and that, when he does, he will think to send the message. What we have here is, presumably, a straightforward causal connection between two mental states (seeing the watch to be upside down and remembering to send the message), but not a kind of connection that cognitive psychology has anything to say about. Roughly, although the mental states are causally connected, they aren't connected by virtue of their *content*; compare the case of the man who is reminded to send a message to his friend when he (a) hears and (b) understands an utterance token of the type 'send a message to your friend'.

I think it's likely that there are quite a lot of kinds of examples of causal-but-noncomputational relations between mental states. Many associative processes are probably like this, as are perhaps, many of the effects of emotion upon perception and belief. If this hunch is right, then these are bona fide examples of causal relations between mental states which, nevertheless, fall outside the domain of (cognitive) psychological explanation. What the cognitive psychologist *can* do, of course, is to specify the states that are so related and say *that* they are so related. But, from the psychological point of view, the existence of such relations is simply a matter of brute fact; explaining them is left to lower-level (probably biological) investigation.

It is, in any event, not a question for a priori settlement which aspects of the mental life can be treated naturally within the sort of theoretical framework that this book has been concerned with. Such a treatment requires of a mental state that it be analyzable as a relation to a representation, and that its causal antecedents (or consequents or both) should be analyzable as relations to semantically related representations. This is, I think, a condition on a *rational* relation between events in a mental life, and I suppose that it's a point of definition that only relations which are in this loose sense rational can have a chance of being analyzed as computational. But not every mental event has a mental cause; a fortiori not every mental event is rationally related to its mental causes. The universe of discourse whose population is the rationally related mental events constitutes, to a first approximation, the natural domain for a cognitive psychology. How large that domain may prove to be is itself a subject for empirical research, but it would be a pretty irony if it proved to exclude quite a lot of what psychologists have traditionally worked on.

The view of mental life I have been proposing may thus be disappointing in the modesty of its ambitions. As I said before, a theory of the structure of rationality is the best that we can hope for with the tools we have in hand; the best, perhaps, that any nonreductive psychology can ever hope for. Though this seems to me to be a lot, it will seem to many to be a lot too little. To those who feel this way, these proposals may be disappointing in still another sense.

It has been a main theme of this book that mental operations are defined for representations. There is, however, a frame of mind in which this seems to be a trap. It is easy to picture the mind as somehow caged in a shadow show of representations unable, in the nature of the thing, to get in contact with the world outside. And it's easy to go from there to an indefinite yearning for epistemic immediacy; a yearning which is none the less impassioned for all that it is largely incoherent. Not being able to say what it is you want is quite compatible with wanting it very much; hence the Bergsonesque fantasies of such West Coast gurus as the late Aldous Huxley.

It is therefore pertinent to insist that this picture *isn't* the one that I have been developing, nor is it implied by anything that I have had to say. To begin with, to assume that mental states are analyzable as relations to representations is not to preclude the likelihood that they are *also* analyzable as relations to objects in the world. On the contrary, in the epistemically normal situation one gets into relation with a bit of the world precisely *via* one's relation to its representation; in the normal situation, if I am thinking about Mary then it's *Mary* I am thinking about. To think about Mary is (*inter alia*) to represent *Mary* in a certain way; it's not, for example, to represent Mary's representation in that way.

So there's no principled reason why a representational theory of the mind need degenerate into solipsism. Moreover, the kind of representational theory that I have been endorsing is specially prohibited from doing so. On my account, the sequence of events from stimulus to response is typically a *causal* sequence; in particular, the sequence of events from distal stimulus to proximal representation is typically causal. If this view is right, then solipsism can't be; there are no effects of things that aren't there.

As for immediacy, it is widely available, though not in any sense that would have satisfied Huxley. Since our epistemic states are typically the physical consequence of physical causes, epistemic relations are typically immediate in whatever sense causal relations are, and that ought to be immediate enough for anybody. On the other hand, such relations aren't, usually, causally explained under the descriptions whose satisfaction makes them epistemic. The same events are thus epistemic and immediate but not, notice, in the same respects. There is no way out of this; it wouldn't, e.g., help to turn and live with animals. They are in the same bind.

Our causal transactions with the world are, I suppose, one and all explicable in the vocabulary of physics. But the epistemic consequences of these transactions can't be, since the properties of the world that we are epistemically related to aren't, usually, its physical properties. This is, I take it, a brute matter of fact. One could imagine a kind of organism which knows about just those features of the world which have to be averted to in causal explanations of *what* the organism knows. But, in fact, there aren't any such organisms. It is indeed, the fact that there aren't which ultimately supports the methodological principle announced in the Introduction: The theoretical vocabulary of psychology is quite different from the theoretical vocabulary of physics. We thus arrive, by a very long route, at a point where the methodological and empirical assumptions of the investigation merge inextricably. That would seem to be a good place to stop.

BIBLIOGRAPHY

Atherton, M. and Schwartz, R. (1974). Linguistic Innateness and Its Evidence. *Journal of Philosophy,* **LXXI,** no. 6, 155–168.

Bar-Hillel, Y. (1970). "Aspects of Language," The Magnes Press, The Hebrew University, Jerusalem.

Bartlett, F. C. (1961). "Remembering." (first published, 1932). Cambridge Univ. Press, London and New York.

Berlyne, D. E. (1965). "Structure and Direction in Thinking," Wiley, New York.

Bever, T. G. (1970). The cognitive basis for linguistic structures. In "Cognition and the Development of Language." (J. R. Hayes, ed.), Wiley, New York.

Block, N. J. and Fodor, J. (1972). What psychological states are not. *Philosophical Review,* **81,** 159–181.

Blumenthal, A. L. (1966). Observations with self-embedded sentences. *Psychonomic Science,* **6,** 453–454.

Bransford, J. D. and Franks, J. J. (1971). The abstraction of linguistic ideas. *Cognitive Psychology,* **2,** 331–350.

Brewer, W. F. There is no convincing evidence for operant or classical conditioning in adult humans. "Cognition and Symbolic Processes." (W. B. Weiner and D. S. Palermo, eds.), to be published.

Broadbent, D. E. (1958). "Perception and Communication," Pergamon, Oxford.

Brooks, L. R. (1968). Spatial and verbal components of the act of recall. *Canadian Journal of Psychology,* **22,** 349–368.

Brown, R. (1958). "Words and Things," The Free Press, New York.

Brown, R. (1970). How shall a think be called? In "Psycholinguistics," The Free Press, New York.

Bruner, J. S. (1957). On perceptual readiness. *Psychological Review,* **64,** 123–152.

Bruner, J. S., Goodnow, J. J. and Austin, G. A. (1956). "A Study of Thinking," Wiley, New York. (Paperback Wiley Science Editions, 1962.)

Bruner, J. S., Olver, R. R. and Greenfield, P. M. (1966). "Studies in Cognitive Growth," Wiley, New York.

Bryant, P. E. (1974). "Perception and Understanding in Young Children," Basic Books, New York.

Bryant, P. E. and Trabasso, T. (1971). Transitive inferences and meaning in young children. *Nature,* **232,** 456–458.

Capranica, R. R. (1965). "The Evoked Vocal Response of the Bullfrog: A Study of Communication by Sound," MIT Press, Cambridge, Massachusetts.

Carnap, R. (1956). "Meaning and Necessity," Univ. of Chicago Press, Chicago, Illinois.

Chihara, C. and Fodor, J. (1965). Operationalism and ordinary language. *American Philosophical Quarterly,* **2**(4), 281–295.

Chomsky, N. (1957). "Syntactic Structures," Mouton & Co., The Hague.

Chomsky, N. (1959). Review of Skinner's "Verbal Behavior," *Language,* **35,** 26–58.

Chomsky, N. (1965). "Aspects of the Theory of Syntax." MIT Press, Cambridge, Massachusetts.

Chomsky, N. (1969). Linguistics and Philosophy. In "Language and Philosophy," (S. Hook, ed.), N. Y. Univ. Press, New York.

Clark, H. H. and Chase, W. G. (1972). On the process of comparing sentences against pictures. *Cognitive Psychology,* **3,** 472–517.

Clifton, C. and Odom, P. (1966). Similarity relations among certain English sentence constructions. *Psychological Monographs,* **80** (Whole No. 613).

Collins, A. M. and Quillian, M. R. (1969). Retrieval time from semantic memory. *Journal of Verbal Learning and Verbal Behavior,* **8,** 240–247.

Cooper, L. A. and Shepard, R. N. (1973). Chronometric studies of the rotation of mental images. In "Visual Information Processing," (W. G. Chase, ed.), Academic Press, New York.

Crowder, R. G. and Morton, J. (1969). Precategorical acoustic storage (PAS). *Perception and Psychophysics,* **5,** 365–371.

Davidson, D. (1967). Truth and meaning. *Synthese,* **17,** 304–323.

Davidson, D. (1970). Mental events. In "Experience and Theory," (L. Forster and J. Swanson, eds.), Univ. of Massachusetts Press, Amherst, Massachusetts.

Dennett, D. C. (1969). "Content and Consciousness," Humanities Press, New York.

Dennett, D. C. (1972). "Skinner Skinned." Unpublished.

Dreyfus, H. L. (1972). "What Computers Can't Do: A Critique of Artificial Reason." Harper, New York.

Dulany, D. E., Jr. (1968). Awareness, rules, and propositional control: a confrontation with S–R behavior theory. In "Verbal Behavior and General Behavior Theory," (T. R. Dixon and D. L. Horton, eds.), Prentice-Hall, Englewood Cliffs, New Jersey.

Fillmore, C. (1971). Entailment rules in a semantic theory. In "The Philosophy of Language," (J. Rosenberg and C. Travis, eds.), Prentice Hall, Englewood Cliffs, New Jersey.

Fodor, J. A. (1968). "Psychological Explanation," Random House, (Smithsonian Inst. Press), New York.

Fodor, J. A. (1970), Three reasons for not deriving "kill" from "cause to die." *Linguistic Inquiry,* **1,** 429–438.

Fodor, J. A. (1972). Some reflections on L. S. Vygotsky's "Thought and Language," *Cognition,* **1**(1), 83–95.

Fodor, J. A. Special sciences. *Synthese,* to be published.

Fodor, J. A., Bever, T. and Garrett, M. (1974). "The Psychology of Language: An Introduction to Psycholinguistics and Generative Grammar," McGraw-Hill, New York.

Fodor, J. A., Fodor, J. D. and Garrett, M. The psychological reality of semantic representations. *Linguistic Inquiry,* to be published.

Fodor, J. A., Garrett, M. and Bever, T. (1968). Some syntactic determinants of sentential complexity, II: Verb Structure. *Perception and Psychophysics,* **3,** 453–461.

Fodor, J. A., Garrett, M. and Brill, S. L. (1975). Pe, ka, pu: the perception of speech sounds in prelinguistic infants. *M.I.T. Quarterly Progress Report,* January, 1975. (Submitted to *Science*).

Fodor, J. D. *Semantics,* to be published.

Forster, K I. and Olbrei, I. (1973). Semantic heuristics and semantic analysis. *Cognition,* **2,** 319–348.

Garrett, M. and Fodor, J. A. (1968). Psychological theories and linguistic constructs. In "Verbal Behavior and General Behavior Theory," (T. R. Dixon and D. L. Horton, eds.), Prentice–Hall, Englewood Cliffs, New Jersey.

Gibson, J. J. (1966). "The Senses Considered as Perceptual Systems," Houghton, Boston, Massachusetts.

Goodman, N. (1965). "Fact, Fiction and Forecast," Bobbs–Merrill, Indianapolis, Indiana.

Goodman, N. (1968). "Languages of Art," Bobbs–Merrill, Indianapolis, Indiana.

Greene, J. (1972). "Psycholinguistics: Chomsky and Psychology," Penguin, Harmondsworth, Middlesex, England.

Gregory, R. L. (1966). "Eye and Brain: The Psychology of Seeing," McGraw-Hill, New York.

Grice, H. P. (1957). Meaning. *The Philosophical Review,* **LXVI**. (Reprinted in "Problems in the Philosophy of Language," (T. Olshewsky, ed.), Holt, New York.

Haber, R. N. (1966). Nature of the effect of set on perception. *Psychological Review,* **73,** 335–351.

Halle, M. and Stevens, K. N. (1964). Speech recognition: a model and a program for research. In "The Structure of Language: Readings in the Philosophy of Language" (J. A. Fodor and J. J. Katz, eds.), Prentice-Hall, Englewood Cliffs, New Jersey.

Harman, G. (1969). Linguistic competence and empiricism. In "Language and Philosophy," (S. Hook, ed.), N. Y. Univ. Press, New York.

Heider, E. (1971). Natural categories. *Proceedings, 79th Annual Convention, American Psychological Association.*

Helke, M. (1971). The grammar of English reflexives. M.I.T. Doctoral Dissertation.

Hull, C. L. (1943). "Principles of Behavior," Appleton, New York.

Hume, D. (1960). "A Treatise of Human Nature," *Vol. I.* (Originally published 1739), Dent, London.

Jarvella, R. J. (1970). Effects of syntax on running memory span for connected discourse. *Psychonomic Science,* **19,** 235–236.

Johnson-Laird, P. N. and Stevenson, R. (1970). Memory for syntax. *Nature,* **227,** 412–413.

Julesz, B. (1965). Texture and visual perception. *Scientific American,* February, 38–48.

Kant, I. (1953). "Critique of Pure Reason," N. K. Smith, (trans.). Macmillan, New York. (Originally published, 1781).

Katz, J. J. (1966). "The Philosophy of Language," Harper, New York.

Katz, J. J. (1972). "Semantic Theory," Harper, New York.

Katz, J. J. and Fodor, J. A. (1963). The structure of a semantic theory. *Language,* **39,** 170–210.

Katz, J. J. and Postal, P. M. (1964). "An Integrated Theory of Linguistic Descriptions," MIT Press, Cambridge, Massachusetts.

Kripke, S. (1972). Naming and necessity. In "Semantics of Natural Language," (G. Harmon and D. Davidson, eds.), Humanities Press, New York.

Lackner, J. R. and Garrett, M. (1973). Resolving ambiguity: effects of biasing context in the unattended ear. *Cognition,* **1,** 359–372.

Lakoff, G. (1970a). "Irregularity in Syntax," Holt, New York.

Lakoff, G. (1970b). Linguistics and natural logic. *Studies in Generative Semantics No.* **1,** Phonetics Lab., Univ. of Michigan, Ann Arbor, Michigan.

Letvin, J., Maturana, H., Pitts, W. and McCulloch (1961). Two remarks on the visual system of the frog. In "Sensory Communication," (W. Rosenblith, ed.), MIT Press, Cambridge, Massachusetts.

Lewis, D. K. (1970). General semantics. *Synthese,* **22,** 18–67.

Liberman, A., Cooper, F. S., Shankweiler, D. P. and Studdert-Kennedy, M. (1967). Perception of the speech code. *Psychological Review,* **74,** 431–461.

Loewenstein, W. R. (1960). Biological transducers. *Scientific American,* August. (Also in *Perception: Mechanisms and Models, Readings from Scientific American* (1972), Freeman, San Francisco, California.

Luria, A. R. (1968). "The Mind of the Mnemonist," Basic Books, New York.

Malcolm, N. (1962). "Dreaming," Humanities Press, New York.

Marslin-Wilson, W. (1973). Speech shadowing and speech perception. Ph.D. Dissertation, Massachusetts Inst. of Technology, Cambridge, Massachusetts.

McCawley, J. D. (1970). Syntactic and logical arguments for semantic studies. *Transcript at the Fifth International Seminar on Theoretical Linguistics (session 2),* Tokyo, unpublished.

McCawley, J. D. (1971). Prelexical syntax. In "Georgetown Monograph Series on Languages and Linguistics," (R. J. O'Brien, ed.).

Mehler, J. (1963). Some effects of grammatical transformation on the recall of English sentences. *Journal of Verbal Learning and Verbal Behavior,* **2,** 346–351.

Miller, G. A., Galanter, E. and Pribram, K. H. (1960). "Plans and the Structure of Behavior," Holt, New York.

Miller, G. A. and Johnson-Laird, P. N. "Perception and Language," to be published.

Neiser, U. (1967). "Cognitive Psychology," Appleton, New York.

Newell, A. and Simon, H. A. (1972). "Human Problem Solving," Prentice-Hall, Englewood Cliffs, New Jersey.

Norman, D. A. (1969). "Memory and Attention," Wiley, New York.

Oppenheim, P. and Putnam, H. (1958). Unity of science as a working hypothesis. In "Minnesota Studies in the Philosophy of Science, Vol. II," (H. Feigl, M. Scriven and G. Mazwell, eds.), Univ. of Minnesota Press, Minneapolis, Minnesota.

Osgood, C. E. (1957). Motivational dynamics of language behavior. *Nebraska Symposium on Motivation,* 5, 348–424.

Paivio, A. (1971). "Imagery and Verbal Processes," Holt, New York.

Penfield, W. and Roberts, L. (1959). "Speech and Brain Mechanisms," Princeton Univ. Princeton, New Jersey.

Perky, C. W. (1910). An experimental study of imagination. *American Journal of Psychology,* **21,** 422–452.

Piaget, J. (1954). "The Construction of Reality in the Child," Basic, New York.

Piaget, J. (1970). "Structuralism," Basic, New York.

Posner, M. I., Boies, S. J., Eichelman, W. H. and Taylor, R. L. (1969). Retention of visual and name codes of single letters. *Journal of Experimental Psychology Monograph,* **79** (1, pt. 2).

Pribram, K. H. (1971). "Languages of the Brain," Prentice–Hall, Englewood Cliffs, New Jersey.

Putnam, H. (1960a). Dreaming and depth grammar. In "Analytic Philosophy," (R. J. Butler, ed.), Barnes & Noble, New York.

Putnam, H. (1960b). Minds and machines. In "Dimensions of Mind," (S. Hook, ed.), N. Y. Univ. Press, New York.

Putnam, H. The meaning of meaning. (To be published).

Ratliff, F. (1961). Inhibitory interaction and the detection and enhancement of contours. In "Sensory Communication," (W. Rosenblith, ed.), MIT Press,

Cambridge, Massachusetts.

Richardson, A. (1969). "Mental Imagery," Springer, New York.

Rosenberg, S. (1974). Modelling semantic memory: effects of presenting semantic information in different modalities. (Ph.D. Dissertation), Carnegie–Mellon University,

Ross, J. T. (1967). Constraints on variables in syntax. (Ph.D. Dissertation), Massachusetts Inst. of Technology, Cambridge, Massachusetts.

Russell, B. (1905). On denoting. *Mind,* **XIV,** 479–493.

Ryle, G. (1949). "The Concept of Mind," Barnes & Noble, New York.

Sachs, J. S. (1967). Recognition memory for syntactic and semantic aspects of connected discourse. *Perception and Psychophysics,* **2,** 437–442.

Savin, H. B. (1973). Meanings and concepts: a review of Katz's "Semantic Analysis," *Cognition,* 2(2), 212–238.

Schlesinger, I. M. (1966). Sentence structure and the reading process. (Ph.D. Dissertation). The Hebrew University, Jerusalem.

Segal, S. J. and Gordon, P. (1968). The Perky effect revisited: paradoxical thresholds or signal detection error? Paper presented at the 39th Annual Meeting of the Eastern Psychological Association

Skinner, B. (1957). "Verbal Behavior," Appleton, New York.

Skinner, B. F. (1971). "Beyond Freedom and Dignity," Knopf, New York.

Slobin, D. I. (1966). Grammatical transformations and sentence comprehension in childhood and adulthood. *Journal of Verbal Learning and Verbal Behavior,* **5,** 219–227.

Sperry, R. W. (1956). The eye and the brain. *Scientific American,* May, 48–52.

Stromeyer, C. F. and Psotka, J. (1970). The detailed texture of eidetic images. *Nature,* **225,** 346–349.

Sutherland, I. E. (1970). "Computer displays," *Scientific American,* **222,** No. 6, 56–81.

Sutherland, N. S. (1960). Theories of shape discrimination in octopus. *Nature, London,* **186,** 840–844.

Teuber, H. L. (1960). Perception. In "Handbook of Physiology," Vol. 3, (J. Field, H. W. Magoun and V. E. Hall, eds.), Amer. Phys. Soc., Washington, D.C.

Thorpe, W. H. (1963). "Learning and Instinct in Animals," Methuen, London.

Tolman, E. C. (1932). "Purposive Behavior in Animals and Men," Century, New York.

Triesman, A. (1964). Verbal cues, language and meaning in attention. *American Journal of Psychology,* **77,** 206–214.

Vendler, Z. (1972). "Res Cogitans," Cornell Univ. Press, Ithaca, New York.

Vygotsky, L. S. (1965). "Thought and Language," MIT Press, Cambridge, Massachusetts.

Walker, E., Gough, P. and Wall, R. (1968). Grammatical relations and the search of sentences in immediate memory. *Proceedings of the Midwestern Psychological Association,* 1968.

Wallach, L. (1969). On the basis of conservation. In "Studies in Cognitive Development," (D. Elkind and J. Flavell, eds.), Oxford Univ. Press, London and New York.

Wanner, E. (1968). On remembering, forgetting, and understanding sentences: a study of the deep structure hypothesis. (Ph.D. Dissertation), Harvard University. Mouton, The Hague: to be published.

Wason, P. C. and Johnson-Laird, P. N. (1972). "Psychology of Reasoning: Structure and Content," Batsford, London. Harvard University Press, Cambridge, Massachusetts.

Werner, H. and Kaplan, B. (1963). "Symbol Formation: An Organismic-Developmental Approach to the Psychology of Language and Expression of Thought," Wiley, New York.

Whorf, B. L. (1956). "Language, Thought, and Reality: Selected Writings of Benjamin Lee Whorf," (John B. Carroll, ed.), Wiley, New York.

Wittgenstein, L. (1953). "Philosophical Investigations," Blackwell, Oxford.

Young, R. K. (1968). Serial learning. In "Verbal Behavior and General Behavior Theory," (T. Dixon and D. Horton, eds.), Prentice-Hall, Englewood Cliffs, New Jersey.

INDEX